From the Banks of the Oklawaha

Vol. III

Facts and Legends
of the
North Carolina Mountains

Frank L. FitzSimons Sr.
1897–1980.

Mr. FitzSimons, 82, was a local historian and the author of three volumes of local lore and historical anecdotes, schoolteacher, school principal, Marine Corpsman, banker, Register of Deeds, football coach, farmer, broadcast personality and winner of the Navy Cross for valor during World War I.

"Mr. Fitz" was best known in Henderson County for more than 5,000 broadcasts he made "from the banks of the Oklawaha" over Radio WHKP in the late 1950s and early 1960s. His rhythmic Southern cadences were heard here nightly at 6 p.m. and early morning telling stories from Henderson County and Western North Carolina's past.

Those radio broadcasts were gathered together and expanded for publication of three volumes, "From the Banks of the Oklawaha," a project that brought him the 1977 Thomas Wolfe award for outstanding work by a Western North Carolina writer.

Mr. FitzSimons was born April 17, 1897, in Grand Rapids, Mich., and at an early age moved with his family to Spartanburg, S.C. He spent his early summers in Henderson County. He was a graduate of Wofford College in Spartanburg.

He came to Hendersonville in 1920 to take a teaching job at Hendersonville High School. In later years he taught at the Blue Ridge School for Boys, Carolina Military and Naval Academy, Dana School, Mt. Vernon (Dry Hill) School and Edneyville School. He also was principal of East Flat Rock School. His educational services here extended from 1920 to 1943.

From 1943 to 1948 he was Register of Deeds for Henderson County, and then joined the former State Trust Co., which later merged with Northwestern Bank. He served in several capacities at the bank, retiring in the early 1970s as a vice president. In 1973, the bank gave funds to the Henderson County Public Library to establish a special local history and writer section to be dedicated to him as a tribute for his years of leadership and service.

He was founder of the Henderson County Curb Market in 1924, and served as chairman of its board of control from its foundation until the 1940s. He sold farm products, which he raised on his farm, Golden Glow Farm, in Hendersonville. He attended the 50th anniversary celebration of the market in 1974, and recently autographed some of his books there.

Mr. FitzSimons was long associated with Henderson County Public Library, successor to the Hendersonville City Library, and was instrumental in having the library become a county instead of a city institution.

During the Depression in 1935 he became the first administrator of the Federal Rural Rehabilitation program for Henderson County.

He was well known as a speaker and from the mid 1940s until the 1960s he was the official speaker at almost every major community function.

One of his hobbies was growing roses, which he began in the 1940s. He was a well-known orchardist.

Mr. FitzSimons was a veteran of World War I, serving with the U.S. Marine Corps. He won the Navy Cross for valor. He fought in three of the greatest battles of that war: Soissons, the Meuse-Argonne and Belleau Wood.

But he said in a recent interview with the *Times-News* that he was most proud of coaching the first football team at Hendersonville High School to win a game. He was originator of the "Arabella Shift," a play he named for his cow.

The list of organizations to which he had given his time, interest and energy would make almost a book in itself.

He was former member and past president of the Rotary Club and was a member of the Hubert M. Smith Post 77 American Legion and Hedrick-Rhodes Post 5206 Veterans of Foreign Wars.

Mr. FitzSimons was married to the former Margarita Kershaw, who survives. They had recently celebrated their 56th anniversary.

He is also survived by a son, Frank L. FitzSimons Jr. of Route 1, Hendersonville; a daughter, Mrs. Donald M. Allston Jr. of John's Island, S.C.; a sister, Katherine Waterfall of Columbia, S.C.; eight grandchildren and six great-grandchildren.

He was a member of St. John in the Wilderness Episcopal Church, where he was buried.

Obituary Hendersonville Times-News 1/29/80

From The Banks of The Oklawaha

Vol. III

by

Frank L. FitzSimons

Drawings by Adèle Kershaw Thornton

Golden Glow Publishing Company
1979

This book is dedicated to
Millie Jones FitzSimons,
whose deep interest and hard work
made this trilogy possible; and to
Adèle Kershaw Thornton whose
sketches give life to the text.

We sincerely appreciate the work of
Theresa Pepin Pace who indexed the three volumes of
"From the Banks of the Oklawaha".

Published by *Golden Glow Publishing Company* in conjunction with **WorldComm**®.
Copyright© 1979, 1998, Golden Glow Publishing Co.
Drawings by Adèle Kershaw Thornton

Second Edition printed 1998

10 9 8 7 6 5 4 3 2 1

ISBN: 1-56664-140-3   Library of Congress Cataloging Number: 98-72963

Golden Glow Publishing Co. RR 14, Box 276, Hendersonville, North Carolina 28792
Phone: (828) 693-6838.

Distributed by **Alexander Books**™ 65 Macedonia Road, Alexander NC 28701.
Phone (828) 252-9515, Fax (828) 255-8719. For orders only: 1-800-472-0438.
Visa and MasterCard accepted.

EDITOR'S NOTE

The editing of a Frank FitzSimons work is a memorable experience. It might be compared to entering a mythical time machine in which one is swept and tumbled about over a period of several hundred years of Western North Carolina history.

We hear again the war cry of Cherokees, the crack of drovers' whips, the stuttering thunder of steam locomotives, the clatter of early automobiles — but we also hear the awesome silence of a magnificient wilderness.

We walk again with pioneers who somehow seem twice the size of modern men and women. We talk with both statesman and thieves, with preachers and murderers, with wide-eyed children and "the old ones" of incredible ages.

We sit again in one room school houses but we also mingle with the educators of today's huge, complex school system. We ride a creaking wagon in one chapter and in another we hear the scream of jet planes dropping down on Asheville Airport. We contrast the grim proverty of hard times with today's abundance.

And then we sit down in a 200 year old log cabin on a mountain side and visit with an authentic 18th Century man. When we reluctantly say goodbye to "my old friend" we must also bid farewell again to the banks of the Oklawaha.

We walk slowly down the mountain with a poignant sense of sadness that even the best of things must end.

But we are immeasurably enriched.

Grady Edney
Coral Springs, Florida
September 18, 1979

Author's Preface

If there is to be an indictment for the writing of this third volume of history, anecdotes and folklore of Henderson County, then let it be laid directly upon the head of my son Frank, Jr. and his very cunning co-conspirator, Kermit Edney.

The very fact that so many people were gracious enough to purchase copies of my first two books was reward enough for an old man to live with the remainder of his appointed days.

But age has a way of making a man gullible about his unique importance in the Master Plan, and the constant flattery and urging of these young men caused me to commit the folly of agreeing to attempt Volume III.

During the cold, blustery days of January and February 1979, with Maggie's help and encouragement, I labored the necessary hours digging back through boxes of notes and old manuscripts. Each story uncovered would bring back a flood of memories of the wonderful people I had known; the recollections would be vivid of those long, tedious climbs up mountain sides, the fording of creeks, the smell of the woods fires, the excitement of finding a new story to tell. It made me relive many wonderful days of my younger years.

Perhaps, some of the stories told in this third volume will have a special meaning to some of my dear friends in the county. That, and the rekindling of the warm memories of the days when the stories were collected, will be ample enough reward for the man who grew rich in years along the Banks of the Oklawaha.

I would like to thank all of you who helped make this trilogy of Henderson County and Western North Carolina possible.

TABLE OF CONTENTS

Part Eighteen   My Old Friend

Part One
The Speculation Lands

Part One

The Speculation Lands

CHAPTER 1

Tenche Coxe

Only the older ones living here who have heard the story from their parents or grandparents know what is meant by the terms Speculation Land Company or the Speculation Lands. Lawyers both young and old who specialize in drawing up deeds and searching land titles also know about the Speculation Lands. Not too long ago, in a remote section of Henderson County, I was sitting on the front porch of his home with an elderly gentleman who was descended from one of the earliest pioneers to settle in the area. Proudly he told me that he was the sixth generation of his family and his son in the cabin just below his was of the seventh generation to live on this boundary of land where the two houses stood.

"This is part of the Speculation Lands," he said as he showed me the original deed to the place which had been given to his ancestors 160 years ago by the Speculation Land Company.

It all started way back in 1796 and the effects and repercussions from it are felt even to this day. It was the most fantastic and colossal real estate project and development ever in the state of North Carolina.

In the beginning it involved more than half a million acres of land in the three counties of Buncombe, Rutherford and Mecklenburg. Through the years, since 1796, the Legislature at various times cut off portions of these three counties to create Henderson, Polk, Gaston, McDowell and Union Counties so that what was in the beginning the Speculation Lands lie in portions of all the counties I have named.

In 1755 a baby was born in Philadelphia to Mr. and Mrs. William Coxe. The proud parents named the boy Tenche and when he was grown he became very active in the political and business affairs of his time. He belonged to the Pennsylvania Militia at the outbreak of the Revolutionary War. Later on he resigned and turned Loyalist and fought with the British forces under Lord Howe. But before the war ended he again became a Patriot, swore allegiance to the Continental Congress and was pardoned for his Royalist British activities.

After the Revolution Tenche Coxe held important positions in the new United States Government during the terms of President Washington and President Jefferson. In 1796 he was connected with the Treasury Department

3

of the United States as Commissioner of Revenue. While holding this position he came into possession of more than half a million acres of land in the counties above named. He got possession of this vast acreage by direct land grants from the State of North Carolina and by purchasing the grants of others, many of whom were war veterans of the Continental Army. This Tenche Coxe is the founder and ancestor of the Coxe family which has played an important part not only in the early history of Buncombe County and Western North Carolina but has continued as a prominent family to this day. This vast boundary of land soon began to be referred to as the Speculation Lands and those connected with it as the Speculation Land Company.

Between 35,000 and 40,000 acres of this land were within the boundaries of what is now Henderson County. The entire half million acres was purchased for less than 12 cents an acre. The portion in Henderson County consisted roughly of the lands drained by the Big and Little Hungry Rivers and the land along Green River from its headwaters. Some of this is now covered by Lake Summitt. Another tract of the speculation land in Henderson County is drained by Reedy Patch Creek below Edneyville.

4

CHAPTER 2

Augustus Sackett

In 1819 approximately 400,000 acres of Tenche Coxe's land was sold to Augustus Sackett who lived in Jefferson County in the state of New York. Mr. Sackett bought the land purely for speculation purposes and he immediately set out to exploit his acreage. He advertised it in the most glowing colors in the weekly and daily newspapers that were published at that time in the United States. He also flooded the mails from New England to Georgia with the large handbills that I will describe in the next chapter. It was the glowing descriptions of the area and its climate that started an influx of settlers who bought a large portion of the land advertised. In 1825 he sold what he had left to four men: James Thompson, Goold Hoyt, James B. Murray and Arthur Bronson.

There are two people who have done the greater share of original research about the Speculation Lands. One of them is the late Clarence W. Griffin who during his lifetime was a prominent newspaperman of Forest City. For many years he was a member of the executive board of the North Carolina Department of Archives and History. He writes about the speculation lands in his book, "Essays on North Carolina History." A copy of this book is in the Henderson County Public Library. The other person who has done much research on this subject is the late Mrs. Sadie (P.F.) Patton, the well known historian of Hendersonville. Mrs. Patton's story about the Speculation Lands was published under the auspices of the Western North Carolina Historical Association. Her booklet is titled, "Buncombe to Mecklenburg — The Speculation Lands."

I tell you this because, as so often happens with events that took place in the years gone by, accounts do not always agree in some details, and there is a difference of opinion of the findings of Mr. Griffin and Mrs. Patton. To quote Mr. Griffin: "the Speculation Land Company originated with Tenche Coxe of Philadelphia in 1796. On August 12, 1819 the assignees of Tenche Coxe deeded to Augustus Sackett a total of 399,090 acres of Speculation Land Company property. Augustus Sackett then incorporated under the laws of the State of North Carolina and henceforth the company was known as the New York Speculation Company."

Now to quote Mrs. Patton: "Nothing appearing in the records of North Carolina would indicate that there was ever a corporation which held title to the property but since the four owners, Thompson, Hoyt, Murray and Bronson, became tenants in common, this vast body of land has continued to be known as the Speculation Company's Land."

Be that as it may, the early series of owners of this land soon found it necessary to send representatives to this area to look after their interests. Among these agents were Judge Joshua Foreman and Jacob Hyatt. Mr. Hyatt spent a large part of the year 1825 traveling over and inspecting the Speculation Lands. He was a fluent correspondent and much that is known about the Speculation Lands and the people living in this area at that time has been learned from his journal and from letters to his wife and his employer, Arthur Bronson, which are still preserved.

CHAPTER 3
The Sackett Ads

The old advertisement was yellow with age when I first saw it in 1964 for it was then 140 years old, having been printed and distributed in 1820. The copy that I saw was owned by C. P. Rhody, a well known antique collector of Henderson County. This advertisement or handbill was the size of a modern newspaper page and back in 1820 it had been distributed to all parts of the eastern seaboard of the United States and in England and parts of Europe. It was something to see and to read.

There were big headlines in bold black type: "For Sale — 400 thousand acres of land in Rutherford, Mecklenburg and Buncombe Counties in the southwestern part of the State of North Carolina."

Through the years down to the present time, the western part of North Carolina has at intervals had land booms but this handbill heralded the start of the first real estate boom in our area. Our present day real estate advertisers could learn much from this ad written and published 150 years ago.

I quote the advertisement as it reads: "Located on the head of Broad, Pacolate and Green Rivers and the heads of the Catawba in North Carolina. The land is not inferior to the lands in any other district of the country in the entire United States. The soil is very strong and productive and the peaches are superior in every respect to those produced in any other part of the Union. The peach brandy of Western N.C. will compare with the best French Cognac or Bordeau Brandy." The handbill tells the world: "In this country there are good roads and goods schools; all the conveniences and most of the luxuries of life. The winters are very mild, so much so that in the winter season the ploughing is generally done."

The large advertising handbill printed and distributed in 1820 was 24 inches long and 19 inches wide and divided in four columns. It goes on to tell how close here in Western North Carolina we are to the seaports of North and South Carolina where a market is found for everything raised and how easy it is to haul the products by wagon or ox carts to these markets.

The safety of living in Western North Carolina in 1820 was pointed out in bold black headlines. Again I quote: "There are not 100 Indians in all of North

Carolina.'' The terms of the sale: ''The price of these lands will be 2 dollars an acre cash, or 3 dollars an acre on credit. The credit will be extended 15 or 20 years if required with interest of 2% the first year, 4% the second year and 7% afterwards until 100 thousand acres shall be sold.''

1820 handbill advertising the Speculation Lands

The last paragraph that I will quote really touches a body's heart strings: "Fellow citizens, I mean not to deceive you. I have a large and fine body of land in one of the best climates. I wish you to participate with me in an improved country where every man may set under his own vine or fig tree. A rise of many hundred if not a thousand per cent in the value of your farm may speedily and confidently be expected and you will receive a rich inheritance for your families and posterity. A clear and indisputable title can and will be given to purchasers."

This elaborate advertisement was signed Augustus Sackett who then gave the name and addresses of his sales agents in most of the large cities in the eastern part of the United States.

Soon afterwards the settlers lured by the vivid descriptions began to pour into Western North Carolina. These 400,000 acres in Henderson, Buncombe, Rutherford and Mecklenburg Counties offered for sale by Augustus Sackett made history and became known through the years to the present day as "the Speculation Lands" and it all started shortly after the Revolutionary War.

CHAPTER 4

James Dyer Justice

Let me retrogress for a few lines. In 1760 two brothers came to the American colonies from Wales and settled in Virginia. These two brothers became neighbors of Thomas Jefferson whose home, Monticello, still stands and today is an American shrine. These Welsh brothers were John and James Justice. John Justice married Mary Stogue and together they raised a large family. One of their sons, Thomas Justice, married Mary Dyer and soon afterwards Thomas and Mary Dyer Justice migrated to Western North Carolina. They settled near the present village of Mill Spring in what is now Polk County. One of their children was a boy who they named James Dyer Justice.

When James Dyer Justice grew to manhood he came through the gap in the Blue Ridge Mountains and settled in what is now the eastern part of Henderson County in the Dana area that is referred to as the Ridge. It is very possible that he followed the same trail through the gap that the first settler, William Mills, followed which later became the Mills Gap Road.* As soon as James Dyer Justice built his log cabin and began to clear his patches of land, he set out to find a wife.

In 1806 he married Anthorit Thomas. Anthorit was the daughter of John Thomas who was the owner of large tracts of land in what is now the western

* Vol. 1 "The Founders"

part of Hendersonville and its vicinity. Pioneer mountain settlers raised large families and James and Anthorit were not exceptions. They raised fourteen children and from them are descended many of the large family of Justices that are today in Henderson County and other parts of North Carolina. James Dyer Justice was highly respected, was active in the public affairs of his day and was widely known.

When Jacob Hyatt returned to the North at the end of 1825 and made his report to the owners of the Speculation Lands, it became apparent to the absentee land barons that a local person who was well acquainted with this area was needed as resident agent. They contacted James Dyer Justice and he accepted the appointment as commissioner. Thus began the connection of a Henderson County family with the Speculation Lands that lasted through five generations for over 100 years.

CHAPTER 5

The Justice Family

James Dyer Justice became the first local person to represent the Speculation Land Company as commissioner, sales agent and supervisor. As the years passed he was succeeded in turn by the Rev. T. Butler Justice, C. Baylus Justice and S. D. Justice. In 1919 George W. Justice of Hendersonville became the fifth generation of the family to be directly connected with the Speculation Lands.

The late George W. Justice is well remembered by older people still living here. He was a successful businessman and civil engineer of Henderson County. At various times he held important offices in our county government. One of the forgotten positions that he held for a short time was that of the first City Manager of Hendersonville.

The Speculation Lands were first advertised for sale in those early days of the 19th Century as the land of opportunity, a land flowing with milk and honey, a veritable Utopia. But no mention was made of the valuable mineral deposits hidden under the ground. These mineral deposits were thought to consist of iron, lead, silver and gold underlying the surface of this vast acreage of land. In fact, from approximately 1820 to 1856, Rutherford County, where much of the speculation lands were located, was the center of the gold production in the United States.

So much gold was produced during this period in Rutherford County that the only privately owned and operated mint established in this country was located there. This was the Bechtler Mint that coined most of the gold mined on the Speculation Lands.* The Speculation Land Company always reserved

* Vol. I "Stories These Mountains Could Tell"

the mineral rights to land it sold and these reservations were so stated in the deeds the company gave. These reservations have given title lawyers a lot of hard work and headaches in rendering title opinions in late years. Many of these lawyers have told me that even today there are thousands of acres of this land owned by people who own none of the mineral rights.

George W. Justice resigned from the company a few months after taking his position. He was then appointed by court order to take charge of the land still owned by the company and to settle the company's affairs.

There still remained unsold 10,000 acres of this land, and by now there were eighty heirs to it living in every state and in several foreign countries. By 1920, after more than twenty years effort, the signature of all of these heirs had been obtained and on March 20, 1920 title to these remaining acres of the Speculation Lands passed to George W. Justice of Hendersonville and to Judge Fred McBrayer of Rutherfordton.

The Speculation Land Company has played an important part in the history of the development of parts of our western counties by making our area known in the very early days and bringing in the first flood of settlers. Little of this history that I have written in these several chapters is known to the present day general public. But there are people still living who even today will tell you that the land they own, live on and farm is some of the original Speculation Lands.

Part Two
Ghosts & Indians

Part Two

Ghosts and Indians

CHAPTER 6

The Flat Rock

There is a legend that persists to this day, a tale that has been handed down by word of mouth through generations. It is a story of an Indian campground in the Flat Rock area of Henderson County and it is about a lost or hidden band of Indians. No written records of it can be found but the old ones tell it to the young ones as it has been handed down through the years.

In the early days, before the white man came, what is now Henderson County was a gathering place for the Cherokee Indians to hold their hunting ceremonies at the large flat rock that gives the name to the present day settlement. Evidences of these rituals have been found over the years.

When the Indians had offered their sacrifices to their gods, praying that these gods would grant them happy hunting, the different bands would find a camping place to leave their women and children to carry on the every day duties of life while the warriors roamed the plateau abounding in game. The kill was brought back to the campgrounds where the meat was dried and smoked for the winter food. The hides and furs were cured for clothes and shelters. When the hunting season was over the various groups returned to their permanent villages further to the west.

Those were happy days for the Cherokees. They had been visiting these hunting grounds and camping places for hundreds of years. But now the white traders were coming into the mountains and permanent settlers were advancing from the coastal areas. They were pushing the Indians slowly but relentlessly back from these favorite hunting and camping grounds.

Early in the spring of 1776, a portion of the Cherokee nation was secretly gathering on the side of Warrior Mountain to attack the block house fort near Tryon, wipe out the garrison and descend on the settlers around Landrum and Mill Springs to wipe them out. The Indian strategy would possibly have succeeded but for a traitor among them.

Skyuka turned traitor by telling Captain Thomas Howard about the Indians' surprise attack. Skyuka led Capt. Howard and his men by a secret path so that they were above and behind the massed Indians. That morning in 1776, just at the break of day, Capt. Howard and his men swept down suddenly on the unsuspecting tribes and overwhelmingly defeated them. Some of the Indians managed to escape the massacre.

*Monument erected in memory of Captain Thomas Howard
just off of I-26 at Howard's Gap near Saluda, N.C.*

The gap several miles north of Tryon where the battle took place has been known as Howard's Gap ever since and the road from Landrum through Tryon and Howard's Gap across Green Riven to Upward and by Ebenezer Church and on to Fletcher has been known as the Howard Gap Road.* All of this is historical fact. Now legend steps in.

It has been told through the generations that one of the bands of Cherokee Indians which gathered on Warrior Mountain came through what is now Henderson County. This group was accompanied by their women and children who were left near the Flat Rock ceremonial grounds. Here they established a camp to wait for the return of their fighting men. Some of the men did return but not as many as had gone forth to fight. And those that did come back were battered, bruised and bleeding from battle wounds and depressed in spirit. There they nursed their wounds to regain strength to make the long rough journey to their permanent homes to the west.

It was while resting here that word was brought that General Griffith Rutherford had led an army of frontiersman gathered at Old Fort to the Indian settlements in the Smoky Mountains, laying waste to villages and crops and killing all in their path. The temporary camp near Flat Rock became a permanent Indian settlement until President Andrew Jackson rounded up most of the Cherokees and moved them to Oklahoma over the passage way that became known as "the Trail of Tears."

Millie FitzSimons and Jane Sherrill Angier examine old Indian camp site.

* Vol. I "Twilight for the Indians"

I drove up the long driveway between rows of towering white pines that led to the home of Mr. and Mrs. Frank Sherrill. The legendary campground was on the Sherrill estate not too far from the flat rock that gives the community its name. It was a perfect autumn day and we walked through the woods until we came to a bold mountain stream which we followed for a mile or so until we came to the place, a spot surrounded by tall majestic trees. The sparkling, rippling water was clear as crystal as it flowed over a bed of white rocks and pebbles, singing a song of happiness.

Three coves between high narrow ridges converge to make the area securely hidden from the sight of a casual wanderer. It was a pretty setting but, as pretty as the place was, nothing will grow there to this day, nor has since the Indians abandoned the camp site. And the old ones tell that where Indians have made a campground for any length of time grass will never again grow.

The day we stood there the only sounds were the rippling of the water and the trilling of the birds in bushes surrounding the place where the remnants of a once proud people camped. Is this really the place? That I can only tell you as it was told to me, told and retold through the generations by the old ones who are now forever silent.

CHAPTER 7

The Ghost House

The two boys were on the way home from a box supper held in the little old one teacher log school house. It was nearly midnight and the night was dark. Broken clouds scudding by in the sky let sudden light from the full moon break through the darkness of the woods but the lights and shadows caused by this made the surroundings seem even more spookey to those teenage boys. Now they were in front of the big gray vacant ghost house and as it loomed up in front of them the abandoned structure seemed twice as large as they remembered it in the daylight hours.

Suddenly a sharp, loud, cracking sound, almost underfoot, froze both of the boys in their tracks. From the old house above them came the most frightful sounds that they had ever heard. The sound like a pistol shot was followed in quick succession by fierce, growling and rattling, scuffling and banging. The boys' feet seemed to be glued to the ground.

A weird, piercing, agonizing scream rent the night air. Then a silent white form drifted out of the house and over the heads of the two boys in the path below. That was more than they could stand. From their throats came a scream more piercing and terrifying than the one that had come a few moments before from the house.

There was a crunching of gravel and the sound of pounding feet. The thoroughly frightened boys took to their heels through the dark woods and they did not slacken speed until, breathless and exhausted, they reached home and plunged into bed, with clothes and shoes on, and pulled up the covers over their heads. They had actually seen the ghost that a short time earlier each had bravely denied they believed existed.

The next day was Saturday and no school. Grown brave by the bright, clear, morning sun, a boldness they really didn't feel, they, with a couple of older friends, invaded the ghost house that did not seem near as large and scary as the night before. Perched on the banister of the stairway at the top of the second floor they found a sleeply old barn owl on a nest littered with the bones of small birds and animals.

As the boys stood looking at the roosting owl, it gradually dawned on them that the eight inch tall, monkey-faced barn owl with its white colored breast and a four foot white wing spread had been the weird ghost that had floated out of the house and over their heads that night and put wings to their feet. But it was a long time before they ever took a short cut home by the ghost house after dark.

Their philosophy after that night was "the longest way around is always the shortest and least frightening way home."

CHAPTER 8

St. John in the Wilderness

It was known as the Wilderness and so recorded on the maps of the region more than 50 years ago; all of that vast area of sparsely settled wild land lying between the little settlements of Knoxville, Watauga and Greenville. Indians still roamed there, hunting, fishing and trading, when Charles Baring, an Englishman and one of the gentry, came seeking a healthy climate to prolong the life of his ailing wife. Living on a rice plantation where swamps and fertile fields were always associated with unhealthiness, Baring had a theory that an infertile soil at a high altitude made for healthy living. So he chose Flat Rock to build his home which he named "Mountain Lodge."

Mr. Baring's theory proved correct because his wife regained her health and lived to be 83 years old and he died at the age of 92. Mr. Baring bought all of the land in the vicinity of the flat rock until he had acquired more than a thousand acres. For many years Mr. and Mrs. Baring lived the life of the English nobility. They maintained an extensive, beautifully landscaped estate. There was a large deer park and a private church or chapel of their own.

Mountain Lodge   (Photo by Barber)

In 1826 or 1827 Mr. Baring had erected a small wooden Episcopal chapel which he named St. John in the Wilderness. Not long after this, the little chapel caught fire and was totally destroyed. In 1832 Mr. Baring started to build the present St. John in the Wilderness and this time he used brick. This church was dedicated in 1836 by Bishop L. S. Ives, Episcopal Bishop of North Carolina, and the church was deeded to Bishop Ives at that time for the Diocese of North Carolina. The church was enlarged and the tower added in 1852.

The minutes of the first meeting in 1836 of the vestry of St. John in the Wilderness are preserved with names of the charter members of the church listed. One of those named was James Brown. Who was this James Brown? How did he happen to come to this wilderness area and become the first person buried in the church yard at St. John in the Wilderness? There is an air of mystery surrounding the man.

At the northeast corner of St. John in the Wilderness, there is an above-ground crypt enclosed in the wrought iron fence. The slab covering the top of the crypt has been there for more than a century and a half and has become so weathered with age that the inscription is no longer legible.

On the side of the crypt there is a plaque inscribed: "James Brown, 1790 - 1840, with Captain Vernor's Troop of the Royal Scots Greys in the Battle of Waterloo."

Tradition tells us that James Brown was the first person buried at St. John in the Wilderness. He was a trumpeter or bugler at the Battle of Waterloo fought near a little village by that name in Belgium. Here Napoleon was overwhelmingly defeated by England and her allies under command of the Duke of Wellington in 1815. It is said that James Brown came to America and Flat Rock from Scotland as a retainer in the household of Mr. and Mrs. Baring. Some stories handed down tell that he was coachman for Mrs. Baring. Others say he was the butler for the Baring family.

Something else has been told by old ones who are no longer alive but who lived in the vicinity of St. John in the Wilderness. On sultry summer nights when the distant horizon is lighted by continuous lightning flashes and crashing thunder becomes an angry muttering rumble, above it all there has been heard a trumpet sounding clearly the battle charge.

Those old ones have said the sound above the wind and rain and thunder is from the trumpet or bugle of James Brown, the first person to be buried in the churchyard high on the hill at St. John in the Wilderness.

(Photo by Barber)

CHAPTER 9

The Headless Horseman

A hundred years ago, the Little River Road that turns off Highway 25 at the Flat Rock Post Office was a spooky route, sparsely settled and for a long period of time never traveled at night because of strange things that happened on it. In those days travelers either waded or drove through Pheasant Branch where it crossed the Little River Road because bridges and culverts had not yet been built.

Today Pheasant Branch goes under the road through a rock culvert and many people cross it every day and are not even aware that there is a stream. The stream flows west parallel to the road until it is joined by the Sallie Capps Branch. The average traveler is still unaware of the combined streams because the ditches through which they flow are deep and the water is hidden by the grass, bushes and wild flowers that grow along the banks.

When the War between the States was declared, renegade bands of draft dodgers and deserters from both armies began to hide out in the areas along the Little River Road and harass, rob, steal and terrify the people and the unprotected homes in the Flat Rock area. They operated generally at night.

Then their activities were halted for a while as travelers began to tell of a headless horseman, seen nightly riding through the woods along Pheasant Branch, the Sallie Capps Branch, and the Little River Road.

Mounted on a large black horse, dressed in a flowing white robe and sitting erect in the saddle, the headless horseman always rode at a slow walk. If a traveler approached too close or was bold enough to try to pass the headless horseman, the horse and rider would vanish before his very eyes. One night when the moon was full and shining exceedingly bright, one of the bolder of the renegades decided to hide in the bushes on the side of the road where it was crossed by Pheasant Branch.

As the headless rider in the flowing white robe came along side the hiding place of the renegade, the hidden man, made brave by the whiskey he had been sipping, rose quickly and with a long pole raised the flowing white robe of the figure on horseback.

A pistol shot! The sound of galloping hoof beats! A few minutes later, when the hidden renegade's companions who had been lurking nearby and now alarmed at what they heard, reached him they found their comrade badly wounded. He was lying in the road and bleeding profusely. The man gasped out his story and told that when he raised the robe of the rider he saw underneath it a man with a tall black silk hat on his head and he was clothed in a black formal dress suit. Before he could finish his story he gasped for breath and died.

For long years afterwards, only the boldest men traveled the Little River Road after darkness fell. The headless horseman continued to ride the road at intervals well into the 20th Century. But since autombiles began to travel the Little River Road the headless rider in the flowing white robe has neven been seen.*

CHAPTER 10

The Haunted Mill

It had been a place to grind corn into grits and meal for centuries. For how long nobody rightly knows; when the first white settlers drifted into the Big Willow River Valley of Henderson County they found the Indians grinding their corn there. This was shortly after the end of the Revolutionary War. Those Indians told that their people had been doing this as far back as the oldest of them could remember.

This is a place where there is an out-cropping of hard rock on Big Willow Creek at the point where the old Indian Trail crosses the creek. It is here the clear mountain water cascades over the rock, singing a song night and day as it dashes to the still water below. This is where Big Willow flows behind the home and the old mill where Mrs. Jesse Pritchard Huggins lives today (1963) and has lived for more than three decades.

The hard, black outcropping rock alongside the creek has a number of smooth, round, shallow holes. It was to these potholes that the pioneers found the 'Indians bringing their corn. They were putting the corn in them and pounding it into meal and grits with smooth rocks, much like the old time druggists ground and mixed their powdered medicines with a mortar and pestal.

When the Big Willow Valley began to fill with settlers one of them was more enterprising than some. He saw that the place would be just right to put a water powered grist mill. Legend tells us that this first miller was a man named White. He built an overshot water wheel to power a pounding mill. In those early days ships began bringing millstones to Charleston and other Carolina and Georgia ports. There these mill stones were loaded on ox carts. After weeks of plodding over the crude trails that served as roads, the millstones reached Big Willow and they took the place of the slow, laborious pound mills. These millstones offered faster service and a better quality of water ground meal and grits.

Those early settlers came from miles around to bring their corn. Some used ox carts or home made sleds pulled by oxen. Those pioneers were a tough, hardy people and many a man thought nothing of shouldering a bushel

* Vol. I "The Founders"

or more of corn and walking with it several miles to have it ground and then walking home with the meal.

For nearly 200 years the old mill has been known by many names: Mace's Mill, Hughes Mill, Allison's Mill and others now long forgotten. All were men who operated it at various times.

Then, as settlers increased in numbers, a blacksmith shop was established nearby. The miller and blacksmith were the most important persons in any community in those early days.

A story has been handed down through the generations until it has become a legend. One of the first of the millers here on Big Willow was mysteriously killed. When found by his family he was dead on the ground in front of his mill. A friendly Indian told the family and friends of the dead man that a murderer always returned to the place of his crime. With the consent of the dead miller's family, the Indian offered to hide in the mill. As predicted, the killer returned in the night and was killed by the watching Indian.

It is told to this day by the old ones that on moonlight nights, when the fog settles over the Big Willow Valley, as it always does between 11:00 and 2:00 o'clock, strange sounds can be heard and strange figures can be seen in and around the old mill. The ghosts of the dead miller, the man who committed the murder and the Indian who watched for and in turn killed the murderer are meeting again at the scene of the crime. Gradually over the years, the now ancient mill on Big Willow became known as the Haunted Mill.

Mr. and Mrs. Pritchard Huggins bought the haunted mill over fifty years ago. He operated it for a score of years. Times change. The tempo of life has become fast. It is quicker and easier to buy corn meal and grits in a paper poke at a super market. When I visited the old mill in the spring of 1963, it stood there as it had for a century and more. The water to turn the mill wheel had been diverted. Mr. Huggins took me down to the mill behind the house but he warned me to be careful as the flooring had weakened with age. Everything was there as it was the last time the mill had operated, but covered now with the dust and cobwebs of time. In front of the mill was the hitching post where the customers in bygone days hitched their horses and mules and tethered their oxen. Nearby was the spot where Uncle Bud Ledbetter had his blacksmith shop.

Mr. Huggins told me that since they owned the mill, on dark nights, especially in July and August, one could look towards the old mill and see a light. On investigation the light disappeared and nobody could be found in the old building. As soon as a body investigating returned to the house, the light could again be seen.

The old grist mill on Big Willow is now only a landmark. Both the mill and the blacksmith shop are relics of another day. Several years ago the Haunted Mill changed hands. The building was restored and operated as an eating place made attractive to tourists. After operating for the summer as a tourist attraction, the Haunted Mill is once again silent.

CHAPTER 11

Princess Twinkling Star

The winter winds howled and screamed across the mountain tops but the Cherokee Indian mother stretched on the bearskin robe in her tepee and was warm in the sheltered mountain cove. Cradled on her arm was the newborn baby, a girl child whose father was chief of his tribe. The newborn baby would grow to be an Indian princess.

The mother had been gazing at the sleeping baby for some time because the infant had yet to open her eyes and the mother was eager for that first sign of awakening. The baby stretched, the chubby, little, clenched fists stuck up in the air. A yawn spread across its wizened face. Then the little Indian princess opened her eyes wide for the first time.

To the young mother, the baby's eyes seemed to sparkle and twinkle, unusual in a newborn child. The mother gasped and called to those in the tepee to see for themselves. "Her name shall be Twinkling Star," they all uttered together. Princess Twinkling Star she became and all through her life she was famous for her lovely smiling face and her flashing eyes that sparkled and twinkled like the brightest heavenly star.

Twinkling Star grew tall and slim with long, shapely legs. She could out run the swiftest boy in the tribe and as she grew older she could out distance the fastest messenger. She could shoot an arrow as straight to the target as the best huntsman or bravest warrior. This was most unusual for an Indian girl but, after all, Twinkling Star was a princess, the only child of the High Chief. Someday, when her father took his final trip to the Happy Hunting Ground, she and her husband would rule the tribe.

The years passed swiftly. Twinkling Star was initiated by the tribe into young womanhood with the ancient tribal ceremonies. Tall and straight as one of the mountain poplars that grew in her native cove, she was a picture of carefree beauty. Her eyes were brighter and more sparkling now than in her childhood. Her long straight black hair flowed free as she raced in village competition on days of the tribal festivals. At other times she wore her hair in two long plaited braids that hung down her back or carelessly slung over a shoulder. At tribal ceremonies the braided hair, black as coal, was twined around her head and held in place by long thorns as pins. It was a shining diadem adding dignity to her beauty which was enhanced by her soft, fawn colored doeskin jacket which was adorned with brightly dyed porcupine quills. Seated beside but slightly below her father, Twinkling Star was a breathtaking Indian beauty.

Princess Twinkling Star was approaching her 18th birthday and it was high time for the princess to be married. Most Cherokee maidens took husbands long before they were 18 but Twinkling Star was the daughter of a chief and she would not be hurried. The fame of her beauty had spread to the tribes throughout the land and for a long time now the braves had been coming to pay court for her hand and to compete in the tribal games to impress the princess and her father. Now as her 18th birthday approached, she must make a choice.

The choice of her hand and heart seemed to rest equally on two handsome young braves. Both were warriors and hunters fit to marry a Cherokee princess and to become chief of the tribe. Running Water, tall and lean, was a great warrior and hunter. He was the fleetest runner on the trail. Falling Rock was as tough as a mountain hickory and as solid as a river boulder. He had the keenest sight and hearing and was the best to track the enemy. In his lodge hung more enemy scalps than in any other lodge in the village.

But Twinkling Star, even at the urging of her father and mother and others of the tribe, could not decide which she loved the best. Each time a hunting party led by Running Water or a war party led by Falling Rock returned, it was thought that now Princess Twinkling Star would make a choice. Then one day a large party on the war path under the combined leadership of Falling Rock and Running Water returned to their village with many scalps of the enemy, but alas Falling Rock was not among those who came back.

He had been seen time and again in the thick of the fight. His war whoop sounded above all the others as he slashed right and left with his war hatchet. When the fight was over Falling Rock was missing. All searching high and low could find no trace of him. The people of the tribe thought that surely now the Princess would marry Running Water but it was not to be. From this time on, each time a war party or hunting party started out Twinkling Star would go among the warriors and beg and plead that they search for Falling Rock. "Look for Falling Rock and bring him back to me." The years went by and Twinkling Star was now a wizened unmarried old woman still begging all travelers to watch for her beloved Falling Rock.

Now all of this happened long before the white man came to our mountains but the story was told through the generations and passed on to the white man. That is the reason that even to this day as you drive on our mountain highways in high powered, shining automobiles, on every curve or overhanging cliff or out cropping of stone you still see the highway markers in big bold bright letters: "Watch for Falling Rock."

Part Three
Memorable Men

Memorable Men

CHAPTER 12

Michael Francis

The first school in Henderson County that we have any record of was started in 1797 in a little old log cabin in the Mills River Valley. The first and only teacher for a number of years was Professor David Haddon who was also an ordained minister. In 1820 a young man by the the name of Michael Francis came to take the place of Professor Haddon and to teach in the log schoolhouse. He taught for six years in this log school that was to grow, expand and become widely known as the Mills River Academy.*

Michael Francis, who was to become one of the great lawyers of North Carolina, was born in Edinburgh, Scotland, and educated there in what, in those days, was known as "the classics." He was only 5 feet 5 inches tall and weighed 325 pounds. It is said that when he walked he waddled like a duck.

One of his pupils was Nicholas Woodfin who later went to live in Asheville, became a lawyer and established a law school. When Woodfin started his law school Francis stopped teaching and with his wife, Erica Johnson Murray, daughter of a pioneer settler, moved to Asheville and enrolled in the Woodfin Law School. Michael Francis, the teacher, became the pupil of his former pupil who was now a teacher.

Michael passed his bar examination and in 1835 was given his license to practice law by the North Carolina Supreme Court. When Henderson County was formed in 1838, he was elected the first Solicitor of the new County Court. He was an astute man, a clear thinker, a student of human behavior, a forceful orator, a master of the facts of law and people came from miles around when it was known that he was to argue a case in court.

He moved from Henderson County to that part of Western North Carolina that became Haywood County. Here his fame grew and spread. His services as a lawyer were in demand all over Western North Carolina. He became a civic and political leader. He represented Haywood as a Representative for one term in the Legislature and for eight years as state Senator. His logic and forceful arguments in which he told of the opportunities and advantages offered here in our mountains attracted state wide attention. He soon became famous and was called "the Great Westerner."

The first client that Francis defended when he started his law practice in

* Vol. I "The Educators"

Haywood County was a Cherokee Indian chief who was in court in the little town of Webster. Francis won the case and the Indian was freed. Six months later the chief brought him a beautiful beaded shot pouch. The beads were handmade by the Indians of the tribe and many of them were made of pure gold.

Michael Francis was the grandfather of Ezra Johnson Francis, known to his friends as John Francis. For nearly half a century John Francis operated one of the largest and finest livery stables in Hendersonville. When he died, the last direct descendant of "the Great Westerner" died. One day in the winter of 1963, I paid a visit to Minnie Francis, the widow of John. I had known her since I was a small boy and her husband often let me ride with him from his home on the Flat Rock Road to his livery stable in Hendersonville.

Mrs. Francis showed me the law license that the North Carolina Supreme Court issued to Michael Francis in 1835. She also let me see the gold beaded shot pouch that the Indian chief gave to him which her husband had inherited. She showed me a full-faced photograph of the 5 foot 5 inch 325 pound lawyer who so loved these mountains of Western North Carolina that he became famous as "the Great Westerner."

CHAPTER 13

Charles William Pearson

Water cascading over sheer cliffs of rock or water rushing in volume over tortuous steep terrain has fascinated mankind since the beginning of time. Waterfalls are things of beauty and at the same time they fill a body with a fearsome awe. One of the most beautiful of the waterfalls in this area is Pearson Falls. A visit to it is well worth the time spent.

Highway 176 goes through Saluda approximately ten miles below Hendersonville. As you drive through Saluda, just at the edge of the town, is a road that turns off of 176 to the right. A sign says this is the Pearson Falls Road and a drive of two miles will bring you to the Pearson Falls Wildlife Preserve. A walk of less than a half mile leads to the falls. Who first discovered the place has been long ago forgotten but it was possibly one of the pioneers who came into the area in Revolutionary times.

The wildlife preserve and the falls are named in honor of and in memory of Captain Charles William Pearson, pioneer, farmer and engineer.

Charles William Pearson was a native of North Carolina and a civil engineer who helped survey the route of the railroad that ran from Salisbury to Asheville, and the one that goes from Asheville to Murphy. During the Confederacy he served as captain in command of Company H, 63rd North Carolina Regiment.

Pearson Falls   (Photo by Barber)

At the end of the War Between the States, he was given the mission of locating the route of the railroad that would run from Spartanburg to Tryon and up the mountains to Hendersonville and Asheville.* In his explorations and surveying the route for the railroad, he found the waterfall that now bears his name and he was fascinated by the falls. Land was cheap in the mountains

* Vol. II "The Age of Steam"

during this period from 1865 to the end of the century. Mr. Pearson bought large acreage of the land between Tryon and Saluda including the land on which the nameless waterfall flowed.

In 1931, long after Capt. Pearson's death, his son, for economic reasons, found it necessary to sell the land. The Garden Club of Tryon raised the money for the purchase of the tract on which the waterfall is located. The Garden Club named the area in honor of Capt. Pearson and set it aside as a preserve for the native mountain flora. A small fee is charged to enter the park and the money is used to defray the expense of maintenance.

The woods and the wild flowers are kept in their native condition as they have been since time immemorial. Naturalists from all parts of America and many foreign countries have visited the park to study the mountain plant life as well as to admire the beauty of the rushing water. The Tryon Garden Club has laid trails through the park so visitors can observe the beauty without disturbing the solitude of primeval surroundings. Picnic tables are provided for those who desire to spend the day.

Pearson Falls and the wildlife preserve is a place of beauty and once visited, the desire to revisit it remains. It is a lasting memorial to a distinguished North Carolinian.

CHAPTER 14

Edgar Porter Alexander

Edgar Porter Alexander, the master gunner of the Confederate Army, is recognized as one of the greatest American artillerists. He was a handsome, dashing figure with a magnetic personality; a natural leader who could inspire men to follow him. He was born May 26, 1835 at Washington, Georgia, the son of a slave-owning planter. He received an appointment to West Point and entered the Academy in July 1853. He graduated in 1857, the third highest in his class.

Alexander was commissioned a second lieutenant of engineers. Because of his brilliant scholastic record he was stationed at West Point as a teacher. While teaching he helped establish and organize the Signal Corps of the U.S. Army and is often referred to as the father of that branch. His next tour of duty was in the far northwest and he was serving there when news reached that isolated area of the fall of Fort Sumter.

He resigned at once. In June of 1861 he was commissioned a captain of engineers in the Confederate Army. So brilliant was his work that he was promoted after the Battle of Bull Run in July 1861 to lieutenant colonel.

He was made chief of ordinance of the Army of Northern Virginia. Soon he was made a colonel and chief of artillery of General Longstreet's Corps. It was as an artillery officer in command of the big guns that he made his record and became recognized as one of the greatest that America had produced.

He took part in all the battles in northern Virginia. In February 1864, he became a brigadier general and was put in command of all of General Lee's artillery. He was severely wounded in the fighting around Petersburg, but returned to duty in time to join in the last days of fighting and was with General Lee at the surrender of Appomatox. An unbiased appraisal by military experts, students and authorities of artillery have rated General Alexander as the best.

His career in civil life after the war was no less brilliant than his record as a soldier of the Confederacy. When the war ended with the defeat of the Southern states, many of the officers and men of the South were destitute financially and many were embittered with the feeling that all was lost.

General Alexander was only 30 years old at the end of the war. He was confident that a new South would rise from the wreckage and destruction that the four years of fighting left in its wake. He intended to make a place for himself in that new South. His achievements for the next forty-five years and the important positions he held read like a page from "Who's Who in America."

He taught for a few years at the University of South Carolina as professor of mathematics and engineering. He organized and was president of the Columbia Oil Company. He was then made superintendent of the Charlotte and Augusta Railroad, vice president of the Louisville and Nashville Railroad; president of the Georgia Railroad and Banking Company, director of the Union Pacific Railroad and several other railroads.

During the years he played such a successful part in rebuilding the South he maintained homes in Columbia, S.C., Louisville, Kentucky, Augusta and Savannah, Georgia as well as a home on a large rice plantation on South Island near Georgetown, S. C. Then in 1890 he built his summer home in Flat Rock which he named the Wigwam. For the next twenty years he spent the summer months of June, July, August and part of September there. On April 28, 1910, at the age of 75, he died in Savannah and is buried in Augusta.

Highly successful in his many business and civic activities for forty-five years following the War Between the States, Edward Porter Alexander yet found time to write extensively. His writing consisted mostly of historical articles. He was an intellectual and a scholar as well as a soldier and business executive.

In 1902 during the summer at the Wigwam he started work on his most outstanding literary achievement. He worked on this book, "Military Memoirs of a Confederate," for five years. It was published in 1907 and was soon recognized as a military and literary classic. Very few of the original editions of this book are now in existence and those that can be found are collector's items. The Department of Archives and History in Raleigh has a copy that is carefully guarded.

General Edgar Porter Alexander
(Photo compliments of Mr. & Mrs. William Jeter)

The Wigwam – now Hillden
(Photo compliments of Mr. & Mrs. William Jeter, the present owners)

In the summer of 1964 I talked to Mrs. Elizabeth Hilton, granddaughter of General Alexander. She came to Flat Rock in June 1890 as a three weeks old baby when the General brought his family there for the first time. I was interested as to why her grandfather had named his place the Wigwam. She told me that he always said that his home was so unpretentious, compared to the other great summer homes in Flat Rock, that his home reminded him of an Indian wigwam.

Mrs. Hilton told me that the Wigwam continued in the family until 1947 when it was sold to Reuben Robinson. It is now owned and lived in year round by Mr. and Mrs.' William T. Jeter.

CHAPTER 15

The Wigwam
(1965)

Only a few of the very old ones still living here remember when the place was built in 1890 and named the Wigwam and even fewer now living remember the man, Edward Porter Alexander, who built the house.

Today the place is called Hillden and it is owned and lived in the year round by Mr. and Mrs. William T. Jeter. Although General Alexander and his family occupied the Wigwam only during the summer months from June to September, it was during these summer months that he wrote the classic, "The Military Memoirs of a Confederate: a Critical Narrative of the War Between the States."

Drive out past the new Flat Rock Post Office and by the historic Woodfield Inn. Just past the south entrance to Woodfield are two gray granite pillars. This is the entrance to Hillden,, formerly called the Wigwam. It is not as pretentious or as old as some of the Flat Rock places but there is an aura of history about it that equals any of them. The white house with the dormer windows can be seen from the highway; it is surrounded by towering white pine and spruce trees.

A paragraph from a letter written to me by Mrs. Elizabeth Hilton, granddaughter of General Alexander, is of interest and I will quote it: "My grandfather built the house in Flat Rock in 1890. He bought the land from a Mr. Farmer who was then running the Farmer's Hotel. My grandfather drew the plans and asked Mr. Farmer to have the house ready by June. Grandfather's family then moved in that June, including my mother and me, a three weeks old baby and my brother, two years old."

Mr. and Mrs. Jeter are remodeling the home for more comfortable year round living but keeping the beautiful wide native pine boards of the original flooring and the old kitchen, connected to the main house by a covered breezeway as many of the early southern homes are built, so that the odors of the kitchen and cooking food are kept out of the main house.

CHAPTER 16

Jerome B. Freeman
(1979)

The rushing water cascades down the mountainside to pour into Rocky Broad River near Chimney Rock 960 feet below. It starts on the back side of Sugar Loaf Mountain in the area that at one time was the site of the isolated settlement that became known as the Lost Colony.* The early settlers called it Hickory Nut Falls but there has been an effort in late years to change the name to Appalachian Falls. About 200 yards from where the water starts its plunge to the valley below, Thomas Marshall built a grist mill and did all the grinding of corn into meal and grits, in the days of the Lost Colony.

In the late 19th Century, all of the area between the Rocky Broad River and the top of the mountain was owned by Jerome B. Freeman, prominent

* Vol. I "Stories These Mountains Could Tell"

James B. Freeman   (Photo compliments of the Freeman family)

farmer, politician and businessman. Jerome Freeman, father of the late Sheriff Bob Freeman and grandfather of Thomas, Robert, Allen, Bert and Catherine Freeman, was known far and wide as Rome Freeman. This land owned by Rome Freeman included the peculiar and spectacular rock formation known as Chimney Rock because of its likeness to a huge smoke stack or chimney.

During the years that this property was owned by Jerome Freeman, the land above and below Chimney Rock was covered with giant virgin black walnut trees, four and five feet in diameter. A firm in London bought the timber on the stump and contracted with Freeman to cut and deliver the walnut logs to the railroad that had recently been completed from Charleston, S. C. to Hendersonville.* It took Mr. Freeman two years to cut and deliver the logs from Chimney Rock to the railroad siding in Hendersonville. The logs were so enormous that often one huge log made a load. Extremely scarce and valuable today, this walnut timber, in the days it was cut by Jerome Freeman, did not bring as much as pulp wood does today.

This magnificent walnut timber was cut by sweat and muscle and the logs were snaked off the mountainside with oxen and loaded on the ox-drawn wagons by the same sweat and muscle. It took from 4:00 o'clock in the early morning until dark for the oxen to make the trip about half way to Hendersonville over the rough, rocky, crooked and often steep dirt road. Here the drivers would camp overnight and the next morning exchange the oxen for

Early picture of Chimney Rock (Photo by Barber)

* Vol. I "The Marvels of a New Age"

mules and horses to complete the trip to the railroad in Hendersonville. Here it was loaded on flat cars to be taken to Charleston and loaded on ships bound for England.

Jerome B. Freeman was an intelligent man with an active imagination. After the walnut timber had been cut and hauled from the area, Rome Freeman was the first person to see the tourist attraction possibilities of the great chimney-like rock standing apart from the mountain behind it, if a way could be found to get to the top of it. Rome Freeman opened a trail from the little village nearby to the base of the massive rock. Then he chiselled a path around the side of the mountain so that people could get to the top of the rock to enjoy the incomparable view that stretched as far as the eye could see.

Rome Freeman charged a fee for the tourists who were guided to the top. They came in untold numbers during the summer months to walk the three mile trail from the village to the base of Chimney Rock and then huff and puff up to the top. Those who did this were so enchanted, fascinated and awed by the view from the summit that they came back summer after summer and brought others with them. Soon Chimney Rock was famous all over the South and the East.

As an advertising and publicity stunt, Rome Freeman once had a small mule put on top of Chimney Rock. It took eight men to get the animal to the top; some in front pulling while the others behind were pushing. Sheriff Bob Freeman, who as a young man helped his father get the mule to the top, told me it was easy to get the mule back down to the valley below. The mule slid all the way down. This project paid off because it attracted wide publicity. Many people who had hesitated to climb to the top of Chimney Rock now decided that if a mule could go to the top so could they.

In the late 1920s the Morse brothers, who were instrumental in building Lake Lure, bought Chimney Rock from Rome Freeman. The deed specified that descendants of Mr. Freeman should always have free access to the top of Chimney Rock. The Morse brothers and Norman Gregg, who operated the attraction after Mr. Freeman sold it, had the means to really develop the attraction for the tourists. In place of the three mile trail that led from the village to the base of the rock they built a well graded, hard surfaced road so that automobiles could move the tourists.

Norman Gregg then had a 196 foot tunnel cut along the bottom of the rock and chiselled a 258 foot shaft through the rock cliff to the top, a total of 454 feet through solid granite and quartz rock, an engineering feat of some magnitude. The tunnel and elevator shaft was completed in 1949. It took eighteen months and 50,000 man hours to carve the stupendous shaft and tunnels; more than eight tons of dynamite was used. Now an elevator whisks visitors to the top of the rock in a matter of minutes.

To get the full thrill of a visit to the top of Chimney Rock, one should go to the top by way of the tunnel and elevator and, after taking in the view, return to the bottom by way of the original trail chiselled around the side of the mountain by Rome Freeman. On the way down you pass by the Opera Box, the Devil's Head, the Hickory Nut Waterfall, the Appian Way (so named by Mr. Freeman after making it possible), on by Inspiration Point and Pulpit Rock, through the Needle's Eye and Moonshine Cave. This cave was actually used, in the days before the tourists came, by old time blockaders to conceal and operate their illegal whiskey stills.

More than a million people have visited the top of Chimney Rock since Jerome B. Freeman saw its possibilities as an attraction for visitors.

On top of Chimney Rock   (Photo by Barber)

First pavilion at Chimney Rock   (Photo by Barber)

CHAPTER 17

Hamilton Glover Ewart
(1964)

In 1888 the Hon. H. G. Ewart announced that he was a candidate for Congress on the Republican ticket and although the election was almost a year off, H. G. Ewart was already campaigning vigorously in Henderson, Transylvania and adjoining counties. In 1889 Judge Ewart, as he was known in later years, was elected to serve in the Congress of the United States. He was the first person to be elected to that position from Henderson County. Two other men from our county have been elected since that time. They were John Grant, a Republican,[1] and Monroe Redden, Sr., a Democrat.

H. G. Ewart was a well-known and prominent citizen in our town and county in his day. In 1878 he served a term as Mayor of Hendersonville. In 1889 he was elected to Congress and in 1896 and again in 1910 he represented Henderson County in the North Carolina Legislature. He then served as a judge of the North Carolina Superior Court and President McKinley appointed him to serve as a Federal judge.

H. G. Ewart married Sarah Cordelia Ripley, daughter of a pioneer Hendersonville family,[2] and shortly after that he built a beautiful home on a high hill overlooking the town. Old ones still living here still call the location Ewart's Hill. The Judge named his home Dun Cragin and it is still standing. Dun Cragin was a magnificent home and for years was one of the show places of Hendersonville. In late years it was operated as an inn and catered to a select clientele. Today (1964) Dun Cragin is called Golfer's Lodge.

At the foot of the hill below Dun Cragin, the Judge built a pond which has always been referred to as Ewart's Pond. On the stream that fed the pond he built a grist mill to grind the meal and grits for the people of the surrounding area. A large portion of the area at the end of Third and Fourth Avenues West and Ewarts Hill and Pond underwent a certain amount of redevelopment during the real estate boom days of the 1920s and was renamed Temple Terrace.

Hamilton Glover Ewart, better known as Judge H. G. Ewart, who married his step sister, Sarah Cordelia Ripley, died in 1918 while on a visit in the North and his body was brought back to Hendersonville for burial. When Judge Ewart died in 1918, Hendersonville and Henderson County lost one of its most prominent and colorful citizens.

---

[1] Vol. I "Some 19th Century Names to Remember"

[2] Vol. I "Vanished Land Marks"

CHAPTER 18

Joseph Cullen Root

It is literally true that scores of people pass by it everyday with scarcely a glance at it. There are many others who have lived here a lifetime who are unaware of it. It is also true that thousands of us living or visiting here have paused there in the years since it was erected to quench our thirst on a hot summer's day. And of those who do stop to drink the pure mountain water that gushes out of the fountain night and day, few pause to read the inscription on the side of the fountain.

It is the drinking fountain on the corner of Main Street and Second Avenue West in front of the Nuckolls Building. It is carved from native stone, a replica of a portion of the trunk of a large tree. The next time you stop to take a sip of the cold sparkling water, that to the thirsty one is sweeter than ambrosia, do take time to read the inscription chiselled on the side of the fountain: "Near this site Joseph Cullen Root, founder of the Woodmen of the World, died on December 24, 1913. Placed by the local camp of the Woodmen of the World." Also carved on the stone tree trunk is the seal of the Woodmen of the World.

Joseph Cullen Root was born in Chester, Massachusetts on December 3, 1844. Soon after his birth the Root family moved to Illinois where he grew up during the turbulent days just before the War Between the States. During that war he was too young to enlist and he went to college and graduated as the war ended. He had a variety of experiences in the business world, read law and was active in local Illinois politics. The remarkable thing about Joseph Cullen Root was that he was always successful in his endeavors.

While he was president of an Iowa insurance society he envisioned a nationwide fraternal benefit organization. In June, 1890 he invited a small group of men to meet with him at the Paxton Hotel in Omaha, Nebraska. By the time this meeting ended the Woodmen of the World Life Insurance Company had been formed. It has grown into one of the largest fraternal organizations in the United States.

Joseph Cullen Root was elected sovereign commander and retained that office until he died. It was through his inspired leadership and his broad vision that the organization has grown to a membership of approximately a million members. Each group of the Woodmen of the World is called a camp which is named for a tree. The Hendersonville camp is the White Pine Camp which has a large membership.

The space on Main Street where the Nuckolls Building stands today was occupied by a hotel from the birth of Henderson County until it burned in 1915. It started as the Ripley House and through the years was remodeled, enlarged and had a series of names. When it burned in 1915 it was known as the

An early meeting of W.O.W. in Hendersonville   (Photo by Barber)

St. John's Hotel and was Hendersonville's largest and most luxurious with more than 200 rooms and a large dance hall.*

In the winter of 1913 Mr. Root came to Hendersonville on a mission dear to his heart. He wanted to move the home office of the Woodmen of the World from Omaha, Nebraska to Hendersonville. There is a letter in the archives of White Pine Camp #213 written to John T. Wilkins, former Mayor of Hendersonville and a member of W.O.W. Camp 213, in which Mr. Root told of these plans.

That day in December 1913, Mr. Root registered at the St. John's Hotel. He had a severe cold that he contracted on the train from Omaha. As soon as he registered at the hotel he went to bed. A doctor was called and he diagnosed the illness as bronchial pneumonia. Every possible medical treatment known at that time was given the sick man. It was of no avail. He died in his hotel room on the corner of Main Street and Second Avenue on Christmas Eve, 1913.

Soon after this, Hendersonville's White Pine Camp 213, in a joint project with the national organization, unveiled and dedicated this drinking fountain to the memory of Joseph Cullen Root, founder and the first sovereign ruler of Woodmen of the World.

* Vol. I "Vanished Landmarks"

CHAPTER 19

Dr. James Steven Brown

The death of Dr. James Steven Brown on Friday, December 26, 1958, marked the end of an era and a way of life in our Blue Ridge Mountains. Dr. Brown, 92 years old, one of the most beloved and respected of men, put aside his little black satchel after fifty two years as a general practitioner and country doctor in these mountains he knew and loved so well.

They were a rugged type, the family country doctors of the years gone by, and Dr. Brown was one of the most rugged. There are only a few left in the entire United States and he was the last of his kind in our area. When he started to practice medicine here in 1906 there was not a paved street or sidewalk in Hendersonville. The few roads in the rural areas were often impassable during much of the winter except on foot or horseback and the outlying mountainous areas were reached by trails.

Dr. Brown knew Henderson County better than any person during his lifetime because he had visited the sick in all sections and he knew the way to the remotest cabin in the most isolated areas. In the early days he made his calls on horseback and as the roads improved he used a horse and buggy and then the automobile.

Often he would be called to the back regions to administer to a patient or deliver a baby. He would go as far as he could with the transportation available and then would continue up a rough mountainside on foot. Regardless of the hour, the weather or the financial condition of the patient, he never refused a call.

Dr. Brown performed many major operations with only the light of a lantern or coal oil lamp, with the patient lying on a crude kitchen table. He delivered many a baby with only the light from the blaze in the the open fireplace to guide him. He brought 6,547 children into the world. The last one he delivered was on his 92nd birthday in the early morning hours before daybreak.

Years ago I had the only telephone in this section of Blue Ridge Township. Often I would be awakened in the dead of night by a neighbor from the vicinity of Dana, Union Hill, Blue Ridge Post Office and Point Lookout and asked to call Dr. Brown because of an emergency in the family. In zero weather with howling winds, rain, sleet or snow, he would always say, "Tell them I will come as soon as I can get there." And he always did.

And yet with all of his far-reaching practice, he was active throughout his life in religious, fraternal and civic affairs of Hendersonville and Henderson County.

He was always behind any movement that meant the progress of town and county. Even while living, Dr. Brown and the things he did for his fellow man had become legendary. Dr. Steve Brown has gone to his reward in the

Dr. James Steven Brown

great hereafter and everyone knows that his reward will be great. If ever a man lived whose soul overflowed with the milk of human kindness, who loved his God with all his soul and who served his fellow man to the utmost, that man was Dr. James Steven Brown.

CHAPTER 20

C. E. Brooks

The headline in *The Times-News* of one afternoon in October 1966 read: "C. E. Brooks, former Mayor, Dies in Florida." It had significance for only the older ones living in Hendersonville and Henderson County. C. E. Brooks was better known to his friends and acquaintances in our area as Ed Brooks and his life span covered more than 75 years of the progress and development and growth of our town. Ed Brooks played an important part in that achievement.

His parents came to Henderson County when he was still a young boy. His first job was working for Major Theodore G. Barker whose home known as Brookland stood on a high hill overlooking Hendersonville. Maj. Barker was the largest land owner in the county at that time. Ed Brooks labored for the Major as a farm hand, often working ten and twelve hours a day ditching the Mud Creek bottom lands for drainage purposes. The standard pay for such work in those years was 25¢ a day.

It was while working at Brookland that he was attacked by a vicious bull that had gotten loose. His cries for help attracted the attention of others near by who rushed up and drove off the infuriated animal with pitch forks.

Ed Brooks was ambitious. He saved his meager earnings and came to town. He opened a barber shop and it was the first barber shop to have facilities for a customer to take a bath, this in the days when a bathroom was almost unknown even in our best hotels and tourist homes. In the barber shop he installed another innovation for those times: a refreshment stand, selling candy, cigars, cigarettes, chewing tobacco and snuff. Bottled cold drinks had not yet appeared on the market.

So successful was this first enterprise that he soon opened a second shop and refreshment stand. Ed Brooks was on his way and was soon regarded as a rising young businessman. In those days older people used an expression when speaking of a young person who showed promise. They said, "He is a person who will go places." That is what was now being said of Ed Brooks.

While he was making a success with his business activities he was also quietly widening his acquaintances with the people of both the town and county. At the same time he was studying the game of politics.

He was elected Tax Collector for Henderson County, serving one term. Banking was beginning to grow in our area so when his term as Tax Collector expired Ed Brooks started as a clerk in the Peoples National Bank. By 1930 he was executive vice president of the Citizens National Bank. He served as Mayor of Hendersonville from 1915 through 1919. He was Mayor when the Sixth Company, Henderson County's own company of fighting men marched to war in 1917 and he was still Mayor when those men returned after the signing of the Armistice, November 11, 1918.*

Possibly the greatest and longest lasting contribution to our area's growth was made by Ed Brooks when he advocated the source for our city water. He was one of the first persons to promote the Pisgah National Forest as the place to get our city water and was instrumental in pushing the water line from the Pisgah National Forest to a successful construction. He also served for a number of years on the first board of the City Water Commission.

Mr. and Mrs. Brooks and their family were very popular. Each of them had children by a previous marriage. A popular humorous bit of gossip of the early twenties in town was told everywhere. It seems that one day all the Brooks children engaged in a family quarrel. Mrs. Brooks frantically called for help. "Mr. Brooks! Oh, Mr. Brooks! Come here quick and do something! My children and your children are fighting with our children!"

In the middle of the Depression Mr. and Mrs. Brooks moved to Florida to live. He died there October 3, 1966. He was 95 years old and right up to the time of his death he was one of the handsomest men that I have ever known.

CHAPTER 21

Louis Williams

In the issue of October 27, 1971 of *The Times-News*, Hendersonville's daily newspaper, there appeared the following advertisement: "Notice - Louis Williams and Sons, Inc., 701 Seventh Ave. East is no longer buying scrap metal as this division of our business has been discontinued."

From those who have come here to live in recent years, the advertisement possibly received only passing, casual attention and the notice meant little. But to those of us who lived here during the years of the terrible Depression of the 1930s it awakened a deep and sincere feeling of nostalgia because it meant the end of an era in our economy. The buying of scrap metal by Louis Williams had an enormous economic effect on the lives of many who were here during the Depression years.

Behind this advertisement is also the success story of a Polish immigrant

* Vol. I "Fateful Years"

Jew who was born Louis Williamosky and came to America as a young man. He changed his name from Williamosky to Williams because there were few in America who could spell or even pronounce Williamosky.

Louis Williams was born in 1889 in Grodno, Poland. Life for a Jewish family in Poland when Williams was born was harsh and restricted.

In 1907 he came to the United States through the help of an older brother who had also come to America with the aid of an older brother who had come to this country a few years earlier. For a time he worked at whatever odd jobs he could find in and around Abilene, Texas. Life was raw in that western frontier country for anyone and it was even harder and rougher for a newly arrived Polish Jew with no special skills and little knowledge of the language or life in this wild western state.

Then one day in Abilene he met a friend he had known in the old country, Ben Cohen. Louis Williams and Ben Cohen established the Western Iron and Metal Company in Abilene. In the beginning the assets of the company consisted of a cloth sign bearing the name of the company and a small empty rented building. An intangible asset of the Western Iron and Metal Company was the burning ambition of Louis Williams to succeed and the fact that the two young partners were not afraid of hard work. Slowly but surely, after months of back breaking work, the business began to grow and prosper.

It was then that Louis Williams made a trip to New York to visit relatives. There he met the charming and pretty girl who was soon to be his wife. He returned to Abilene and built a house. He furnished it and sent to New York for the lovely young lady, Minnie Goldstein, to come to Texas. Louis and Minnie were married in their own home and it was here in Abilene and in this same house that their first child, Jacob, was born.

In 1919 the family moved to Detroit, Michigan where Louis Williams was engaged in the real estate business for a short period of time, and where another son was born whom the family named Sam. In 1920 he went back to Poland to visit relatives and while he was there the Bolshevik Revolution occurred. He was caught in the upheaval and for more than a year nothing was heard from or about him. The only news out of Poland were the horror stories of the persecutions of the Jews.

But Louis Williams was a resourceful man. He managed to survive and returned to America, bringing with him other members of his family. One of them was his sister, Mrs. Morris Weisberg, who lives here in Hendersonville. The hardships of the Bolshevik Revolution broke his health and he was now a sick man. The doctors advised the Williams family to move to Western North Carolina, preferably to the Asheville area. There now were three children: Jake, Sam and their sister, Anne, who became Mrs. Morris Kaplan.

The year 1922 found the family in Asheville and there Louis established Williams Men Shop on Biltmore Avenue. Then came the land boom of the Roaring Twenties and Hendersonville was the center of the real estate explosion. He sold his business in Asheville and in 1926 the family came to Hendersonville. Like so many, he was going to make his fortune in the

Mr. and Mrs. Louis Williams – 1966   (Photo by Barber)

escalating real estate market. For a time it looked as if his dreams would come true.

Then the boom collapsed. Louis Williams and hundreds of others lost everything.* He managed to borrow $200 and opened a small junk yard. He began to buy scrap metal at his business on Seventh Avenue East. The firm grew from the beginning and began to expand. Used auto parts, new automobile parts and glass were added to the business. In 1937 a plumbing division was added, then structural steel. From a small lot where he started to buy and trade in scrap metal, his business has expanded until it occupies an entire block of Seventh Avenue.

Older ones living here will remember the Henry Hyder building, Brown's Cafe, Harry Hill's chicken house, the Pace building, Walt Hyder's garage; all

* Vol. I "The Roaring 20s"

now replaced by Louis Williams and Sons. Now Jake and Sam were members of the firm along with Morris Kaplan.

The years brought prosperity. Louis Williams began to turn more and more responsibilities over to the junior members but he remained active even as he grew older. He found time to make a trip to Israel and the Holy Land.

Louis Williams died in June 1971. He was 82 years old. He had forty five successful years in Henderson County. He was an outstanding citizen of Western North Carolina.

CHAPTER 22

A Friend In Need

Louis Williams started his junk yard with $200 that he borrowed after losing everything in the collapsed land boom of the Roaring Twenties. Little did any of us living here at the time realize what lay ahead of us. All banks had closed, people were out of work, wages were 7½¢ to 10¢ an hour if a body could find a job. Many people who were able to find jobs on a farm were working for these wages and were taking their pay in chickens, eggs, potatoes or any farm produce that could be eaten because there was little or no cash in Hendersonville or Henderson County. The banks had closed in 1930, never to open again. The Depression was on.

Louis Williams' scrap yard began to grow until it extended from Beech Street to Ashe Street. Black and white, young and old, men, women and children were searching the town and county for scrap metal of all kinds. Iron, brass, aluminum, copper, jar lids, cast off farm machinery; the word had gone out that Louis Williams was paying cash money for such material. For several years there was a parade from early morning to late at night. Streams of people converged on the junk yard. The scrap metal was brought in horse drawn wagons and carts, broken down Model T Ford automobiles. Some brought the scrap metal in toe sacks across their shoulders. There were rickety wagons made at home with roller skates for wheels. I remember vividly a little old red tin wagon pulled by a mangy billy goat. The wagon would be piled high with junk of every description and headed down Seventh Avenue toward the junk yard several times a day.

It was the worst period of the Depression years and this was the main source of cash money for many people. Prominent citizens living here today were among those who gathered scrap metal; the only way to get money to buy groceries. There are grown ones today who as children earned their first money selling scrap to Louis Williams.

The Depression ended with World War II and in the years that followed,

Louis Williams' business grew and prospered and expanded with many new departments. An era ended when the scrap iron division was closed. Urban renewal has taken over the site of the original scrap metal yard. Soon only the old ones will remember the part that Louis Williams played in the economy of our county when hard times were on us. He built a successful career based on honesty, integrity and fair dealing in a time of adversity. Louis Williams was a man who above all else, regardless of color or creed, loved his fellow man.

Part Four
A Family Chronicle

Part Four
A Family Chronicle

CHAPTER 23

The Reese Family

They were early rulers of that country known to you and me as Wales. The family dates back to antiquity. The Welch spelling of the name Reese in those ancient days was Rhys. Long after the Norman invasion of England and William the Conqueror had subdued the Anglo-Saxons, the Welch people under Rhys leadership were still resisting the Norman-French invaders.

The date on the family coat of arms under the original spelling of Rhys is 1171. Sometime during the centuries following 1171 the Welsh family married with the English branch of the family which lived just across the border from Wales because the next date on the coat of arms is 1599 and the spelling of the family name had taken the English version which was Rees. In 1700 the Rev. Mr. David Rees, a Presbyterian minister from Wales, came to America. Since that time the name has been spelled Reese, as it is today in Western North Carolina. But through the years to the present day, there have been many variations of spelling the name in the many branches of this large family.

A son of the first David Reese who came to America was also named David and it was this second David Reese who was one of the signers of the Mecklenburg Declaration of Independence in Charlotte, May 20, 1775. The Reese family is spread through all of Western North Carolina and it is a prominent family in Henderson County.

On August 7, 1807 a baby was born in South Carolina and was named William Reese. The exact year this baby came to what is now Henderson County is not known but it was not too long after 1807 because family tradition tells that William Reese was brought here as a very young child. William lived in or near the village of Sumter and was troubled with asthma from birth. The doctor advised the mother, Mrs. David Reese, that a higher altitude would help the child.

Mrs. Reese had a son by a previous marriage who owned an inn that was a stagecoach stop on the original Buncombe Turnpike near where the little village of Mountain Home is now. Mrs. Reese brought the young child William over the crude, rough roads of that time to the inn operated by Ben Richardson, the half brother. William Reese was the first Reese to come to live in what is now Henderson County.

The mountain air and altitude did prove beneficial and William grew strong and sturdy as the years went by and he became a man of parts, highly respected by his pioneer neighbors who were beginning to settle this wilderness area.

From ancient times in Wales the Rhys clan, now spelled Reese in Western North Carolina, had been master craftsmen, workers in iron and other metals, artisans skillful in the use of their hands. At an early age it became apparent that William Reese had inherited the skill and ability of his Welch ancestors.

In the pioneer days in these mountains, one of the most highly respected of men in any community was the blacksmith, a skilled craftsman to whom all turned for aid. As a young man William Reese bought land on the Howard Gap Road. There he built his log house and set up a blacksmith shop, one of the first in our county. William Reese then married Margaret Caroline Plumblee, the daughter of an early settler in the Fletcher area who gave the land where Patty's Chapel was built and where the cemetery is still used.*

The young couple worked hard. The fame of the skill of William Reese spread because he was equally as good working with wrought iron, copper, brass and wood as he was with general black smithing. As the years went by William and his wife bought land at every opportunity until they owned property that ran all the way from Featherstone Creek, where it crosses the Howard Gap Road, to the top of Couch Mountain.

During these years William and Caroline Reese raised a family of six boys and three girls. While William was busy at his forge Caroline was raising the family of nine children. Caroline Reese was also overseeing and managing farm operations on their increasing land holdings. William Reese established a grain mill on Featherstone Creek to grind the corn, wheat, barley and rye for his neighbors. He then built one of the first saw mills run by water power. The Reese Mills were long a landmark in their area of Henderson County and are still remembered by a few of the old ones still living because the grain mill continued to be operated by William and Caroline's son James.

For the times, William Reese was considered a learned man and he believed in education. One of the first rural schools in Henderson County was built on land given by William and Caroline. It was called the Reese School and was attended by students until consolidation of our county schools in the late 1920s closed the little school forever.

During all of those years and despite his many activities in the years before the War Between the States, William Reese was serving as commander of a company of state militia. When the war started in 1861 he was too old for military duty. In his place, three of his boys fought in the Confederate Army: James, who operated Reese Mill after the War; Henry, who gave his life; and William, who returned home at war's end and became a doctor.

As soon as the pioneer settlers in these mountains cleared the land and built their log houses, their most important task was to clear and plant their patches of land to raise food for their families and livestock through the long

* Vol. II "Mysteries"

cold winter months. The only farm tools they possessed were the ax, the adz, and the hoe. Fortunate was the settler who had an ox and a bull tongue plow to scratch the soil. Many of the crude implements were made of hard wood. Some few were tipped with soft wrought iron. William Reese, pioneer master craftsman, is credited with making the first metal mole board turning plow to be used in Henderson County.

William Reese, whose ancestors of royal blood ruled the land of ancient Wales, one of the first blacksmiths to set his anvil and forge in what is now Henderson County, a man who contributed much to the early development of this area, died in 1885. He lies peacefully in his grave in Patty's Chapel Community.

CHAPTER 24

Some Reese Descendants
(1963)

About the time William Reese built his log cabin and blacksmith shop on the Howard Gap Road, another pioneer took up land on the same road. His name was Bradley Johnson and the acres he acquired joined the land of William Reese. Bradley Johnson married one of the Plumblee girls, even as William Reese had done. Bradley Johnson and his wife operated a large inn built of logs and it became a famous stopping place to pen and feed the large droves and flocks of livestock and fowl from Kentucky and Tennessee on the way to market in the Carolina and Georgia low country.*

This old inn was built in 1833 and it was a landmark until it was demolished in the early 1960s. The tall rock gate posts and the huge old English boxwoods are all that were left to mark the place. Charlotte Johnson, daughter of Bradley Johnson, married Samuel Stroup. Samuel and Charlotte Stroup became the parents of Joseph Stroup. Mary, the oldest daughter of William Reese, married James Dunlap and they became the parents of Carrie Dunlap. Joseph Stroup, grandson of Bradley Johnson, married Carrie Dunlap, who was the granddaughter of William Reese. This was a romance of our Blue Ridge Mountains that lasted for six decades. In 1963 Mr. and Mrs. Stroup were still living on part of the original land of their pioneer ancestors.

In November 1963, I visited Mr. and Mrs. Stroup to talk to them about their pioneer ancestors, Bradley Johnson and William Reese. At the time of my visit they were well past the allotted three score and ten years and were living in semi-retirement after a lifetime of activity in the agricultural, civic and religious life of our county. Still in use on the Stroup farm were wrought iron gates and door hinges, gate latches and other artifacts made more than a

* Vol. "Stories These Mountains Could Tell"

55

century ago on the forge and anvil by William Reese out of iron ore mined on Forge Mountain.*

In the early days the mountain blacksmiths had no coal so they used charcoal to heat the metals to be worked. Mr. and Mrs. Stroup pointed out the pit where William Reese made his own charcoal. Traces of the ashes from the old blacksmith shop could still be seen.

After an enjoyable hour spent with Mr. and Mrs. Stroup, I drove back to Hendersonville and stopped at the home of James Reese on Highland Ave. James Reese inherited the skill of his grandfather and his Welch ancestors of ancient times. He was a master carpenter and cabinet maker, as many houses he built and cabinets he fashioned will attest.

Jim Reese had in his workshop (in 1963) the first iron moldboard plow used in Henderson County, made by his ancestor from iron ore dug on Forge Mountain. Wooden pins made from locust and hand-forged nails and bolts held the plow together. Crude in comparison to our modern steel plows, this ancient plow in its day reflected the skill of the maker. It was then a wondrous thing that speeded the advancement of our agriculture.

CHAPTER 25

The Dufour House

The records of Henderson County show that in August 1883, A. Dufour and wife, Marie M. Dufour, bought a large tract of land along the French Broad River from G. H. Trenholm, Mary E. Ladson, D. R. Myers and A. L. McCall. Mr. and Mrs. Dufour were from Geneva, Switzerland and the initial A. was for his first name which was Alfred. Sometime ago, through a mutual friend, I was given the address of Mr. Harry Morton, a grandson of Mr. and Mrs. Alfred Dufour who once lived in the French Broad Valley. Mr. Morton, the grandson, now lives in France on the edge of Switzerland. In response to my inquiry Mr. Morton gave me this information about the Dufours.

"The Dufour family is quite an ancient one, tracing its ancestors back to the 14th Century which would be more than 600 years. The family is descended from Girard du Four of Dom Martin, Canton de Vaud of Switzerland. Girard held the village oven for the chapter of Lausanne. This was a feudal right handed down from generation to generation. The people of the village were compelled to bake their bread in the village oven for which they paid a fee. Girard collected the fee, took his commission and passed the remainder to the proper authorities.

"Girard was a commonly used Christian name in Switzerland six or seven hundred years ago. DuFour is the Swiss-French meaning in English 'of

* Vol. II "Mysteries"

the oven.' Hence the beginning of that family named Girard du Four. This translated into English is 'Girard of the Oven.'

"The family, through the past six or seven centuries, became notaries, magistrates, local councillors, priests and land owners of Dom Martin. One of the ancestors of Alfred Dufour held a commission in the Swiss Guards of the King of France and was killed in the massacre of the Swiss Guards in the Revolution in 1784.

"Alfred Dufour was born in 1840, the son of Claude Dufour, at the family estate at Mont Cherand, Canton of Vaud in Switzerland. When he was a teenage boy he visited the United States and became strongly attracted by the country. He returned to Switzerland and became a successful lawyer, a poet, a member of the Grand Council of his canton. When he was a young man he successfully fought several duels."

There are times when a family from a long distance away will move into a community. That family will live there for a short time and depart, never to return, yet it will leave an impression that will last long after its departure.

Such a family was that of Alfred Dufour which came from Switzerland to the French Broad - Mills River Valley in 1883, lived there for ten or twelve years and then departed.

When you drive out Highway 191, which is locally referred to as the Mills River Road or the Haywood Road, you cross the French Broad River. On the right hand side of the road was a large white two story farm house. In 1968 the late Guy Jaynes lived in it. (The house in late years has been torn down.) The Jaynes family owned the house and farmed the land. Guy Jaynes and his brothers Edgar and Arthur were raised there as was their sister, a Mrs. Hall who operated the store and Sinclair service station next to the big old house.

Before the Jaynes family acquired the property the house was owned and lived in by another prominent family, the Francis family. Bob Francis, a retired New York executive, his brother William Francis, owner and operator of Francis and Wright, and their sister, Margaret, the wife of Jean Williams, retired executive of the Duke Power Company, were raised in that old white farm house.

They lived there when they attended Mills River High School and later when they came to Hendersonville High School by bus in 1921 and 1922. This was after the high school at Mills River had burned and was being rebuilt.

All of this that I have written happened over a period of three quarters of a century since the Dufour family left the area but the house where they lived was still referred to as the Dufour house and property until it was torn down.

Alfred Dufour and his beautiful wife Marie Maure Dufour brought their son Jules Claude Dufour and their daughter Marguerite with them when they came to the Mills River farm. Soon after coming to Henderson County, Mr. Dufour became seriously ill but finally recovered. He made no attempt to operate the large farm that he bought but was content to live the life of a well to do gentleman of that period.

Highly educated and cultured, he delivered lectures on literary subjects and spent much time translating French and Swiss literature into English during the years here. It is possible that the family became homesick and yearned too strongly for the old country because in 1896 they returned to Switzerland. They settled in Geneva where Mr. Dufour became a professor at the University of Geneva. He died there in 1915.

Although the Dufour family returned to Europe in 1896 the records at the Court House show that they did not sell the property here in Henderson County until 1901.

CHAPTER 26

The Levi Family

A short distance south of Cedar Springs Baptist Church a stream of water rises and meanders through a beautiful area in the southern part of Henderson County. In its course the stream flows in a southerly direction, then east for quite a distance, then north until it empties into Green River not too far from the Highway 25 bridge below Tuxedo. A road parallels the stream from its source to its mouth. The creek is known as Bob's Creek and the road is Bob's Creek Road.

The Bob's Creek Valley is narrow and the fields along its banks are small but extremely fertile. The drive through the Green River Valley and the Bob's Creek Valley is beautiful at any season of the year. The Bob's Creek area is famous for the finest flavored pole beans that are raised. Bob's Creek and Green River pole beans are in demand all through the southern states during the growing season. The two valleys produce most of the pole beans that are raised in Henderson County.

Just south of Bob's Creek Panther Mountain rises to an altitude of 2,800 feet and Corbin Mountain towers slightly over 3,000 feet. The two mountains are separated by Panther Gap. The view from either mountain is magnificent. Corbin Mountain has a fire observation tower which serves both North and South Carolina. The state lines cross both mountains.

In this area that is bounded by Bob's Creek on three sides and Green River on the northern side lives one of the large families of Henderson County that began with one man and his wife, early settlers whose descendants have spread over Western North Carolina, South Carolina and Texas. The Levi family is one of the most interesting, intriguing and fascinating families in the county. There is an aura of romantic mystery surrounding them. While there are Levis and Levi descendants in other parts of Henderson County, this family for more than a century and a half has populated the same area of Bob's Creek and its vicinity, where it started. In fact, Bob's Creek and Levi are almost synonymous and it is a person ignorant of our county heritage if the mention of one of these names does not immediately bring to his mind the other.

The Levi family and Bob's Creek have been woefully neglected in what has been written and recorded in the years gone by. In research it has been impossible to find much information. As a result, many legends and traditions about this family have emerged through generations. These have been handed down and have become interwoven with the known facts. It is hard now to tell fact from fiction, as each branch of the family has their own versions. The stories are always interesting but do not always agree. There is one legend that all branches of this family do agree on and about which every Levi or Levi descendant that I have ever talked to is extremely proud. The first person by the name of Levi to come into the Bob's Creek area of Henderson County was a Jew from the city of London, England.

Long before the time of Christ, the sons of the tribe of Jacob were those of the children of Israel whose duties were taking care of the sacred utensils and vessels of the temple. As time went by a Jewish priest became known as a Levi. The best known Levi of all time was the patriarch Moses who led the children of Israel out of bondage from Egypt. As the children of Israel moved westward and into the British Isles, the priest or rabbi became known as a Levi. It was natural when family names were being developed in England for Levi to become a family name.

One story is that the first Levi to come to America was with the British Army under Major Ferguson. He was captured by the American colonists at the Battle of Kings Mountain, escaped and traveled west until he came to the Bob's Creek area and settled. He is supposed to have married a Gentile girl.

Another legend is that there were two Jewish brothers from London, England. When they came to America soon after the end of the Revolutionary War they landed in Charleston, S. C. There they invested what money they had in cheap jewelry, trinkets, ribbons and such. They started walking through South Carolina as pack peddlers. One of the Levi brothers stopped and settled in what is now the Pickens area of South Carolina and established the South Carolina branch of the Levi family. The other brother is said to have continued on until he reached the vicinity of Bob's Creek where he married a Gentile and established the Bob's Creek branch of the family.

These two accounts have been handed down through many generations and there seem to be no recorded facts to substantiate either legend or variation of the two legends. This is the one that is generally accepted as true and has been substantiated by known facts, family and Bible records and old letters.

John Levi served in the British Army as a drum major. When his time of service was ended he was still a young man. He came to Charleston, South Carolina. He did some extensive traveling in those early years soon after he landed in Charleston. It is known that at least twice he came through South Carolina into the mountains of Western North Carolina and on one of these trips he met and married Sarah Bailey. As we shall see, this was the beginning of the Levi family in Henderson County although it would be a number of years before it was established.

It is known that soon after his marriage John Levi went to Texas and fought under General Sam Houston for Texas independence from Mexico. He also served in the United States Army with the rank of captain against Mexico when those two countries fought in the middle 1840s. For his services Captain John Levi was granted a large boundary of land in the Rio Grande River area and from that period on he was always referred to as Captain John Levi.

Capt. John Levi did not like the hot flat Texas country and soon sold or traded his land. Records show that his Texas land grant was the land that the town of Brownsville, Texas was later built on.

The next we hear of Capt. John Levi was when he came back to Charleston and then headed for the mountains. He found himself on the top of Panther Mountain where he built his home and acquired not only Panther Mountain but a large section of the Bob's Creek Valley. This was in the late 1840s or early 1850s.

It is presumed that soon after his marriage to the Gentile Sarah Bailey and while still in Texas he and Sarah started a family because by 1861 they had five sons old enough to fight in the War of the Secession when North Carolina joined the Confederacy.

On Panther Mountain Capt. John and Sarah Bailey Levi raised five sons and a daughter. There was Wade Hampton Levi, Johnnie Levi who was killed at the Battle of Gettysburg, Calvin Levi who married Margaret Batson, Robert Perry Levi whose son was Zebulon Vance Levi. Zebulon Vance Levi was the father of Ben Levi who operated an automobile business in Hendersonville and now lives here in retirement. Lafayette Levi married Francis Beddingfield and had five sons and two daughters. The sons were Ezekial, Robert Hampton, David, Carter and Wacinirva, called W. C. The girls were Mary and Arcida.

Robert Hampton Levi was the father of Fannie Levi who married Clyde R. Morgan. A son of Robert Hampton Levi was Robert Glenn Levi who was killed in World War II. The Levi family is proud of their record: there have been descendants of Capt. John Levi in the armed forces of the United States in every war since the Captain fought for the independence of Texas and against Mexico.

Clyde R. and Fannie Levi Morgan live in the Green River Valley near the Green River Baptist Church. Mr. Morgan's grandfather, Frank Pace, a Confederate soldier, died in a prisoner of war camp in Douglass, Illinois, where nearly 10,000 other Confederate prisoners perished.

I recently paid a visit to the home of Mr. and Mrs. Morgan to obtain information about the area and the family. Mr. and Mrs. Morgan at one point in our conversation took me into the living room of their home. They quietly pointed out to me a bust of the Hebrew Patriarch Moses. It was a replica of

60

Michelangelo's famous statue of Moses. Their daughter Evangeline had married Don Freeman and had lived several years in Italy where Mr. Freeman was an electrical engineer with Westinghouse. While in Rome she had visited the Sistine Chapel in the Vatican where the original Michelangelo's statue of Moses can be seen.

Evangeline Morgan Freeman had been startled because the head, face and features of Moses looked exactly like those of her mother's grandfather, Lafayette Levi, in a picture which the family possesses.

Mr. and Mrs. Morgan have a son, Robert Ray Morgan who is a professor of creative writing at Cornell University in Ithaca, New York. He holds a master's degree of fine arts and has written and published several books of poems. The titles are "Zirconia Poems," "Red Owl," "Land Diving," and "The Small Farm." Copies of these books are in the Henderson County Public Library.

Capt. John Levi was a large man physically. He had to be because he started as a drum major in the British Army and a man had to be big to hold such a rank. His Gentile wife was a pretty woman with delicate features. Although Capt. John Levi is the only ancestor of Jewish extraction in the Henderson County Levi family, the patriarch left his physical characteristics for his descendants. That is the reason that through the five or more generations of descendants from the Jewish Captain Levi and his Gentile wife Sarah Bailey, all of the women who have Levi blood in their veins have been pretty and attractive. They have inherited to the present day the delicate refined features of Sarah Levi stamped with the Hebrew facial characteristics of Captain John Levi.

The most widely known member of the Levi family in Henderson County and one of the most popular is Elden Leland Levi, Jr. He is the son of Elden Leland and Ezma Laughter Levi and is better known as "Smokey" Levi. He is a master tonsorial artist, operating his famed establishment on Church Street.

"Smokey" Levi is a direct descendant of Captain John Levi who was his great, great grandfather. His great grandfather was the Confederate veteran Calvin Levi and his grandfather was Frank. As this is being written in the spring of 1979, Elden Leland Levi, Jr. is a ruggedly handsome man in middle years of life, black hair and clean shaven.

In the years to come, as a body strolls down Church Street in Hendersonville, he will see a gray haired man with a flowing, luxurious beard sitting on the green bench in front of Bob Freeman's News Stand. The old gentleman will have the benevolent dignity of a patriarch. A closer look will show a striking resemblance of the dignified old gentleman on the bench to the Michaelangelo sculpture of Moses that rests in the Sistine Chapel in the Vatican in Rome. And then a body will recognize a friend of many years. It will be "Smokey" Levi.

Lafayette Levi   (Photo compliments of Mr. & Mrs. Clyde Morgan)

Part Five
War & Peace

Part Five

War and Peace

CHAPTER 27

A Time of Terror
(1979)

Lindsey Baker Anders was a mountain man in that period of unrest prior to the War between the States. Like so many men here in Henderson County and the other counties of Western North Carolina, he sincerely believed in the dignity of the individual and the freedom of man. It was natural that he and so many other men of his time who were opposed to slavery liked the way the young Illinois lawyer, Abraham Lincoln, talked. And when he ran for the office of President of these United States and preached the freedom of man, Lindsey Anders voted for Lincoln and he opposed slavery and the secession of the Southern states from the Union.

When the war started Lindsey Baker Anders and his wife Nancy Capps Anders had seven children, but his state was calling. He answered that call and joined the Confederate Army. Soon after he marched off to defend his homeland, a baby was born and the mother named it Elbert Lindsey and Elbert Linsey Anders became the eighth child in the family.

Nancy Anders had a hard time for the next several years providing for her family. Her oldest son was a frail, sickly boy. unable to help much with the farm work. Mrs. Anders and the younger children worked the farm which was located in the Echo Mountain area of what is now part of Laurel Park. Many were the nights when the family went to bed exhausted from the hard grueling work with hunger gnawing at their stomachs.

It was during this time and until the war was finished that the people in Henderson County were robbed and continuously harassed by lawless bands of renegades. These gangs combed the countryside looking for anything of value that they could steal: gold, silver, food, horses, cattle and hogs.* When not in the fields her only horse was kept hidden in a thicket and only Nancy Anders knew where she kept hidden the few gold coins she possessed.

Mrs. Sadie Anders Williams, granddaughter of Nancy Anders, told me what happened as it was told to her by her grandmother.

"One day a band of lawless men rode to the farm and surrounded the cabin. My grandmother saw them coming and called the children to hide what food they could in the loft of the cabin. The men had attempted to disguise

* Vol. I "The War Between the States"

themselves by blacking their faces but my grandmother recognized the leader as a seemingly respectable man in the community.''

"The horse hidden in the thicket neighed and was easily found. The smoke house and pantry were stripped of all the food they contained. The bushwhackers demanded money, ransacked the house and found a tin box with valuable papers but no money, gold or otherwise. The leader jerked Mrs. Anders out of the doorway.''

'Woman! I know you have money! I know it is gold! Tell us where you have hidden it or we will hang your son standing there by you!'

"The boy standing by his mother was Frank Anders, her oldest son, only 14 years old, but the one she depended on since her husband had departed to fight.''

"The leader went to the bed where the baby was asleep and threw baby, covering and mattress on the floor while the mother pleaded with him not to kill the infant.''

'I'm only looking for a rope to hang your son, Frank,' "the leader of the band growled.''

"The outlaw leader ordered the men to mount their horses with all of their loot with the boy Frank marching ahead of them, the outlaw band disappeared over the hill with a final threat. 'When you hear a gun fire you will know your boy is dead, because we will shoot the rope from around his neck when we have finished hanging him.'''

"There in her log cabin, Nancy Capps Anders clutched her baby in her arms. The children huddled around her, the terrified woman waited fearfully. She was praying that she would not hear the shot that heralded her son's death. Then in the distance she heard not the sound of one gun shot but several in rapid succession. The woman sank to the ground sobbing bitterly.''

"How much time passed she never knew. Then she was startled by the hysterical voices of the children.'' 'Ma! Ma! There comes Frank! Ma! Ma! He's all right!'

'They just hung me by my thumbs to make me tell where the gold was hid,' "he panted when he could catch his breath.'' 'When I told them I didn't know they shot the rope in two and let me come back.'''

"The few coins of gold had been hidden beneath the house under a loose brick in the base of the chimney, near where a small flock of chickens roosted at night out of the weather.''

While all this was happening to his family, Lindsey Baker Anders was fighting in the battles of northern Virginia. He was captured by the Yankees and sent to a prisoner of war camp in New York state. Soon after this the war ended. Lindsey Anders was released, sent by train to Salisbury, N.C. From there he walked home.

He finally arrived at his cabin on the side of Echo Mountain with frost bitten feet and there he saw for the first time his son who had been born just after Mr. Anders marched off to war. The baby boy had been named Elbert Lindsey Anders but like his father he went through life called Lindsey.

The Confederate veteran was happy to find his family had survived the war because of the strength and courage of his wife and children.

Some twelve years after his return home, he sold his farm on Echo Mountain and bought a tract of land along Finley Creek in the Valley Hill section of Henderson County. He bought the land from the State of North Carolina, paying 30¢ an acre for it. It was on this land that the baby boy Lindsey was raised to manhood, fell in love and married Lucy King, his childhood sweetheart.

Lindsey Anders, a son of the Confederacy, inherited a part of his father's Valley Hill land and lived on it until his death in 1935. His bride, Lucy King Anders, was 95 years old at her death.

Four of the grandchildren of Lindsey Baker Anders who are the children of Elbert Lindsey Anders live to this day in March 1979 on portions of this land for which their grandfather paid 30¢ an acre. They are: Mrs. Sadie Anders Williams, Mrs. Madge Anders Edney, Mrs. Ada Anders Brittain and Homer Anders.

CHAPTER 28

A Time of Rejoicing
(1957)

George Potts was a happy man that year following the spring of 1865 because he was a free man, now that the fratricidal war had ended. He savored his freedom much more than you and I who take our freedom for granted. George Potts had spent his life in bondage; it was possible for him to be bought, sold or traded as chattel. The bondage of George Potts and several million others had ended when General Lee surrendered at Appomatox Court House.

George Potts had further reason to be happy because Lavinia Moultrie looked on him with favor; Lavinia with the snapping, sparkling eyes and the cheerful smile, the willing hands when it came to work, the comeliest girl in the settlement and already famous around Flat Rock for the delicious rusk that she cooked. That delectable sweet bread was enjoyed at breakfast and supper by past generations but alas is no longer seen on our Southern tables.

And so George and Lavinia were married in the parlor at Glenroy, one of the oldest estates at Flat Rock, the home of Dr. Mitchell King.* Glenroy was long known as Kenmure and was the home of the late Gordon McCabe, Jr. It is now being developed as a golf and residential area.

The young couple were married by the rector of St. John in the Wilderness. George and Lavinia Potts went to live on the flat land on top of Glassy

* Vol. I "Some 19th Century Names to Remember"

George Potts   (Photo compliments of Potts family)

Lavinia Potts (wife of George)   (Photo compliments of Potts family)

Mountain, eighty five acres they had managed to buy through the help of Judge King.

George Potts felled the trees, hewed the logs with an adz and built a log cabin and covered the roof with hand-split, white oak shingles. With the help of Lavinia, he laid out roads, cleared the land and tilled it with oxen. The long years that followed 1865 was a hard life but a happy one because George and Lavinia Potts were free and their children, ten in number, were born free. With the money they saved they came off of Glassy Mountain and bought fifty five acres of land in East Flat Rock. That land is still owned and lived on by the descendants of the hard working couple.

I knew George and Lavinia Potts in my young days when they had grown old. Though they are now dead these many years, I can still taste the delicious rusk that she fed me when I visited at their home. They led a full and worthwhile life and, as leaders and advisors of people of their race, were held in high esteem by all.

Their son and my good friend Fred Potts went with me to Glassy Mountain where I saw the roads, now abandoned, that were built by his father using oxen and a drag pan. I saw the fields cleared and farmed by George and Lavinia Potts that are now grown up in timber, and I saw the large piles of rock picked up in the fields by Fred and his brothers and sisters to make cultivation easier for their parents. This was in 1957 and the hand hewed log cabin was still standing but time and the elements were rapidly taking their toll.

I spied in the undergrowth and picked a sweet smelling moss rose and saw a few others blooming, tame flowers, planted there decades ago by loving and free hands. All of this had now returned to wilderness but the memory of George and Lavinia Potts lives on in the hearts of those who knew them, a family that made the most of their opportunities.

CHAPTER 29

A Faded Photograph
(1961)

The picture was old because it was taken in 1904 but the people in it and the building that it was taken in front of would be much older if they were still in existence. Yet the picture covers a period of the history of our area that is rapidly being forgotten except by the oldest ones now living and soon they will be gone and all will be forgotten except what I am recording in this chapter.

The scene was in front of Hendersonville's first City Hall and Opera House that stood on the east side of Main Street between Fourth and Fifth Avenues where the J. C. Penney Company's store building is today.* Mrs.

* Vol. I "Vanished Landmarks"

Confederate Veterans' Reunion
(Photo compliments Miss Martha Shepherd)

John Francis, who before her marriage was Minnie Potts, showed me the picture. It is a photograph of the Confederate veterans of Hendersonville and Henderson County who were attending the Confederate Veterans' Reunion of 1904. All of the old soldiers and the City Hall and Opera House are gone now.

As Mrs. Francis and I looked at it, nostalgic memories were kindled. She and I were able to identify a large number of them we remembered and who were prominent in the affairs of our area in the years following the War Between the States and many of whose descendants still live here.

The Confederate veterans in the picture of 1904 stand proud and erect even though 39 years had gone by since General Lee had surrendered at Appomatox. When the picture was taken some of the old soldiers needed the help of walking canes and practically every man in the picture had a flowing white beard and the few who did not have beards had luxurious moustaches.

Well remembered in 1961 by older ones living here was Jesse Shepherd who was wounded in the head at the Battle of Chancellorsville and left for dead on the field of battle. But it took more than a minnie ball from a Yankee gun to end the life of the young Confederate mountain man from Henderson County. Jesse Shepherd recovered, returned home at the end of the war and was active in city and county affairs for a long number of years.

One of his sons was M. M. Shepherd, a pioneer merchant of our town who operated a general merchandise store in the building on the corner of First Avenue East and Main Street, the oldest building in the city until it was torn down.*

Another son, Thomas Shepherd, established the Shepherd and Son

* Vol. I "Vanished Landmarks"

Jesse Merrill Shepherd at Age 47   (Photo compliments of Cecil Kessler)

funeral home that is now operated by the third generation of the family. V. C. V. Shepherd, known to his friends as Vol, was long active in the political and business affairs of both the town and county. All of the sons of Jesse Shepherd and his daughter, Mrs. Kate Bowen, are now dead.

Jesse Shepherd, the stalwart Confederate veteran who carried the Yankee minnie ball lodged in his skull until the day of his death, had many grandchildren: William Shepherd, Martha Shepherd, Mrs. Nanna Shepherd West, Mrs. Cecil Kessler, who for many years was librarian at Hendersonville High School; and Mrs. James T. Fain, Jr. All were the children of Mr. and Mrs. Thomas Shepherd. Miss Catherine Shepherd, Ruth Shepherd, Louise Shepherd and John Patton Shepherd were the children of Mr. and Mrs. M. M. Shepherd. The children of Mr. and Mrs. V. C. V. Shepherd were Arthur Shepherd, who was City Attorney for many years; Mrs. Hazel Shepherd Shannhouse of Charlotte, M. M. Shepherd also of Charlotte and Mrs. Marian Shepherd White of Jacksonville, Florida.

Samuel Hardin who fought in the three day Battle of Gettysburg has two granddaughters living here: Mrs. Virginia Wright Harrell and Mrs. Lula Wright Jones. Nancy Hardin Dotson who is with the county school system is a grand-niece of Samual Hardin. Virginia Harrell has a large picture on one of the walls of her home that is 51 inches by 33 inches in size. It is a print of a panoramic view of General Longstreet's repulse at the Battle of Gettysburg in which her grandfather fought.

Another one of the veterans that we recognized in the old picture was Captain Tom Shipman. Capt. Shipman lived to a ripe old age and was active mentally and physically to the time of his death. He was the father of Jim Shipman, one of Hendersonville's leading attorneys for over half a century. He was also the father of Mrs. Kate Durham who has for many years been a leader in the Daughters of the Confederacy.

Captain W. Preston Lane lived on the corner of the Chimney Rock and Dana Roads. Although Capt. Shipman and Capt. Lane were near the same age and served in the same army and war, Capt. Shipman became the father in law of Capt. Lane.

During the 1920s Capt. Lane lived on the Chimney Rock Road and Capt. Shipman lived with his daughter and son-in-law, Mr. and Mrs. R. P. Freeman, on the Sugar Loaf Road. Although the two old veterans were advanced in age they were both still active. Regularly, during good weather, they would meet at Harrison Brown's country store at the junction of the Chimney Rock Road and Sugar Loaf Road. Each time they met there they would spend the morning reliving their experiences in that far off war and comparing the activities and glories of their respective companies. Sometimes their arguments would become quite heated and the old soldiers would get so mad they would shake their walking sticks at each other as they hurled verbal threats. People in the community would often stop by Brown's store to hear the old soldiers argue and quarrel and to listen to their accounts of the terrible conflict. No matter how violently the two old soldiers disagreed, the daily meetings always ended peacefully with each agreeing to meet again the next pretty day.

From the Mills River Valley in the picture was Dr. Lister L. Johnson. Dr. "Lis" Johnson, was known far and wide. He became a doctor following his return from the battlefields and was beloved through his many years of practicing medicine. This was in the days when doctors were scarce and the rural doctor found his patients living far apart. His visits to his patients were made with horse and buggy when the roads were passable but oftentimes in bad weather he made his calls on horseback, carrying his medicine and instruments in saddlebags. There are old ones still living in the Mills River and French Broad Valley who were ushered into this world by Dr. Johnson.

In the picture taken in front of the City Hall that day in 1904 were also a number of young ladies who were Daughters of the Confederacy and who helped entertain the veterans at their reunion. They were lovely and charming but to the present day generation they would be a sight at which to wonder. All of the ladies were young and were dressed in the fashions of the early 20th Century. They wore large, sweeping, broad-brimmed hats held on their heads by long hat pins, an unheard of instrument today. The large hats with ostrich plumes and bright colored stuffed birds on them were the latest fashion and were called Merry Widow hats. The blouses and jackets worn by the ladies had bulging sleeves and their skirts reached the ground in front and were a little longer at the back. Not even the toe of a shoe peeped from beneath the long, ground-sweeping dresses.

CHAPTER 30

The Whitakers
(1963)

Joshua Whitaker came through the gap in the mountains to Henderson County nearly 150 years ago. He came from the valley of Crooked Creek in McDowell County. The first official record of his arrival is a deed that is a prized possession of his great granddaughter, Frances Freeman Honeycutt, former head of the U.S. Agricultural Stabilization and Conservation Office of Henderson County. The old deed is dated April 5, 1856, although it was not recorded in the office of the Henderson County Register of Deeds until October 1887, in Deed Book 23, page 458. The deed transfers 640 acres of land on both sides of Clear Creek from David Miller to Joshua Whitaker for the sum of $1240, a price of less than $2 an acre.

When Joshua Whitaker brought his family to live on the headwaters of Clear Creek in the area where Laurel Creek flows into it, he already had four sons well on their way to manhood. When the War between the States began five of his nine sons marched away to war. Julius, Ben, Robert and Burgin joined the Confederate army and one son "Fate" (Lafayette) fought for the Union. Burgin Whitaker was the only son to survive. He was the first man to volunteer when Captain Baylus Edney started to raise a company of Henderson County men to fight for the Confederacy. This company officially became part of the 25th North Carolina Volunteers but before the end of the war it was known far and wide as Edney's Greys.* His brother Julius was killed by a bushwhacker named Tom Miller on Terry's Gap while home on leave.

Burgin fought through the entire four years of the war and was the only one of Joshua's boys to return home. When he came back from the war his father gave him a tract of land on Laurel Creek. Burgin was a hard working man and was skillful with his hands and the few tools available in those dark days of Reconstruction. He went to work to build himself a home. He cut the logs for it on his own land and snaked them out of the woods to the little valley with a yoke of oxen. Burgin Whitaker hewed them to the proper size and shape and he raised them until his log cabin was finished.

When I visited the old log cabin in 1963, it was still lived in and was on the road that runs by Laurel Creek. Today it stands between the homes of the late John A. Freeman and Charles Washington Freeman who are descendants of Burgin.

* Vol. I "The War Between the States"

JOSHUA WHITAKER

Born Oct. 4, 1809   Died Jan. 22, 1886
married
LYDIA BURGIN
Born July 27, 1815   Died Feb. 24, 1889
(Her father was a lawyer and a state legislator)
Children:

Julius B. Whitaker   Born Nov. 18, 1835
    Married Matilda Ann Lyda
    Served in Edney's Greys. Killed by a bushwhacker named Tom
Miller on Terry's Gap while home on leave.
William Ben Whitaker   Born Dec. 19, 1836
    Served in civil war. Died in service.
Elizabeth T. Whitaker   Born Mar. 11, 1838
*James L. Whitaker   Born Nov. 1839
Robert I. Whitaker   Born Apr. 24, 1841
Joshua Burgin Whitaker   Feb. 1, 1843
    Married Lizzie Freeman - one survivor of Civil War
*Joseph L. Whitaker   Sept. 23, 1844
Rosamond Whitaker (female)   Dec. 13, 1846
Elizar C. Whitaker   Mar. 19, 1849
Dr. J. Whitaker   Sept. 27, 1852
Marcianne Whitaker   Nov. 29, 1854
Calvin S. Whitaker   Nov. 25, 1856
Thomas A. Whitaker   Mar. 14, 1859

*One of these two was named Lafayette and was known as "Fate" Whitaker.
He served on the Union side in the Civil War. Julius B.; Ben; Robert I; and
Burgin joined the south.

CHAPTER 31

The Carlisles

James Carlisle was a strong and sturdy Henderson County mountain
boy. In 1863 James Carlisle was 16 years old and North Carolina and its ten
sister states were desperately defending themselves against a vastly superior
enemy force. As soon as he reached his 16th birthday James Carlisle enlisted
in Company H, 58th Regiment, North Carolina Infantry. Sixteen years old is
mighty young for a boy to march off to war but he knew that his state was
endangered by an invading enemy and needed him.

Soon after he enlisted he was sent with his outfit to Virginia and was in the
continuous fighting around Richmond as part of the Army of Northern Vir-

ginia and he was with General Lee when Lee surrendered at Appomattox. During one of the battles young Carlisle was wounded in the shoulder by a minnie ball that passed through his body and killed one of his comrades behind him.

An indication of the suffering that the soldiers endured in those Civil War battles is illustrated by the first aid given to him. The wound was cleaned by his commanding officer drawing a silk handkerchief back and forth through the bullet hole in the shoulder. The young soldier was then put on a horse to go to the field hospital in the rear. When the horse was killed by enemy fire, he walked the remainder of the way to the hospital tent. After General Lee surrendered Carlisle returned to his home in Henderson County by walking the entire distance from Virginia, as most of the Confederate soldiers were forced to do. He raised a large family in the Galamore Gap section of the county and is buried in the Refuge Church Cemetery at Dana.

On a Sunday afternoon, June 15, 1958, an impressive ceremony was held at the grave site of James Carlisle. The Hendersonville chapter of the Daughters of the Confederacy unveiled and dedicated a monument and marker on the grave. Following the dedication Mrs. Thad C. Jowitt and Mrs. Albert Beck, representing the Daughters of the Confederacy, decorated James G. Carlisle, son of the Confederate veteran for his service in World War I; Hilliard and Steve Carlisle, grandsons of the Confederate veteran, for their service in World War II; and another grandson, Charles B. Carlisle, who fought in the Korean War.

These descendants received the Military Crosses that are only presented to direct descendants of Confederate veterans who have served their once again united country in active warfare.

James Steven Carlisle Sr. and James Steven Carlisle Jr.
at the Grave of James Carlisle   (Photo compliments of the Carlisles)

CHAPTER 32

Armistice Day

November 11, 1918 was Armistice Day. It was a day of rejoicing not only in Henderson County but all over the United States and most of the world. It was the day that the bloodiest war of all time up to that date ended. It was the First World War that had inspired the free nations of the world to fight "A War to End All Wars." The end came abruptly on the eleventh hour of the eleventh day of the eleventh month.

Armistice Day became a national holiday and for three score years November 11th was celebrated throughout our land. It should have been. For more than four years, the larger and more powerful nations of the world, as well as some of the weaker, had been locked in battles across all of Europe involving millions of fighting men. The big guns roared and growled, pouring out death and destruction such as the world had never seen before, right up to the very minute of that eleventh hour.

And then there was sudden silence along the far flung battle line that was almost as terrifying as the noise of battle. It was so sudden and so silent.

The War to End all Wars for all times was over and on that November 11, 1918 a very weary world believed it and so rejoiced. Here in Hendersonville, for three decades, Armistice Day became the biggest holiday of the year with county wide observances. Every store and business closed. In the morning on those Armistice Days were the largest and most colorful parades ever seen here up until those times. In those days the parades started at the Court House and ended at the High School where patriotic services were held. These were attended by overflowing crowds, after which the schools of the town and county closed for the day.

In the afternoon at the High School athletic field, the football game of the season was played with Hendersonville High School playing its greatest rival of that period. Armistice Day celebration ended with a great display of fireworks, followed by a dance in the old gymnasium that stood at the end of the athletic field on Ninth Avenue. This was Hendersonville's first gymnasium, a long wooden structure built in the autumn of 1921 but now remembered only by the elderly who were living here then.*

Hitler, Mussolini and Pearl Harbor disillusioned a new generation. Armistice Day lost its meaning when the Second World War started. At the end of that war Congress changed November 11th from Armistice Day to Veterans Day to honor all men and women who have fought in all wars that our country has engaged in.

* Vol. I "The Educators"

CHAPTER 33

Hendersonville's First Armistice Day

How was that first Armistice Day, November 11, 1918 celebrated here in Hendersonville and Henderson County? *The French Broad Hustler*, the weekly newspaper published here in 1918, reported, "The signing of the Armistice by Germany was celebrated to an extensive degree in Hendersonville on Monday."

That was a rather mild and stilted way to describe it. Those who were here at the time will remember it as long as they live. The celebration was wild and hilarious and exciting. It was not confined to the town but was county wide. The news that the war would end at 11:00 o'clock that November morning was received here at 5:00 a.m. It was a chilly dawn and pitch-black dark but shrill whistles crashed through the early morning darkness followed by the softer tones of the church bells throughout the town and county to herald the glad tidings.

It brought everybody out of bed and wide awake. Above the din could be heard the clanging of the big bell that hung in the tower of the old City Hall on Main Street, the bell that rang only on occasions of emergency. Within minutes, hundreds of people gathered on the streets, shivering from cold and excitement, laughing, back slapping, calling back and forth to one another as the wonderful news spread.

When daylight came people were in no mood to go to work. All schools and places of business were closed and plans were quickly made for an appropriate celebration which began with a parade down Main Street that afternoon.

In the line of march were numerous automobiles. With such a short time to prepare, it was astonishing how many gaily decorated floats had been made ready, most of them displaying the national colors and the flags of the Allied nations. Every kind of thing that would make a noise was put to strenuous service for the next two hours. The streets were full of moving vehicles and the sidewalks crowded with thousands of people who poured into town from all parts of the county to take part in the celebration.

When the parade ended the crowd gathered at the bandstand near the City Hall on Main Street. Mayor C. E. Brooks, Ed Brooks to his friends, opened the ceremonies with a prayer. W. A. Smith and E. W. Ewbank, leading citizens of that period, were called on and each spoke briefly. "America" and "The Star Spangled Banner" were sung by the large crowd and the Rev. Mr. G. W. Belk closed with a prayer.

So ended the first Armistice Day in Hendersonville. It was a long, strenuous, happy day and the tired people of Hendersonville and Henderson County slept soundly that night, rejoicing in the knowledge that the boys would soon be coming home and that the "War to End All Wars" had come to a victorious end.

W. A. Smith

Part Six
Education Honor Roll

Part Six

Education Honor Roll

CHAPTER 34

The Good Shepherd School

It was a one room log schoolhouse covered with rived boards instead of the usual hand-rived shingles used in those days. The board roofing was rived and the logs hewed by the men and boys of the community. Few people now living know about that log schoolhouse and those who do are the senior ones now but they were children who attended that school nearly 75 years ago. The school was located on the northmost side of Point Lookout in the eastern part of Henderson County. It was beneath the pinnacles of Sugar Loaf Mountain and near the headwaters of Little Creek. It was known as the Good Shepherd School.

My friend G. B. Stepp, who was called by his friends and widely known as Bly Stepp, was a prominent farmer and apple orchardist of the Point Lookout area. Mr. Stepp brought me a picture of the little log school and told me the story about it. It is a contrast of the educational opportunities in our county as the new century began with those we have now in our modern rural schools.

The picture is that of the Good Shepherd School No. 2; there was an earlier smaller school also called the Good Shepherd. This picture of the school was taken in 1910 when the new log building was dedicated.

Standing in the schoolhouse door is Mrs. Sharp, sponsor of the school and Miss Bertha Williams, the teacher. Most people will remember Bertha Williams as Mrs. Bertha Hagan who taught for so many years in our county public schools. Mrs. Hagan was regarded as one of the finest teachers in our school system.

Bly Stepp told me that Mrs. Sharp had come into the Edneyville - Point Lookout area as a missionary working under the auspices of the Episcopal Church. She and the church sponsored and helped build the schoolhouse. (She is remembered only as "Mrs. Sharp.") The county schools only operated three months of the year but the Good Shepherd ran for four months and sometimes longer. This was a godsend for those boys and girls who thirsted for education. Mrs. Sharp was a graduate pharmacist. She was helped by her friend Ruth Gottlieb who was a medical doctor. These two women were among the first women college graduates to be licensed to practice in their field in the entire United States.

Lined up in front of the school are fifty or sixty boys and girls and some of their parents. Bly Stepp is in the picture, then a twelve year old boy. He knew all the others and named them for me. Some of the parents in the picture are no longer living. Many of the boys and girls in that 1910 picture are today the old ones of the Point Lookout - Edneyville community.

Among the parents that I recognized were Gabriel Laughter, known everywhere as Gabe. Gabe and Leander Laughter were pillars of their community during their lifetime. With them you can see their wives. Their dresses were so long that the ladies' shoes cannot be seen. In the picture are also Mr. and Mrs. Tommie Jones, Hunter Lamb, Corrie and Charlotte Lamb, Frank Gilliam and his sister Mollie.

In the center of the picture, dressed in white with ribbons in their hair, are three pretty little girls. These are the Justice triplets who were six or seven years old when the picture was taken. Triplets were rare in our mountains and they caused a sensation when they were born. In January, 1969, when this was written, the Justice triplets, Essie, Dessie and Bessie, were still living. Essie was the wife of Rome Williams. Bessie married Barzellie Nix and Dessie became Mrs. Cecil Nix. They all lived in the same general area where they were born, raised and attended school.

One of the young men in the picture is Ben Jones who in 1969 lived on Duncan Hill Road. He and his family were well known in our county for their singing ability.

Times were hard in the early 1900s when the picture of the Good Shepherd School was taken. The children sat on benches, four to six to a bench. The grades were from the first through the seventh and one teacher taught all seven grades in one room.

It was a day's journey from the Point Lookout - Sugar Loaf community to Hendersonville and back in the days of the Good Shepherd School. Mrs. Sharp established a small drug store in the area near Edneyville so people did not have to go so far to obtain medicine when there was sickness. Mrs. Sharp is still remembered for the good things she did for people in the area.

Bly Stepp and I agreed that times have changed in many ways since the picture of the Good Shepherd School was taken.

CHAPTER 35

Mount Vernon School

It was a beautiful school or so the grownups and the boys and girls of the area thought. It sat there gleaming in its new coat of white paint on the hill above Haunt Branch on the road that went from Hendersonville to Dana. It

Mount Vernon School – About 1909
(Photo compliments of Mr. & Mrs. Carroll Pettet)

Front Four (Left to Right): *Loree Maxwell, Donald Maxwell, Willie Pettet, Frank Pettet*

2nd Row (Left to Right): *Teacher-Salley Osborne, Elsie Osteen, Sue Maxwell (Merrill), Helena Dermid (Duckett), Drama Blythe, Junie Pettet, Glenard Harris, Cora Maxwell (Laughter), Essie Corn (Newman), A. Shipman, Odell Maxwell, Volney Corn, Hubert Maxwell, Belvin Shipman*

3rd Row (Left to Right): *Ocie Shipman, Lillie Hill (Morrison), Bertha Hill (Love), Ethel Maxwell (Warren), Karo Henderson (Donahue), Angelia Jones, Alice Hill (Jones), Josie Corn (Lanning), Vincent Maxwell, Seldon Shipman, Deck Jones*

4th Row (Left to Right): *Glenard Harris, Unknown, Wallace Henderson Victoria Taylor, Bertha Maxwell (Frazier), Maude Maxwell (Brown), Bertha Maxwell, Albert Corn, Elbert Corn, Unknown, General Henderson*

Student Body of Mount Vernon School — About 1930
F. L. FitzSimons, Principal, Upper Right Corner

was the only road in those early days at the beginning of the century. The road is still there but now it is referred to as the Old Dana Road. A new road was built in later years.

Mrs. Collie Crawford Hill suggested the name Mount Vernon for the new school, after the ancestral home of George Washington. It has been fifty years since Mount Vernon closed its doors and the two restrooms burned. They had stood hidden in the woods, separated by some distance, one for the girls and one for the boys.

There are many still living who went to school at Mount Vernon and whose children also went there. These same ones will have a vague expression when Mount Vernon School is mentioned but suddenly the faces will brighten. "Oh, you mean Dry Hill!" And Dry Hill School it was called unofficially through the years.

The only source of drinking water for the large number of one and two teacher schools scattered over Henderson County was either nearby springs or hand dug wells which were comparatively shallow in comparison with the drilled wells of today. The source of drinking water at Mount Vernon was a dug well 25 feet deep at the top of the hill. Every time there was a prolonged dry spell in the area the school well would go dry until wet weather started the water flowing again. The students began to call it Dry Hill and Dry Hill School became the popular name everywhere.

Miss Eleanor Plank and I taught at Dry Hill School the last four years before it was consolidated with Dana School. We had been preceded by some very prominent teachers. Some that I remember were Elva Pressley, Mrs. Nannie Mitchell, her daughter Irene Mitchell and Scott Young.

Teaching in those days was much more informal than now. The teachers and pupils had more fun and the school was the focal point of a community. Dry Hill School closed in the middle of the six and seven month terms in the fall of the year so the boys and girls could help on the farms to cut tops, pull fodder and harvest the hay crops. The students walked to school, some of them two, three and four miles each way to and from school regardless of the weather. They brought their lunches. In cold weather the lunches were eaten huddled around a pot bellied, wood burning stove in each of the two rooms. There was always an hour for midday recess and if an exciting baseball game was being played, the hour would often stretch beyond that time.

It has been 75 years since Mount Vernon or Dry Hill School was dedicated and half a century since it was consolidated and the same families are still living in the area: the Hendersons, Paces, Capps, Hoots, Browns, Kitchens, Flemings, Hills, Corns, Blythes and others. The present generation of these families now go to the modern consolidated schools and ride buses where their parents walked.

The big day every year at Dry Hill was the last day of school. Those finishing the 7th grade were given certificates after they had spoken their pieces. It was an all day affair with the parents attending and bringing picnic dinners. After dinner the exercises were held. These were followed by a baseball game between Dry Hill boys and the team from Tracy Grove School. Rivalry was hot between the two schools and the games were exciting. Often fights between supporters of the teams would break out. When

Baseball Team of Mt. Vernon School
Back Row L to R: *F.L. FitzSimons, Coach John Gibbs, Emmot Capps, Curtis Hill, Bill Pace* **2nd Row:** *Clarence Hill, Elmer Capps, Ector Capps, Edison Pace, Austin Newman* **Front Row:** *Glover Pace, Leroy Henderson*

these fights were between students of the two schools they were easily broken up by the teachers or parents. After all of these years, I vividly remember a fight that took place between two grown young women. It could have been serious but when it was over it was amusing.

The argument started between the two ladies as to whether a player was safe at first base or was out as called by the umpire. It started with words, some which I dare not quote here. It developed into a slapping and hair pulling affair. I was the host and school principal. The large crowd at the game began to appeal to me to stop the fight.

I was young and naive. I had never been faced with such a situation but I felt my responsibility. At that exact moment the two pretty young gladiators were locked in mortal hair pulling combat.

I bravely and gallantly stepped forward to separate them, but to my amazement they separated themselves, turned and glared at me with fists drawn back. In a loud, harsh, threatening voice, one of them said, "You touch me and I'll slap hell out of you!"

I stepped back and said, "Ladies, go to it."

Very often the problems of the teachers in the small rural schools of that day were quite different from those of present day teachers. The first few days of the term, large numbers of community dogs of all sizes and descriptions began to appear at school. The weather was hot so the doors and windows were left open. Dogs wandered aimlessly in and out of the building. Nothing could keep them out except shutting the doors. This made it too hot in the classrooms.

I finally told the boys and girls they would have to leave their pets at home. The children told me they tried to do this but their dogs would follow them. Then one morning I walked to school. Much to my surprise a few minutes after I got to school, there appeared in the school room my large, rather aggressive Airedale, Tommy. The next few days this was repeated. After that there was no more trouble at school about dogs.

CHAPTER 36

The Hills

Frank C. Hill was a true native son, born and raised in Henderson County. He married Lillie Lee Osteen whose ancestors had settled in the county in pioneer days. Mr. and Mrs. Hill raised and educated a family of ten boys and girls. If my memory has not failed me, I taught all of these children except one and the only reason I didn't teach the tenth is because I no longer was teaching when he reached the 7th grade.

C. Frank Hill & Lillie Lee Osteen Hill
(Photo compliments of Mr. & Mrs. Curtis Hill)

Mr. and Mrs. Hill and family have been neighbors of mine for over fifty years and finer neighbors a body never had. I always enjoyed talking to them and did so every chance I had. I was interested in the early schools in the area where we lived. Mr. Hill told me that the first school in the community was a one teacher cabin known as the Ace School. It stood just off the present Dana Road where the late Everette Love built a fish pond years after the little school closed forever.

On the hill behind the house where I live stood the Hood School. This school took its name from the Lemuel Hood family who donated the land where the schoolhouse was built. The Hood School was later moved to a site on the Old Dana Road. The one room log Hood School was eventually torn down and replaced by a two room school house. This new two teacher school was named Mount Vernon. This was the school I told about in the last chapter. It was named by Frank Hill's grandmother. Mount Vernon served the community until 1928 when it was consolidated, along with all the other one and two teacher schools, with Dana grammar and high school.

Johnson Hill, the grandfather of Frank Hill, brought his family to the area where they and their descendants have lived for decades. They came from Fodder Stack Mountain in Transylvania County just before that area was cut off from Henderson County in 1861 to form Transylvania County. Andy and Thomas Hill, who were grandsons of Johnson Hill, became school teachers. They are still remembered by old ones of the Ridge section because of their musical ability, especially their fiddle playing.

Johnson Hill served as a County Commissioner from 1870 through 1872. He believed in education and contributed generously to help build Judson College*. The other sons of Johnson Hill were Dock, George, Milas and John H. who was the father of Frank. The remarkable thing is that the land owned and farmed a century and a half ago is still owned, lived on and farmed by the descendants of Johnson Hill.

Curtis Hill, a retired foreman of Duke Power Company, a son of Frank Hill and a great grandson of Johnson Hill, lives on a portion of the original Hill farmstead. Other descendants are scattered all the way from here to Florida and west to California.

As the years passed the population of the area between Dana and Hendersonville increased. The original road between the two communities could no longer serve them all. Around 1910 the new Dana Road to Hendersonville was opened. The rights of way for the new road were given to the county by the owners of the land. These public spirited men were C. A. Watterson, the father of the late popular Register of Deeds, Marshall Watterson; P. T. Ward, Blake and Robert E. Ward, Robert V. and E. M. Osteen, John H. and Milas Hill and W. T. Capps.

The older generation of Henderson County realized that progress required better schools and better roads. The present generations are in agreement.

* Vol. II "Schools of Distinction"

John & Lanette Hill – Parents of C. Frank Hill
(Photo compliments of Mr. & Mrs. Curtis Hill)

Adams Run School

Left to Right: *Frank Clark - Teacher, Mary Stepp, Agnes Paris, Curtis McCraw, Lauri Davis, Hobert McCraw, Fannie Bell Bradley, Alice Paris, Cary Lively, Bob Paris, Ella Davis, Pink Stepp, Dovie Stepp, Mintie McCraw, Jink Stepp, Lou Ella Stepp, Will Case, Rosie Hyder, Minnie Paris, Pearlie Stepp, Ken McCraw, David Furman Stepp (with tie), Fate Stepp, Joe Stepp, Terrill Stepp, Clayton Stepp, Frank Paris, John Case, Arnold Paris*

Standing in Doorway: *Jay Paris, Tom Paris, Burg Paris*

CHAPTER 37

Miss Lanning and Mr. Young

Miss Sue Lanning has long rested peacefully in eternal sleep but there are those still living who well remember as I do the calm, quiet, gray haired lady who made her influence felt in the lives of so many boys and girls in Henderson County. The Parent Teacher Association of Fletcher High School met on April 29, 1957 and devoted the entire program to honoring Miss Sue who had just completed fifty years of teaching in the rural public schools of Henderson County. Most of those fifty years she taught in the Fletcher area. And during that half century she missed only five days from her teaching duties, a most remarkable record.

The only person I have been able to find who has a record that is comparable to Sue Lanning's achievement is that of Scott Young who taught in the Henderson County public schools for fifty three years. Mr. Young retired in 1929 when the schools of the county had been consolidated.

The last one teacher school in Henderson County was Adams Run, deep in the Big Hungry section. It was here that Mr. Young taught. He died a few years after he retired. He was the father of Mrs. Louis Roper of a prominent Mills River family. When Scott Young started teaching in 1876, the conditions of our schools were even more primitive than when Miss Lanning started in 1907.

They are wonderful records, those of Miss Lanning and Mr. Young. The progress of education in Henderson County has been phenomenal. Much of it has been due to the sacrifices made by Miss Lanning, Mr. Young and others like them who taught in those long ago days. I consider myself fortunate that I knew both of them and many other dedicated teachers during their active years.

CHAPTER 38

Ernest L. Justus
(1960)

Ernest L. Justus is considered to be one of the outstanding school men in Western North Carolina by the Department of Public Instruction. During his half century with the schools of Henderson County, he has served as a teacher at Balfour School, principal of Flat Rock High School, supervisor of the Flat

E. L. Justus   (Photo by Barber)

Rock Administrative School District which consists of the Flat Rock High School, East Flat Rock, Tuxedo and Valley Hill grammar schools; principal of the Consolidated East Henderson High School, and since his retirement from active teaching and administrative duties, he has been elected to serve several terms on the Henderson County School Board.

Ernest Justus is proud of his Blue Ridge Mountain heritage that can be traced back to pioneer days. A remarkable fact is that his school career has all been in the area settled by his ancestors, and that he and his brothers, George and Drayton, have lived and are living on lands that have been in their family for more than 175 years.

Professor Justus is the son of the late Frank and Julie Jones Justus. One day in January 1960 he invited me to go on a trip with him. He and Bill Jones were going to visit some of the early landmarks of their ancestors in South Blue Ridge Township. Captain Robert Jones, veteran of the Continental Army, was the first of the Jones family to arrive in what is now Henderson County and was the great grandfather of both Bill Jones and Ernest Justus.

We drove through East Flat Rock to Ollie's Grocery at Five Points and stopped to talk to Jim Jones who at 85 years of age lived on land where Captain Robert Jones built his first log cabin and cleared the land before moving into the Upward area. We went by the Oak Grove Church and stopped at the original Justus homeplace.

John Justus had bought a large boundary of land from John McMinn who had acquired it in 1793 through a state grant. This John Justus was the great, great grandfather of Ernest, and one of the first settlers and the first Justus in that area. Some of the land is still in the family after all of these years, owned by Professor Justus who has the original deed for the property in his possession. The deed is now nearly 200 years old.

John Justus built his log cabin, cleared the land and raised his family. The original log cabin is no longer standing but at the time of our 1960 visit the three room house that took its place was still standing although it was more than a century old. It was in this three room house that Ernest Justus was born. While we sat and talked, Mr. Jones, 84 years old, had a far away look as he told of the good times he enjoyed in the fall of the year when he was a boy. "In those days," he said, "this place was owned by W. D. Justus, the grandfather of Ernest. He always had the biggest corn shuckin in these parts. I came as a boy and folks would come from miles around. Nobody has corn shuckins anymore in these times," he sadly commented.

The W. D. Justus mentioned by Mr. Jones was a prominent and leading citizen in the early days of our county. At one time he served as Sheriff and in 1868 he represented the county in the State Legislature. He was a devout Christian who believed in the literal application of the Biblical admonition, "Be ye fruitful and multiply." In the little three room house we were standing beside he raised a family of 24 children. He and a number of his offspring are buried in the Jones Cemetery. His tombstone tells that he was born in 1819 and died in 1892.

William Davenport Justus – Grandfather of Ernest Justus
(Photo compliments of E.L. Justus)

We next parked our car on the Howard Gap Loop Road in front of Paul Surrat's home. We were looking for the original pioneer burying ground of the Justus family. After much searching through the thickets of briars and underbrush we found it on top of a hill, hidden by the overgrowth of nature. No one has been buried here for more than a century although we counted more than forty graves. There was only one grave with a headstone that was legible. The

Nancy Pittillo Justus – wife of William Davenport Justus
Grandmother of Ernest Justus   (Photo compliments of E.L. Justus)

crude lettering read, "Isabellar Justus, born October 29, 1809. Died September 8, 1851." Her given name was spelled in the old fashioned manner ending with an "r" instead of an "a" as spelled now.

No one now living knows who occupy the graves other than the one with Isabellar's name on it, except that most of the graves hold the remains of pioneer members of the Justus family. All but forgotten, now untended, they quietly sleep there on the lonely hilltop. Who knows of the sorrow, the heart breaks, the tragedies of life buried there?

Few now living remember Ben Laughter whose old homeplace was then owned and lived in by Professor Henry Davis, a former principal of Hendersonville High School. Every year at harvest time, Mr. Laughter bought all the apples produced in the Upward area at the standard price of 20¢ a bushel. In those days a body could get a government license to make whiskey in Henderson County. Mr. Laughter made brandy with the apples. It was famous and sold for $1.50 a gallon.

In this same vicinity we stopped to speak to Jim Suttles who lived at the Elias Gibbs homeplace. Elias Gibbs was a Confederate veteran whose fame as a miller lives on in the memory of many still living.* He was the father of Pack Gibbs and grandfather of Lawrence Gibbs, three generations of mountain millers.

On this trip Ernest Justus and Bill Jones talked of the days gone by and the pioneer members of their families who had passed with those years.

East Henderson Consolidated High School is one of the largest schools in Henderson County. In recent years a modern stadium has been added to the school. To honor Professor Justus for his many years of dedicated service to several generations of the young people of our county, the stadium has been named and will always be known as the E. L. Justus Stadium.

CHAPTER 39

Bruce Drysdale
(1959)

In January and February of 1959 a body riding or walking north on Main Street passed the St. James Episcopal Church. On the hill could be seen the foundations and steel girders of a building under construction. This was the beginning of a long needed new school in Hendersonville. When completed and equipped it would be one of the most modern schools in any city in Western North Carolina. There would be twenty classrooms, an auditorium, a library, a cafeteria and office space for administrative personnel and the plans were so drawn that additional classrooms could be added as the need arose because of the continued growth of our population. Such a building had been needed for a long time to relieve the over-crowded conditions of the city schools brought about by the rapid growth of our population since the end of World War II.

In 1959, on motion by Roy Johnson, seconded by Cal Kuykendall and unanimously passed, the Hendersonville School Board voted to name the new building "The Bruce Drysdale School." At this time, Mr. Drysdale had

* Vol. II "The Confederacy"

been an outstanding citizen for more than forty years. During these forty years he had been active in every type of endeavor that made for the growth of our town and county.

The first week in January 1959, Bruce Drysdale resigned from the city School Board because of ill health. He had served on the board for approximately 25 years, the last thirteen years as chairman. There had been no one person who had given as much time, deep study and work for the advancement of education in Hendersonville. The time had always been given freely and cheerfully.

The interest of Mr. Drysdale in the proper educational facilities and opportunities for children had not been confined to our area alone. While serving on the local School Board he had also served on educational committees and boards of Western North Carolina and the entire state. The high standards of the public school system in North Carolina are in a large measure due to the work and interest that he had given so willingly and often at personal sacrifice.

The action of the School Board in recognizing and honoring Bruce Drysdale while he was still living was met with the unanimous approval of our entire community.

Part Seven
The U.S. Mail

The U. S. Mail

CHAPTER 40

Pump, N.C.

In 1892 *The Hendersonville Times* was a weekly newspaper and the only newspaper published here. In its issue of March 9, 1892 *The Times* announced that Miss Minerva Laughter and J. A. Rhodes were married at the home of the bride's father at Pump and that the officiating minister was the Rev. F. C. Hamric.

Only the elderly still living in that beautiful area along the Hickory Nut Gorge Road above Bat Cave remember that at one time there was a community in Henderson County called Pump. The settlement had grown to such size and importance that in 1883 a post office named Pump was established there.

The name came from the fact that in the center of the community there was a pump that supplied water to all the people in the settlement. Legend tells us also that Pump was important because there was a spot near the water pump in those days where a body could leave a quarter or half dollar and return later to find a jar of a clear white liquid the color of water, but unlike water it had a bead and was much more potent.

The first Postmaster at Pump was Joseph H. Freeman, the great grandfather of Bob Freeman who operates Freeman's Newsstand in Hendersonville. The Rev. F. C. Hamric who officiated at the marriage of J. A. Rhodes and Minerva Laughter at Pump in 1892 also later served as Postmaster.

In 1902 the name of the post office was changed from Pump to Gerton and Gerton it is to this day. There is a legend that the change was made because of a cancellation stamp that was sent to the Postmaster at Pump. When the cancellation stamp was used it was found that the letter "P" in Pump had been changed to "R" and the stamp read "Rump, N.C." When the word spread it caused much amusement except for the people of Pump who were indignant. A meeting was called and it was decided to change the name of the post office at once.

In his delightful book "Postmarks", published in 1970, Lenoir Ray verifies this legend as an actual fact. He also states that the name Gerton was selected in place of Pump to honor Gertrude Freeman, a highly respected school teacher and descendant of Joseph Freeman, the first Postmaster. Gertrude Freeman was a bashful woman and thought that a post office named

Gertrude would be unbecoming for a lady. The name Gerton was a contraction of Gertrude and everybody was happy.

CHAPTER 41

A Post Office Named Horace

At the turn of the century there was no Rural Free Delivery of mail in Henderson County. In fact the first R. F. D. route was established in Henderson County in 1902. Farmers and others who lived in the rural areas went to the nearest post office to mail letters or to get their mail. This was not too inconvenient because there was a post office every few miles and they were scattered all over Henderson County.

My friend the late B. T. Nix was a prominent apple grower who lived on the Lamb Mountain Road. This is a portion of the original Sugar Loaf Road that went from Hendersonville to Point Lookout and on to the top of Sugar Loaf Mountain. Mr. Nix and I were talking about some of the post offices that used to serve the county. I asked him if he had ever heard of a post office in his section in the early days named Horace. He said that only he and a few older ones still living remembered Horace and those few were ones who lived in Edneyville, Point Lookout and Sugar Loaf Mountain areas of the eastern part of the county.

The post office, Horace, North Carolina was established in 1901 with James M. Jackson as Postmaster. He served as Postmaster until Horace was closed by the Post Office Department in November 1913. Who gave this little mountain post office the name Horace and why I have been unable to find out. This post office was first located on Point Lookout where Roland Jones, a well known apple orchardist, now lives. Later on Mr. Jackson opened and operated a store about where Clyde and Weldon Stepp now live and the post office Horace was moved to that store.

Along in our conversation Mr. Nix began to talk about the Ottanola Post Office further up the mountain from Horace. The Ottanola Post Office was located where the late Howard Gilbert lived at the fork of the road that goes to the top of Sugar Loaf and the road to World's Edge. A large hotel or boarding house catering to the summer tourists was located here and went by the name of Ottanola Inn. The Ottanola Inn was destroyed by fire and the post office was moved to the Will Merrill place near where Mountain Home Church is today.

In the days when these isolated post offices existed, the mail was brought from the Hendersonville Post Office by wagon or buggy or, when the roads were impassable in the winter, by horseback to Edneyville Post Office where the mail for Horace and Ottanola was picked up by Gabe Laughter.

Gabe Laughter carried the mail from Edneyville to Horace and Ottanola on foot. It was a common sight to see Mr. Laughter with the mail sacks on his shoulder climbing the mountain walking barefooted. The round trip amounted to fifteen or twenty miles and Mr. Laughter did not want his feet cramped by shoes in hot weather. Barefooted or with shoes on, Gabe Laughter was quite a man in his day.

When Rural Free Delivery of mail came to Henderson County scores of little post offices such as Horace and Ottanola were closed. They had served their time.

CHAPTER 42

Some R.F.D. Pioneers

In the first score years of this century there were no paved roads in Henderson County. There were few if any all weather, crushed rock roads as the unpaved roads are called. The roads then were what were known as top soil roads, a mixture of top soil, sand and clay which were kept in condition by scraping them with split log drags. In dry weather they could be traveled successfully in horse drawn vehicles. In the winter the rain, snow, ice and alternate freezing and thawing often made the roads hub deep in mud when a few warm days came. When frozen, the deep ruts left by the wagon and buggies made travel an ordeal.

John Redden
One of Henderson County's First Rural Mail Carriers

The early mail carriers used horses and buggies to deliver mail on their rural routes. All of the rural mail carriers kept two or more horses that were used on alternate days because routes of twenty to thirty miles a day were too hard a work day, day after day, for one animal. I talked to Roy Johnson, a career postal service man who started as a rural mail carrier. He told me that he kept two horses. He used one for the first half of his route and the other for the second half.

I remember several of those rural mail carriers in those early days. One of them was John Redden, father of Monroe and Arthur Redden, both of whom are prominent lawyers today. I remember the white mule that John Redden often drove on his route. Jesse Johnson often drove a large high headed, high stepping bay horse that was beautiful to see in action.

These men used horses until the middle of the 1920s. John Redden, Jesse Johnson and Tilden Hill were the last ones to use horses on their mail routes out of the Hendersonville Post Office. In the early 1920s a few of the younger and more adverturesome rural carriers began to experiment with automobiles on their rural routes. At first they would use their automobiles in good weather and would use horse and buggies in the winter time or during long spells of wet weather in the summer.

Two of the first ones to use automobiles that I remember out of the Hendersonville office were Glover Jones and Milner Flack. Milner Flack's car will always be remembered by those on his route at that time. It was a stripped down Model T Ford, painted yellow, and it could be heard by a patron waiting at his mail box long before it could be seen.

And when all of the rural carriers switched to automobiles it was a lucky, a very lucky carrier who did not have a flat tire and often several flat tires every day while delivering mail.

CHAPTER 43

R.F.D. 1
(1970)

Robert Alvin Hall delivers the mail on Hendersonville's R.F.D. 1. He has been doing it for a score of years and then some. He is the son of Mr. and Mrs. Robert P. Hall of East Flat Rock. Alvin Hall is a dedicated career postal employee and one of the most conscientious persons that I have ever known. Mr. Hall invited me to go with him on his route while he delivered the mail. Frustrated through all these years because I have always wanted to be a rural mail carrier, I quickly accepted the invitation after it had been cleared at headquarters. On Friday, December 4, 1970 I rode the entire route with Mr. Hall and so finally achieved my long secret ambition.

Alvin Hall delivering mail at Rt 1 Box 399
The home of the Author, October 1979

Alvin Hall's Rural Free Delivery route is a long one. He travels 79 miles in the summertime and 74 miles in the winter. More than 40 miles of the roads he travels are gravel covered dirt or rock roads. The five mile difference in the length of the summer and winter delivery route is because only summer visitors live on one five mile stretch.

Mr. Hall drives a Land Rover jeep type of car: four wheel drive with heavy duty, six ply tires. The car has the steering wheel on the right hand side which makes delivery easier because all mail boxes are required to be on the driver's right hand side of the road. A body really gets "shook up" traveling those 40 or more miles on the unpaved portions of the mountain roads on Mr. Hall's route. There are approximately 400 patrons on this mail route and some of them live in places that are unknown to many people who have lived a lifetime in Henderson County.

The first stop was at Huntsinger's store and cottages. Mrs. Huntsinger was waiting to get some information about the mail. Mrs. Huntsinger is the former Bell Whitesides, daughter of the late Whit Whitesides. Her father was on the Edneyville School Board in 1923 when I was principal of that school and Bell Whitesides Huntsinger was a high school student.

I soon learned that a rural mail route is a complicated thing, as we often turned, twisted and backtracked along the way. We turned up the Pressley Road and delivered mail along the way until the road ended at the Pressley homeplace. On this road at her mail box we chatted with Mrs. Reedy Patch Moon. Mrs. Moon is well known for her thoughtfulness and attention to those in her community who are sick or injured. Before marriage, Mrs. Moon was

Reedy Patch Hill, daughter of Greenberry Hill and the sister of my friend Tilden Hill, who is a retired rural mail carrier. Mrs. Moon told me that she was named for the "Reedy Patch" area where she was born during the flood of 1898.[1]

I knew her father who was a prominent farmer, businessman and Republican Party leader for several decades before and after the birth of the new century. There are only a few left who remember that Greenberry Hill was one of several men in the dark days of December 1930 who had the courage to organize and charter the State Trust Company which opened for business ten days after Hendersonville's three banks closed their doors never to open again. For the next 28 years the State Trust Company was the only bank here until it merged in 1958 and became part of the Northwestern Bank.[2]

On Highway 64 East we passed the large, rambling wooden building operated for many years by the Lowrance family. This was a popular stopping place for summer visitors before and just after World War I. It is typical of the boarding houses that were scattered all over Henderson County before automobiles and motels put them out of business.

Mr. Hall was now putting mail in boxes of patrons who were living in an area rich in the pioneer history of Henderson County. When we stopped to deliver mail at the Western Carolina Apple Packers building, I looked across the road where a young orchard had recently been set.

This area is known to the old ones as the Lucien Edney place and the Lucien Edney house had only recently been torn down. Until a few years ago a cart road led from the Edney home through the woods to the spring besides which William Mills and his wife Eleanor spent their first night in what was to become Henderson County. Some distance from here at the end of the old abandoned cart road, William Mills, his wife and several of their children are buried.[3]

As Alvin Hall and I moved along I could see in the distance where, at one time, stood the home of Samuel Edney. He and his brother Asa came into the area soon after William Mills did. Samuel and Asa Edney each married daughters of William Mills. The village and township of Edneyville take their names from these Edney brothers.[4]

We went past Edney Inn, another one of the popular boarding houses in past years. It was operated for a long time by Mr. and Mrs. Ralph Edney, the parents of Cecil Edney who for a number of years was a clerk in the Hendersonville Post Office. Just beyond here we stopped at the new Edneyville Post Office. Mrs. Joyce Wingate, an attractive and gracious young lady, was Postmistress at the time of our visit. She is the daughter of Jim Rhodes who was Fire Warden of Henderson County for a long number of years.

Here at the Edneyville Post Office we were in the center of the apple country. We stopped at the store next to the post office and had Manuel

[1] Vol. II "Name Lore"

[2] Vol. II "The Builders"

[3] Vol. I "The Founders"

[4] Vol. I "Twilight for the Indians"

Pressley, Jr. fill the gasoline tank. Sixty years ago I bought 1,000 locust fence posts, each one six feet long, cut and delivered to my farm, from Manuel Pressley, Jr.'s father. As we talked, I reminded young Pressley of this and told him I paid his father 20¢ a piece for those fence posts and that today I would have to pay at least a dollar a piece for them. Some of those locust posts are as sound today as the day they were delivered.

From the Edneyville Post Office to the end of the mail route there were apple trees everywhere and apple packing houses, one after the other. We went by Mount Moriah Baptist Church to Point Lookout up the Gilliam Mountain Road. The rock quarry on Gilliam Mountain is no longer operated. It was closed down soon after a security guard named Bowman was killed by several of the rebellious prisoners working in the quarry. The killers escaped, were captured, tried and electrocuted.

When Alvin Hall and I started on the route that December morning in 1970, it was cool but the wind was beginning to blow. By the time we reached Point Lookout it was cold and the wind was howling.

On Point Lookout the early settlers built a fort for refuge when Indians came through the area raiding, killing and burning.[1] This part of the route went almost to Cliff Fields and World's Edge. When we stopped to put mail in Bill Martin's box we talked to Mrs. Martin whom I had known for many years. When I was teaching at Dana and Edneyville, Mrs. Martin was teaching at Point Lookout and Balfour. Bill Martin and I served together on the Farmers Home Administration County Advisory Committee. Only a few nights before this, Mr. and Mrs. Martin had the harrowing experience of being shot at by a migrant laborer in an attempted robbery. Some of the other well known apple growers who live on Route 1 in the Point Lookout area are the Gilberts, Stepps, Roland Jones, the Daltons and Williams, to name a few.

Not too far from the Mountain Home Baptist Church we put mail in the box at the Howard Gilbert home. As noted in Chapter 41, this area is known as Ottanola because for several decades there was a hotel here called the Ottanola Inn for the entertainment of summer visitors. Near here also was the Ottanola Post Office in the days before the coming of R.F.D. From the Gilbert place we started the 2½ mile drive up Sugar Loaf Mountain. No mail boxes along here until we reached the summer colony just below the top of the mountain.

Here also on the edge of the colony were the remains of that large summer hotel that was so popular in the years before World War I. It was called Salola Inn, built by John Williams whose son Henry drove a hack to and from Hendersonville to carry the guests in the days before automobiles.

Entire families from the deep South came to spend all summer at Salola and Ottanola Inns to enjoy the cool invigorating mountain air and to eat the fine foods that made the two Inns famous.

On top of Sugar Loaf Mountain there is a large round white building in an

[1] Vol. II "Scrapbook"

area that is closed to the public but to which we were admitted. This is an installation of the U.S. Government. Jim Rabon, an official of the Federal Aviation Administration, was on duty and invited us into the building which contained some of the most complicated and intricate machinery and instruments that I had ever seen.

Mr. Rabon explained that this station was called the Asheville Vortac, two different facilities sending out signals in all directions to properly guide airplanes. He explained very patiently how everything worked but it was all just too complicated for my feeble mind to comprehend.

When we left the top of the mountain we traveled the Ball Rock Road, the Hog Rock Road, the Slick Rock Road and the St. Paul Episcopal Church Road. At the end of the route we had traveled over eighty measured miles delivering mail. To say I was "shook up," tired and stiff is putting it mildly. But I thanked Postmaster Quinn and Robert Alvin Hall for making it possible to achieve a life long ambition even if it was only for a day.

Alvin Hall & the Author
Discussing their travels on Route 1

Part Eight
Tintypes

Tintypes

CHAPTER 44

Brookland

The large, stately pebbled dashed house has stood with silent dignity for nearly a century and a half on the high hill overlooking Highway 176 and Hendersonville. The place has been known as Brookland and it was witness to the first Court House being built and years later saw that Court House torn down and the present structure erected in its place. And now there is talk that Hendersonville and Henderson County need a still larger hall of justice.

From the high hill over looking a vast wilderness, Brookland watched with interest in 1842 as Charles de Choiseul, County Surveyor, laid out the streets and avenues and building lots and platted the map of the little village that would be chartered in 1847 as Hendersonville, the county seat of Henderson County.* Through the generations the big house with the white columns has acquired a serene dignity and character of its own.

Edmund Molyneau was English Consul with an office in Savannah, Georgia and one in Charleston, S. C. He was also a wealthy man of culture and education. Brookland, also known as the Barker place for more than a century, was bought by Federick Rutledge in 1828 or 1829. Rutledge soon afterwards sold the land to Charles Edmondston who in turn sold it to Edmund Molyneau. Molyneau built the fine house on the hill in 1841 and began to develop the land like an English estate, as a summer home to escape the sweltering low country climate of Savannah and Charleston.

Billie Jones, who lived past his 100th birthday, took me as a young man to Oleetah Falls near the headwaters of Little Hungry River. He showed me the site of the first water power sawmill in that entire area. It had been built and operated by his grandfather as a sash sawmill, commonly called an up and down saw. Mr. Jones told me that his grandfather sawed from the heart of virgin timber all the original lumber to build Brookland. The lumber was hauled from the mill to the Brookland site by ox cart, a round trip taking all day and taking less than 300 board feet at a load. The sash or up and down mill was a crude affair although much faster than sawing lumber by man power.

"If a man put in a full day from the break of day until it was dark, when the days were longest, he could saw possibly 300 board feet of lumber if he didn't rest too often," said Mr. Jones when I asked him how much lumber such a mill could produce in a day. One of the legends about Brookland is that while

* Vol. I "A County and a City Are Born"

Charles Edmonston – Early Owner of Brookland
(Photo compliments of C.S. Staton, Jr. - Present Owner)

hauling lumber from the Oleetah Falls saw mill one day a linch-pin broke on the ox cart while it was going down a steep hill near Upward. The heavily loaded cart, rushing down hill out of control, killed the driver, the yoke of oxen and scattered lumber along the road for nearly half a mile.

When the War Between the States erupted the British Consul was recalled to England. For a period of years the great house overlooking Hendersonville with a superb view of Mount Pisgah stood empty and began to deteriorate.

Another legend about Brookland had its birth during the war period just after Mr. Molyneau was recalled to England. Mr. Molyneau employed a Charleston woman of German descent at Brookland as housekeeper. When he received his orders he returned to Savannah and Charleston and left the housekeeper to follow after she had prepared the house to be closed.

Some say it was a band of bushwhackers while others tell it was a group of Union soldiers with General Stoneman's army.

Whichever it was, a group one day surrounded Brookland and found only the housekeeper in charge. They began to search the house for valuables such as table silver, cut glass, jewelry and money. Finding nothing, they accused the housekeeper of hiding or burying the valuables. She denied the charges and the men began to torture her. Finally they threatened to hang her. The poor creature was frantic with fear but continued to refuse to give any knowledge of what they sought.

Taking her outside among the giant white pines nearby, they put a noose around her neck and threw the other end of the rope around a tree limb. They pulled until her feet were off the ground and she had passed out. She was let down and cold water was dashed over her until she came to. The ritual was repeated several times before the raiding party gave up and rode away.

The unfortunate housekeeper was left a physical and mental wreck. She caught the first stagecoach going towards Charleston. The horses became frightened going down the mountain and plunged over a cliff. The coach was demolished, killing all its passengers. It has been told by the old ones that since that time around Brookland, when the wind is blowing on dark nights, one can hear a woman screaming in fright and pleading for her life. It is said to be the spirit of the housekeeper begging with the hangmen, her pleas mixed with her last screams as the stagecoach plunged down the mountainside.

Brookland was sold in 1882 by Edmund Molyneau's estate to Major Theodore Gaillard Barker, adjutant and chief of staff of the famed South Carolina Confederate calvary leader, General Wade Hampton. Maj. Barker became a successful lawyer of Charleston, S. C. after the war and was active and successful in restoring and operating some of the rice plantations that had been ravaged by the invading Union armies.

Brookland was in very rundown condition when it came into Maj. Barker's possession. He started immediately to restore the grand old white column house for his summer home. The restoration of Brookland was completed in 1892 when the house was pebble dashed. This type of outside finish for homes was just becoming fashionable and popular in Henderson County.

Maj. Barker had now become the largest land owner in the county and was operating Brookland as a successful farming operation, with the help and advice of Dan McCall, Bob Stepp, members of the McGraw family and others. The Major built the county's first dairy barn with concrete floor and stanchions. He imported purebred Devon cattle, a dual purpose breed to improve the milk and beef producing abilities of local cattle. He gave land all the way from East Flat Rock to Hendersonville to the railroad company for a right of way.

In appreciation the railroad established a flag station at the point where the driveway from the big house crossed the tracks, near where Francis and Wright has a store today. For several decades all passenger trains stopped there to take on or let off passengers who were guests or who lived at Brookland.

After living and entertaining lavishly six months out of the year for nearly four decades at Brookland, Maj. Barker died in 1917 and is buried at St. John in the Wilderness. Brookland was bought as a summer home by Henry Ficken, a prominent Charleston banker and businessman. The extensive acreage was later subdivided and sold by the heirs of Mr. Ficken and is today one of Hendersonville's most beautiful residential areas.

Since the early 19th Century the big house has overlooked the city, its

Brookland   (Photo compliments of C. S. Staton, Jr.)

brilliant lights shining in the darkness and its view of the sunset behind Pisgah a magnificent nightly occurrance. The house, surrounded by ten acres and beautifully landscaped, was bought by Mr. and Mrs. Christopher Eugene Staton, Jr. in 1977 and is lived in by the family. Mr. Staton is the son of Christopher Eugene Staton and Helen Katherine McGraw Staton. John F. McGraw, grandfather of the present owner, was at one time caretaker at Brookland and his grandmother, Jannie Lee Gurley McGraw, had also lived there as a child. The first place that Eugene Staton, Jr. came to after his birth at Mountain Sanitarium was his father's home, also on Brookland property.

With such a background, it is most appropriate that Brookland should be owned and lived in by Eugene Staton, Jr. and his family. Recently this author was invited to visit Brookland and he spent several delightful hours touring the house, the out buildings and grounds where as a boy he played in the summertime. There has been little change in the buildings through the years and Mr. Staton told me proudly that what changes have been made are restorations slowly of the original architecture.

CHAPTER 45

The Oklawaha Land Company

Today Hendersonville and Henderson County have a large number of major real estate firms and an even larger number of individuals acting independently as real estate brokers and sales persons. There was a time when only men dealt in real estate but now there are nearly as many women engaged in the business as men. It has been estimated that there are at the present time 500 or more firms and individuals engaged in the business in some shape or form here in Henderson County.

But it was not always so. In 1887 the first real estate firm in all of Henderson County was organized. That would be only eight years after the railroad came to the county. And do you know the name of that first realtor? It was the Oklawaha Land Company. The biggest advertisement ever published up to that time in a Hendersonville newspaper ran in several issues.

A whole page in big bold type tells the story: "Oklawaha Land Company!" screamed the headlines. "W.A. Smith, President; D.M. Hodges, Secretary and Treasurer, Hendersonville, N. C."

The newspaper advertisement goes on: "For the purpose of placing those who have lands for sale in Henderson County and Western North Carolina in direct communication with purchasers we have formed an association in the real estate business and will style ourselves the Oklawaha Land Co. with headquarters in Hendersonville, N. C."

The announcement of the new firm continues: "We have made arrangements to advertise land and will as soon as practical have our agency advertised in the leading journals north and south. Parties wishing to sell their land might do well to see us. If we make no sales, we make no charges. In our advertising we will give the selling price and not the asking price. Call on us or address us, The Oklawaha Land Co., Hendersonville, N. C."

I hope you caught the "call on us" in the above paragraph. You must remember there were no telephones when the Oklawaha was organized. Some of the prices quoted by the real estate firm in 1887 will make one's heart race. "A new house with 8 rooms and 5 acres of land with splendid water in a very desirable part of town on Shaws Creek Street only ½ mile from the Court House for $1,700.00."

The Shaws Creek Street of 1887 is today Sixth Avenue West.* Can you imagine a new eight room house and five acres of land within the city limits for less than $2,000? It is interesting to note that there was no mention of bath rooms. Why? Because bathrooms had not come into existence in 1887 and there was no city water system.

"A vacant lot and one full acre on Church Street for $400 and a two acre lot near Judson College for $220. A new house with two stories, six rooms, stables and ten acres of land, ½ mile from the city, $1,700. A house and lot on Fourth Avenue West containing ⅞ acre. One story house, four rooms, shade trees and a good well of water under the back piazza, garden in high state of cultivation, $750."

And don't you wish you could buy a farm today at the prices quoted by the Oklawaha Land Company? "72 acres, six room house, barn and orchard, 3½ miles from town, price $1000." Another one offers "220 acres, well timbered, eight room house and out buildings, large orchard of young apple trees, eight miles from Hendersonville, $1,800."

The values of real estate have changed since the Oklawaha Land Company was organized in 1887 by W.A. Smith and associates. And the number of people dealing in real estate has increased proportionately with the increased values and the growth in population.

CHAPTER 46

Branson's Business Directory
(1978)

Very few now living have ever seen or heard of Branson's North Carolina Business Directory. It was the Dunn & Bradstreet of its day. I recently came into possession of a copy that was published in 1890. Branson's

* Vol. I "The Marvels of a New Age"

Directory describes Hendersonville as "a beautiful and thrifty town with a population of 680 people. The location of Henderson County could hardly be surpassed for elegant scenery and good land."

V.L. Hyman was Mayor of the city and the City Commissioners were P.E. Braswell, W.A. Hood, J.S. Barnett, H.Y. Gash and Jonathon Williams. In that year of 1890 there were 23 post offices serving the people of Henderson County; most of them no longer exist. As noted in earlier chapters on the U.S. Mail, many had such picturesque names as Angeline, Delmont, Gypsy, Pink Bed, Pump and Splendor. Justice must have been dispensed in a rapid manner in those days; Branson's Directory listed 45 magistrates or justices of the peace.

There were 27 churches served by eighteen ministers throughout the town and county. There were only four denominations. The denominations listed were Baptists with thirteen churches, Methodists with ten, two Presbyterian churches and two Episcopal. It had only been eleven years since the railroad from Charleston to Hendersonville had been completed but already in 1890 there were 23 hotels and boarding houses in the town and county and plans for more were being made. One of these is still operating today nearly a century later. At that time it was known as the Flat Rock Hotel. It had been built before the War Between the States and operated as Farmer's Inn. Today it is in the same location in the same building with much of the same furniture and furnishings which are now antiques. It is now Woodfield Inn and is a luxury hotel famous for its delicious food, catering to a high type of clientele. It is operated by Mrs. Gladys L. Clemmons.

Woodfield Inn   (Photo by Barber)

In that first year of the Gay 90s there were thirteen lawyers practicing here and seventeen doctors in the town and county. There was only one dentist and one barber but there were seven blacksmith shops, five livery stables and Gullick and Ficker Company was manufacturing carriages, buggies and wagons. There were 22 stores in the county listed as general stores, five of them in Hendersonville. For the information of the present day generation, a general store was one selling everything from hairpins, needles, thread and ribbons to saddles, harness, ox yokes, plows, cheese, crackers and sardines; even shoes and men and women's ready to wear.

There were 27 corn and flour mills scattered through the county. Twenty six of them were run by water pouring over the large mill wheel but T. J. Carland of Mills River was very proudly advertising that his grist mill was powered by steam. There were 24 saw mills turning out lumber for building purposes. All were operated by water power except three which were steam driven.

There were 44 public schools in Hendersonville and Henderson County and six private schools. As I told in an earlier chapter, most of the county schools were in session for only a few months each year and were one teacher schools; there were only fifty teachers serving all 44 county schools.

There was only one bank, The State Bank of Commerce and *The Hendersonville Times* was an independent weekly newspaper; J.D. Davis, editor and proprietor. The Oklawaha Land Company was the only real estate firm.

Levi Branson, editor of Branson's Directory of North Carolina, 1890 edition, made this statement in his foreward: "This 7th edition of my directory shows great prosperity in all lines of business and is issued in a time of prosperity in North Carolina."

CHAPTER 47

The Carl Blythe Pictures

When Carl Blythe went to work for the first time in 1913 he was 13 years old. His job was with *The Western North Carolina Times*, a weekly newspaper that was published here. Type setting was done by hand in those days and it was a slow, tedious, messy way but it was the only method used by small newspapers of that era. Carl Blythe retired from newspaper work after more than 40 years experience. When he retired he was with the Hendersonville *Times–News*, our city's modern daily newspaper. He had seen the printing business develop from the days of setting type by hand to the offset printing press that is now used by *The Times–News*.

Carl Blythe and I have been friends for probably sixty years. It is sometimes hard to remember exactly how long because time goes by so fast.

The Jockey Lot

As a boy starting to work when he was only 13 years old and while growing into manhood, he worked at a number of different jobs until he realized that his real calling was newspaper work.

But one of the things that he did in his late teens and early twenties was delivering milk. It was called "peddling milk." I was doing the same thing.

In those days milk was delivered early every morning, so people would have it fresh for breakfast. There were no modern plants like Coble and Biltmore and no supermarkets where people went to buy their daily needs of milk. When Carl Blythe and I were delivering milk, there were a dozen or more people milking from two to twenty cows.

The milk was put into glass pint and quart bottles and capped with waxed pasteboard and paper caps and distributed around town to the homes. There were as many different types of vehicles used to haul the milk as there were people delivering. All were horse drawn buggies, carriages and wagons. Now that I think back to those days, I can't remember ever seeing a milk vehicle pulled by a mule. Carl Blythe and I get together once in a while and reminisce about those horse and buggy days when we meet at Bob Freeman's Newsstand on Church Street.

One day Carl Blythe sat down at my desk in the Northwestern Bank and opened a small package.

"See how much of this you remember," he challenged me.

The package contained four pictures, each four inches square. They were scenes taken at various places in Hendersonville many years ago.

All of them were taken in the days when there were nothing but dirt streets and sidewalks; not even a single square foot of pavement or hard surface. In the pictures showing the streets in Hendersonville, there was not one automobile because there were none in those days. Only horses and mules pulling the vehicles. There are others besides Carl Blythe and me who remember when Hendersonville was that way.

One picture shows the Depot on Seventh Avenue East. By the large crowd gathered there it must have been nearly train time because everybody who could went to the railroad station to see the passenger trains arrive. Looking up Seventh Avenue from the station, you could see the Dotson House, one of the better hotels or boarding houses of that day. The Dotson House was operated by the mother of the late Kate Dotson. For years Kate Dotson taught music here and played the piano and organ at churches and other public gatherings. The Dotson House stood on the corner of Seventh Avenue and Locust Street. It burned down in another of our spectacular fires.

Still looking up Seventh Avenue from the Depot, could be seen the large Victorian style house on the corner of Seventh and Grove Street. This was the house that Bob Freeman and his brothers Tom and Allen and sister Catherine Freeman were raised in. The house is still lived in by Tom Freeman although it has been moved about a half block to where it is on Grove Street. Before World War I Seventh Avenue East was a residential street. Carl Blythe and I can remember when three other prominent citizens lived on Seventh Avenue. They were Judge Hilliard Staton, Judge Jim Shipman and Dr. Walter Carpenter and their families.

There was a picture of Main Street taken in the last decade of the 19th century. Carl Blythe and I could tell this because the pictures were taken from

Depot on 7th Ave. East   (Photo compliments of Carl Blythe)

Main Street Hendersonville In the 1980's
(Photo compliments of Carl Blythe)

the tower of the then new City Hall on Main Street, built in the 1890s. It showed the trees growing down the middle of Main Street and the street car tracks along side of the trees.

But the picture I like best of all was the one of a circus parade going up Main Street. The parade was led by a couple of huge elephants with gorgeous ladies under white umbrellas riding them. The rear of the parade showed the big bandwagon pulled by four large white Percheron horses. The driver wore a uniform and white helmet and the musicians were dressed in bright fancy uniforms.

Carl Blythe and I knew that this picture was taken before November 1915 because the picture showed the parade passing in front of the St. John's Hotel which burned to the ground in November 1915 in one of the most spectacular fires we ever had here.

Lead Elephant of Circus Parade
(Photo compliments of
Carl Blythe)

The End of the Parade
(Photo compliments of Carl Blythe)

CHAPTER 48

Bat Cave
(1957)

Drive out Highway 64 East and you eventually come to the swift, boulder-strewn waters of the Rocky Broad River. Here you cross the river on the wide new concrete bridge that spans the river within yelling distance of the Bat Cave Post Office. It is in the center of the village that is built along both sides of the Hickory Nut Gorge road that goes from Charlotte and Rutherfordton to Asheville.

The post office and town of Bat Cave takes its name from Bat Cave Mountain, on the right as you turn toward Chimney Rock. And Bat Cave Mountain gets its name from a huge dark cave running hundreds of feet back under the mountain. This cave is inhabited by literally thousands and thousands of bats that roost in it during the day before setting forth on their nocturnal search for food at sundown.

This cave has been visited, in the years now gone by, by scientists who came to study the life and habits of the strange flying mammal.

In the early 1900s, in the years before World War I, people spending the summers in and around Hendersonville always visited the Bat Cave area. Regular scheduled trips were made by horse drawn two, three and four seated carriages from Hendersonville. Hacks, the vehicles were called. These livery stable hacks would start just after an early breakfast. The trip to Bat Cave and back would take all day with a picnic lunch on the side of the mountain. The by now weary sight seeing tourists would often not get back to their hotels and boarding houses until late at night.

The river below the bridge was crossed by wading or using stepping stones. A steep, narrow path led up the mountain side from the bank of the Rocky Broad to this cave. Here the older boys of the village below would offer to guide the visitors for a small fee. Only the boldest would go very far into the cave when the pine knot torches showed the thousands of bats hanging upside down from the ceiling and sides of the cave.

But with the passage of time the interests and recreations of our summer visitors change. The cave filled with bats that at one time was a great attraction for our visitors was gradually forgotten. Now only occasionally a curious visitor back packing in the area pays the cave a visit, much to the annoyance of the thousand of bats that make it their home.

The road from the village of Bat Cave is today a hard surfaced, well graded highway, lined on both sides by dwellings, motels, summer hotels, eating places, gift shops and picnic grounds all the way below Chimney Rock to Lake Lure. For a score or more years after the turn of the century there was no Lake Lure; only the road crossed the Rocky Broad River. It was a narrow dirt road going from Rutherfordton through Henderson County and into Buncombe County and Asheville, and there were few houses on it.

This early dirt road was once a toll turnpike and the tollgate stood across it a mile or so below Bat Cave and just across the Henderson County line in Rutherford County. The tollgate and tollhouse was kept by Joe Williams, dead now these many years.

I talked to Mrs. Frank Hudgens, a daughter of Joe Williams. In 1957 she was 94 years or more old, yet she was strong physically and alert mentally. She well remembered that when she was a girl her father operated the tollgate across the road at a point that was called by several names: Parris Gap, Humphrey Hill or Hunklary Hill. It only depended on who was talking in those early days as to which name was used.

There was a narrow path beside the tollhouse through which a person on foot or horseback could go free around the tollgate. But to raise the gate, said Mrs. Hudgens, there was a charge of 25¢ for a wagon pulled by two horses or a yoke of oxen. This road by Bat Cave and Chimney Rock was a passage way to markets south and east of our mountains for cattle, horses, mules, hogs, turkeys and sometimes even ducks and geese raised in Kentucky, Tennessee and Western North Carolina. Droves and flocks of these creatures were continually using this tollroad.

A charge of 5¢ per head was made for the droves of animals like cattle, horses, mules, sheep and hogs but no one now recalls the charge per head for the flocks of turkeys, geese and ducks.

These large bodies of livestock could make their approach to the tollgate known for miles before they reached it by the clouds of dust stirred up by the hundreds of animals and by the shouts of the drovers and the cracking of their blacksnake whips that kept the animals moving.*

Mrs. Hudgens chuckled and told me of the time her father was hoodwinked out of his toll. A drove of several hundred mules came through Hickory Nut Gorge one morning and down the road to the toll gate. The owner rode in front of the mules on a white horse that the mules had been trained to follow. The owner told Mr. Williams that he did not know just how many mules he had with him but he agreed to let the gatekeeper count them as they passed and would then pay for them.

The gate was raised. The rider on the white horse passed through the gate; the rider gave a loud, shrill whistle, spurred his horse into a gallop and the mules stampeded after horse and rider. They all disappeared down the mountain in a cloud of dust.

The people of Rutherford County finally revolted against the toll. Joe Williams moved the gate to the Henderson County side of the road and continued to operate the tollgate and collect the toll for several years more. It was finally discontinued and the use of the road became free. All that remains is the log tollhouse, still standing by the roadside at Parris Gap on Humphrey Hill. It has been restored and is now privately owned.

* Vol. I "Stories These Mountains Could Tell"

CHAPTER 49

Cow in the Well!

The late Frank Waldrop, a prominent and successful man of Hendersonville, retired in 1966 although he was well beyond the age that most men retire. Frank Waldrop had a rare distinction. He was born within the city limits of Hendersonville, always lived within the city limits and was the oldest native born citizen still living within those original city limits. Mr. Waldrop was a descendant of pioneer Henderson County families that have been prominent in city affairs for several generations. Frank Waldrop told me an amusing and interesting episode that happened when he was a boy. It was one that could only happen in a small southern town such as Hendersonville was in the first year of the 20th Century.

In the year 1900 that block in our town that is bounded by Fifth Avenue West, Sixth Avenue West, Main Street and Church Street was owned by W. A. Smith. This is the area that today is occupied solidly by business buildings

Looking West from Main Street from Tower of old City Hall along what is probably 5th Ave. about 1900   (Photo compliments of Carl Blythe)

including First Federal Savings and Loan with its large parking lot. In 1900 this block was a field of grass and corn and the only building on it was a large barn. The land on Seventh Avenue East was also pasture land where J. M. Waldrop, Frank's father, grazed a very fine milk cow which he had recently bought from his brother Dr. J. G. Waldrop.

Just before milking time that day, Frank Waldrop, a bare foot boy of 12, led the cow from the pasture to the barn where First Federal Savings and Loan is now. On the way to the barn, Joe Israel saw the cow and offered to buy it for $75, an unbelievable price at that time. The offer was turned down and Frank led the cow on to the barn and tied her to the corner of the barn with a long chain.

The cow realized that the length of the chain gave her some freedom and she started for the corn field. Nearby was an old dry well covered with boards, about 75 feet deep. The well was where the back of Ed Hartnett's Electric Service Company is now. In her stroll to the cornfield the cow stepped on the rotten boards covering the well and down she plunged, head first into that deep dark well hole.

There was much confusion and much running back and forth, shouting and yelling as the news spread that Waldrop's cow was in the well. John Davis, Frank's uncle, brought his ropes, pulleys and blocks and tackles from his brickyard, located where the railroad crosses Brookland Avenue. A man climbed down the well and tied a rope around the cow's body. Everything went fine until the cow was pulled nearly to the top. Then the rope broke.

Again the rope was taken down and tied to the cow but this time around the animal's neck. Finally the unfortunate beast was pulled to the surface but the poor thing was dead.

Bill Lyda ran a meat market where Morris Kalin has his furniture store now. It was the only meat market in town. For days after the cow was pulled from the well Mr. Lyda sold no beef. The rumor started the next day and spread around town that Bill Lyda had butchered Waldrop's dead cow that night and hung the carcass in his butcher shop to sell. Nobody wanted to eat the meat of an animal that had come to its death in a well.

CHAPTER 50

First City Manager

In 1913 M. M. (Roe) Shepherd, a pioneer merchant of Hendersonville, was still operating a mercantile business only a little further north on Main Street than where he had started a score of years earlier, in the Flave Hart

Early Hendersonville Businesses
Left to Right: *M. M. Shepherd, Thomas Shepherd*
(Cecil Kessler in carriage), with Flave Shepherd

Building that later became known as the Drake Store Building.* In 1913 Roe Shepherd was elected Mayor of Hendersonville to serve until the next election in 1915.

In the spring of 1913 the City Council had revised our city charter and the Legislature of North Carolina, which was in session at that time, approved the new charter. Those few that are still living here and were living here in 1913 have forgotten that the new city charter authorized the City Commissioners to appoint a city manager if and when they so desired.

The records of their June meeting show that the Mayor and the Commissioners voted to have a city manager and George Justice was appointed to that position. His salary was $150.00 a month which was a munificent income in those days. Hendersonville thus became the first town in Western North Carolina to have a city manager form of government.

It was reported in *The Hendersonville Democrat*, the weekly newspaper published here in 1913, that this action of City Commissioners has met with the approval of the majority of the citizens and the first year under a business manager will be watched with interest by all.

How long Hendersonville kept this type of government no one now seems to remember. I have searched the minutes of the Council meetings and have been unable to find any further reference to the matter. However, we do know that it lasted several years because the March 15, 1915 issue of *The Western North Carolina Times* carried a quarter page advertisement in big bold black type: "City Taxes must be paid. April 1st is the limit of time for the

* Vol.I "Vanished Landmarks"

130

Hendersonville's First City Manager, George W. Justice

payment of City Taxes. Don't postpone the payment on the assumption that arrangements can be made for a future time." This was signed by George Justice, business manager.

How soon after this and why the City Council did away with this type of government can only be conjectures. The key to the reason possibly lies in the election of 1915, several months after the March advertisement signed by the city manager. In that election C. E. (Ed) Brooks was elected Mayor and the city administration changed hands.

This change had nothing to do with either the efficiency or popularity of George Justice. In the years that followed he served the people in many ways and was elected to other important offices.

This was Hendersonville's first experience with a manager type of government and it would be more than a half century before we had another city manager, La Vern Bechtel who took office in 1978.

CHAPTER 51

"Five Months in the Old North State"

In 1962 Noah Cochran was a long-time member of the Hendersonville Lions Club. He was very active in working with and helping the blind, a major activity of Lions International where ever there is a Lions Club.

One day he asked if I had ever read a book, "Five Months in the Old North State." The book has long been out of print and today is a collector's item. It is about Hendersonville and Henderson County and Noah Cochran told me where I could see a copy. The local library had never heard of it.

The small concrete block building that stood for many years at the lower end of Seventh Avenue East is no longer there. In 1962 it was lived in by Wilson Watson, often referred to as "the Old Blind Preacher." Wilson Watson has been blind since he was a boy. One day, mixing mortar, the quicklime splashed into his face, searing his eyes so that permanent blindness followed.

Wilson Watson has an autographed copy of this rare book and he knew the author personally. On the flyleaf of the book in the handwriting of the author is the notation: "To Mr. and Mrs. Watson and Wilson Watson with best wishes of Roland F. Holloway, January 18, 1915." And on page 52 of the book is a picture of Wilson Watson with his mother and father in front of the Watson's small log cabin with the caption "A Mountaineer Family."

The entire five months of "Five Months in the Old North State" were spent here in Hendersonville and Henderson County and the book tells much about things as they were then.

The book was written by Roland F. Holloway and published in the early part of 1914. It is dedicated to the memory of his mother, Martha F. Holloway, who died here while she and her two sons were here for their health. The book was published by the Lakeside Press, R. R. Donnelleys and Sons Co., Chicago, Ill. The remarkable thing about this well written book is that the author was only 16 years old when he wrote it and the numerous pictures illustrating the volume were all taken by him and his brother.

Roland Holloway, his younger brother and their mother spent the winter of 1913 and the spring of 1914 here. The author states that "the bright, balmy weather brought joy to the heart and health to the body."

The three people from Chicago found the climate, the lay of the land and our people and customs strikingly different from those of a big city like Chicago. They spent their five months walking, riding horseback and driving over the entire county in a buggy. And the two boys found the joy, happiness and health they came here to seek, saddened only by the death of their mother.

The Post Office was described as a delapidated little building. They rode the Dummy Line out Fifth Avenue West to Laurel Park and walked the path that led from the end of the Dummy Line to Crystal Springs, referred to as Cupid's Path. They were fascinated by the beauty of Osceola Lake which was destined to be washed away by the flood of 1916 and restored in the early 1920s.*

The author describes a carriage trip to the summer estate of Major Theodore G. Barker, the largest land owner in the county at that time. The place was known as Brookland then but today as Brookland Manor. On the same trip he visited St. John in the Wilderness. And here I quote the author: "Hidden in the pines and oaks stood a quaint little structure that was ever beautiful, snuggled quietly in a little knoll with tall waving pines dipping their green heads above it; half covered with ivy; neglected and apparently abandoned. This little church was the most beautiful, the most quiet and most interesting place of worship we ever found in the mountains. Now the old church is only in use for a few weeks during the summer. Its quiet beauty makes it an ideal spot to visit at any time. Time will obliterate the inscriptions on the graves and will crumble the old church into ruins."

How wrong was the author's predictions about St. John in the Wilderness! The little Episcopal church is not abandoned and time has not crumbled it into ruins. Beautifully kept and preserved, the church is now open for services twelve months of the year with the Rev. Mr. Walter Roberts as rector.

The author visited the lodge that was built in the late 1820s by Charles Baring. The author describes it in 1913 as a large frame structure sadly in need of paint, with the windows barred, the shutters swinging to and fro on rusty hinges, the roof of the wide front porch sagging in the middle. Today the lodge is called Mountain Lodge, lived in by the Albert Moreno family. Mountain Lodge today belies the author's description. It is the most beautiful estate in Flat Rock and is the show place of our area.

The thing that fascinated Roland Holloway more than anything else when he visited Mountain Lodge was the little rock spring house. Raised in Chicago, he had never seen a spring house. The large pots and kettles hanging

* Vol. I "The Marvels of A New Age"
  "Fateful Years"

in the spring house and the pans sitting in the cold stream from the spring fascinated him. He had not realized until he visited the spring house at the Mountain Lodge that the only refrigeration in the summer available to a rural family to keep milk, butter and other perishables from spoiling was those rock spring houses with the nearly ice cold water constantly flowing around the utensils.

Who remembers Roland Holloway, his brother and mother who spent five months here in the winter of 1913 and early spring of 1914? Mrs. Fred Corn, who before her marriage was Pauline Pace, daughter of Mr. and Mrs. Winfield Pace of East Flat Rock, told me that her father and mother had known them. At the time Mr. Pace was operating the livery stable on Third Avenue West behind the Justus Drug Store.

When I went to see Mr. Pace he told me that he drove the family in a hack or carriage on all of the trips they took. "I never saw better behaved boys," he said. "After every trip they tipped me a dollar and that was a big tip in the days when a man worked from daylight until after dark seven days a week for five dollars a week."

Mr. Pace was also given an autographed copy of the book by the author but he had given it to his son Leon Pace who lives in California. Mr. and Mrs. Pace and Wilson Watson, the Old Blind Preacher, never saw or heard from the author after he left here except when they received autographed copies of the book titled, "Five Months in the Old North State." But we all agreed that the author, Roland F. Holloway, would hardly believe the many changes that have taken place over the years since he spent five months here in the winter of 1913 and spring of 1914.

CHAPTER 52

1914

In 1914 Hendersonville's newspaper was a weekly called *The Western North Carolina Democrat and French Broad Hustler*. In the last week of the January issue appeared a news item announcing that H. B. Sholar of Columbia, S.C. and Ella R. Peebles of Salisbury, N.C. were married at the Methodist Church parsonage by the Rev. W. F. Womble. The young couple spent their honeymoon at the Kentucky Home. The Kentucky Home no longer exists and the land where the hotel stood on Fourth Avenue West between Church and Washington Streets is now a city parking lot.* John P. Sholar, a son of that marriage, lives in Hendersonville.

In January 1914, there were fifteen livery stables in our town. It was big business and J. B. Brookshire Stables on King Street was carrying a full page

* Vol. II "The Inns of Yesteryear"

F. G. Shepherd in front of M. M. Shepherd's
(Photo compliments of Martha Shepherd)

advertisement in the newspaper: "For Sale or Trade - 25 horses and 25 mules. All are sound, well broken and young." All the livery stables are gone now and their places have been taken by garages, gas stations and used car lots, all of which service automobiles and other motor vehicles instead of horses, buggies and carriages.[1]

Those who today have trouble with remembering zip codes, Social Security numbers and five to eight digit telephone dial numbers should have lived in 1914 because M. M. Shepherd's store across from the Court House had telephone Number 2 and Charles Rozelle Furniture Store's phone was number 4. In 1914 you cranked the bell on your wall telephone to get the operator who was referred to as "Central." When the operator answered you told her the phone number you desired. It didn't matter if you forgot the number because you also told her the name of the person you wanted to speak to. The operator would still connect you and could possibly tell you whether that person was at home or gone shopping or visiting.[2]

The town and county was thrilled by the news that January 1914 that "The excavation for the new Federal post office will begin at once." This was announced by the contracting company who said that the new post office would cost the staggering sum of $60,000. This post office building was the one that was erected on the corner of Fourth Avenue and Church Street and is now called the Federal Building.

The newspaper that last week in January 1914 announced a prize contest sponsored by the paper in which the first prize would be a $75 Rock Hill Buggy.

[1] Vol. I "Days of Yore"
[2] Vol. II "Wonders of the New Century"

The Federal Post Office at Corner of 4th Ave. & Church Street
Just After It Was Built   (Photo by Barbers)

For the information of the young people who might read this, the Rock Hill Buggy was not a baby buggy; it was a vehicle pulled by a horse or mule and was the most popular form of transportation of that time. The Rock Hill Buggy was the elite of those long vanished days.

CHAPTER 53

The First City Directory

Did you know that the first city directory for Hendersonville was published in 1915? I recently saw one of them. It was printed on coarse paper and time has yellowed the pages. There are scores of people listed in that first city directory who are still living here but the vast majority of them have scattered to the four corners of our nation or have passed on to the "Great Hereafter." A number of the family names listed in that directory are still found in the latest one published. This first little old directory is an interesting small volume and as I thumbed through it the memory of those days of 1915 flood my mind with a feeling of nostalgia.

"Hendersonville is located upon a broad, level table land around which winds the Oklawaha," reads the introduction which goes on to say, "There are thousands of opportunities awaiting the right man to develop them." When that first directory was published, the Post Office was still on the southwest corner of Fourth Avenue West in the building that in later years became known as the Rose Pharmacy Building. The new Post Office Building was nearly finished. It is now known as the Federal Building. Hendersonville's Post Office today is on Fifth Avenue West.

The City Hall and Opera House was on the east side of Main Street between Fourth and Fifth Avenues. It would be ten years before this first City Hall was condemned as unsafe, torn down and work was started on the present City Hall on the corner of Fifth Avenue East and King Street.[1] The street car tracks ran down the middle of Main Street from Second Avenue to the railroad station on Seventh Avenue.[2] When the first directory was published the Confederate monument which today stands on the Court House lawn was in the middle of Main Street at First Avenue.[3]

Charles Rozelle, the furniture man, had his store across from the Court House in 1915 but he later moved it farther up Main Street between Third and Fourth Avenues. And only a few still living here remember, as the directory puts it, "It pays to trade at the Bee Hive where every day is a special day." Calico was selling for 5¢ a yard and a new shipment of oil cloth for the dining room and kitchen tables had just been received. Frank Israel was advertising his livery stable service on Third Avenue.

There was a full page advertisement advising everybody to ride the trolley car to Laurel Park.

This was the old Dummy Line that started at the corner of Fifth Avenue West and Main and ran on the tracks out Fifth Avenue to Crystal Springs where you could take the Swiss Cog railroad to the observation tower several hundred yards above the spring.[4] There was also in that first directory an advertisement announcing the services of Miss Purkey. I wonder if anyone now living here remembers Miss Purkey who advertised her services in 1915. She was quite a person. "Miss Purkey - dress making - Graduate of the American College of Dress Making in Kansas City, Missouri - Fashionable Dress Making and Ladies High Class Tayloring a specialty."

"The Central Cafe, 225 N. Main St. Regular Meals 35 cents. Private Dining rooms for Ladies and Escorts." Hendersonville was a little town in 1915 and everybody knew everybody else. Tongues would wag with gossip if a local girl made so bold as to enter such a place. Only the summer girls with escorts would dare use a private dining room.

Gallamore Drug Company was on the corner of Seventh Avenue East and Locust Street and the Candy Kitchen was across from the Depot. It was a mouth watering place for young people to gather while waiting for the passenger trains to arrive.

[1] Vol. I "Vanished Landmarks"
[2] Vol. I "The Marvels of A New Age"
[3] Vol. I "The War Between the States"
[4] Vol. I "The Marvels of A New Age"

Early Business of Hendersonville – Danny Dogan in Front

Some of the leading merchants listed were M. M. Shepherd at the monument across from the Court House, H. Patterson, E. Lewis and Son, Lott's Cash Shoe Store, Justus Drug Store, J. G. Williams and Hunter's Pharmacy.

Hendersonville has changed through the years and has grown a lot since that first directory was published in 1915. I hope that some of those who read this will remember some of the things that I have told in this chapter.

CHAPTER 54

Indian Cave Lodge
(1969)

In 1969 it was a ramshackled derelict, ravaged by the creeping decay of neglect during the passing years. There was a time though that it was a place of splendor, filled with the gay, rippling laughter of young people and of the old ones who were still young in spirit. Even in 1969, although it had been vacant and unattended for nearly two score years, the echo of dancing feet could almost be heard through the deserted halls of the old building.

Very few of those who have come here to live in late years have ever heard of or know where the old hotel was located and there are those who have lived a lifetime here who did not know how to get to it. There are two ways to go to Indian Cave Lodge and Indian Cave high on the side of Mount Hebron.

The View From Indian Cave   (Photo by Barber)

When you get there you have a magnificent view of the Big Willow and Little Willow River Valleys.

One way is to drive out Fifth Avenue West through Laurel Park. When you come to the sign which directs you to Poplar Lodge you are on the Jones Gap Road. This Jones Gap Road was surveyed and built by Solomon Jones, the Road Builder.*

At the Jones Gap Baptist Church there is a road that turns sharply left up the mountain. This road goes to Indian Cave Park and the Lodge.

Or you can drive out the Willow Road and take the Finley Cove Road which is named after a pioneer settler who came to the area from Ireland. The Finley Cove Road will bring you to Jones Gap. It is a pleasant drive to go one way and come back the other route.

Indian Cave, Indian Cave Park and Indian Cave Lodge were all on the side and top of Mount Hebron. Solomon Jones, who died in 1899 at the age of 97, owned all of this land during his lifetime. He lived on it and raised his family on this mountain. He named it Mount Hebron because he was a religious man and when he acquired this nameless mountain Solomon Jones remembered how the children of Israel had come unto Mount Hebron where the land flowed with milk and honey. He built an observation tower on top of Mount Hebron that was a famous tourist attraction in the horse and buggy days.

* Vol. II "Scrapbook"

Virgil Jones, Jr., who is a prominent building contractor and a great great grandson of Solomon Jones, helped me gather much of the information about Indian Cave Park and Lodge.

At the beginning of the century Hicks Jones, son of Solomon, sold 100 acres of land to Reginald Sumner from St. Petersburg, Florida. There was a building on this property known as the Farm Cottage. Sumner added a dining room and erected tents in the vicinity of the Farm Cottage. These tents were rented to summer visitors who were fed at the Farm Cottage dining room.

Sumner was unable to meet the terms of the mortage on this property and after a few years lost the land. Another Floridian who was originally an English sea captain by the name of Gilbart bought the land. In the early part of 1917 Gilbart started to build Indian Cave Lodge. Two Henderson county natives, Ben Orr and Ernest Drake, supervised the building of Indian Cave Lodge.

Capt. Gilbart operated the hotel during the summer months until his death several years later. During the period that he operated the lodge he sold a number of building lots to friends from Florida for building their own summer homes. The captain gave the area where he sold the lots the name Indian Cave Park. The name came from the large cave high on Mount Hebron. Legends handed down tell that the cave with its awe-inspiring view was used by the Cherokee Indians to hold their religious rites and ceremonies. Legend also says that the cave was used as a place to hide by deserters and draft dodgers during the Civil War.

When Capt. Gilbart died the Indian Cave, Park and Lodge were acquired by Joe Davis and F. I. Kithcart who operated it as a partnership. It was during this period that Indian Cave Lodge reached the peak of its glory. In 1926 it became nationally known because it was where Jack Dempsey trained for his fight with Gene Tunney.

Dempsey stayed at the Lodge while training and thousands flocked to Mount Hebron to see him work out with his sparring partners, Tilley Kid Herman and Pete Angelos. With him that summer at Indian Cave Lodge was Dempsey's wife, the glamorous moving picture star, Estelle Taylor. She was as famous in her own right as was Dempsey.

Every morning, as part of his training, Jack Dempsey ran all the way from the Lodge to the Hendersonville Post Office and back. When Dempsey and his retinue left, Young Stribling, "the Boy Wonder from Georgia," came to Indian Cave Lodge to train for his fight with Berlenback for the light heavyweight championship.*

Sometime in the late 1930s Kithcart and Davis sold Indian Cave Lodge to Jack Hearst, a reputedly wealthy Miami baker. Mr. Hearst built a large horse and cattle barn behind the lodge. In the big barn loft he put a dance floor. He named it the Golden Bull Barn Dance Hall. All summer, every summer, the Barn echoed to the stamping feet of the square dancers until the wee hours of morning.

* Vol. I "The Roaring Twenties"

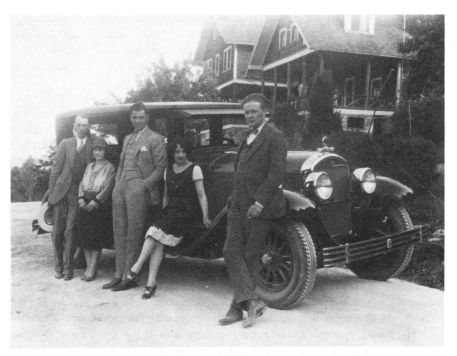

Jack Dempsey & his wife in Laurel Park, Walter Smith on Right
(Photo by Barber)

Mr. Hearst proved to be a better bakery man than an operator of a resort hotel. When he died the property went into receivership and the Indian Cave Lodge closed. There it sat, idle, empty and rapidly falling into decay, high on the side of Mount Hebron. It was a rotting symbol and reminder of the gay times of the Roaring Twenties and the years that followed in Hendersonville and Henderson County. Today Indian Cave Lodge no longer exists.

CHAPTER 55

The Brenner-Penny Fire

The real estate boom of the Roaring Twenties was at its height here in our mountains. Property of all kinds changing hands daily at undreamed of prices that a few years earlier would have been considered fantastic. Suburbs were springing up like mushrooms overnight. This was the period of time when Laurel Park, Druid Hills and Sylvan Heights were developed. Land that was covered with scrub timber, briars, bushes and underbrush suddenly - overnight it almost seemed - would be cleared, subdivided into lots and paved streets and put up for sale on the auction block.

People were scrambling over each other to buy before the building lots increased in value. The town and county were booming and there seemed to be no end in sight.* Hunter's Pharmacy was on the corner of Fifth Avenue West and Main Street. Next to it, in the space now occupied by Sterchi's Furniture Store, the Brenner-Penny Department Store had recently been opened. It was stocked with high priced, top quality merchandise.

The fashionable men, women and children's clothing were the latest styles from New York, London and Paris. It was a dream store such as we had never before had here.

Just south of the Brenner-Penny Store was the Hendersonville Book Store operated by Yates Little whose wife taught in the city schools.

It was cold that Friday night of November 12, 1926 when the whole town and a large part of the county was awakened just after midnight by the shrill screaming of the recently installed fire siren that took the place of the big old fire alarm bell that had been in the recently condemned tower of the City Hall.

The Fire Department had just done away with its horse drawn equipment and in its place there were two shining red motorized vehicles whose clanging bells added to the bedlam as men and equipment rushed to the scene of the fire. Those awakened that cold November night hurriedly dressed and made their way to the fire. In a short time, Main Street and Fifth Avenue were packed and jammed by eager spectators. All wanted to help fight the now roaring fire but most were only hampering the efforts of trained, professional fire fighters.

The smoke billowed high in great black clouds. Then the flames began to dart skyward as the fire got out of control. It looked as if all of Main Street was doomed to go up in the flames that autumn night in 1926. The Asheville Fire Department was frantically called on for help and Asheville rushed over men and a fire truck equipped with the latest fire fighting equipment. When the Asheville truck reached here it had trouble reaching the fire, so densely packed were all the streets with spectators.

It was long after dawn before the fire was brought under control. Hunter's Pharmacy had been damaged by smoke and water. The Brenner-Penny Department Store, the pride and joy of Hendersonville, was gutted by fire and Yates Little's Book Store was also badly damaged. The reported loss amounted to $250,000, which would be equivalent to a million dollars today. More fire fighting equipment was used to put out the fire than had ever been used before in the history of our town.

Hendersonville had had a big scare and a night of excitement. Only the valiant efforts of our fire fighters saved the town from total destruction.

* Vol. I "The Roaring Twenties"

CHAPTER 56

Brookshire's Stable
(1961)

The old building has served its purpose, a relic that changing times had made useless. It was being destroyed in the name of progress. It was not so old as age is numbered in years yet for more than half a century it had been a landmark in Hendersonville and there are old ones who cannot remember when it had not stood there on the northeast corner of King Street and Second Avenue East.

During its years of usefulness it served a way of life that completely disappeared with the development of the machine age. It was the center of a way of life that our present younger generation knows nothing about. And it is such a pity.

On a January day in 1961, Roy Williams and I were riding down King Street when we came to the huge old wooden building at Second Avenue. Around it were a swarm of workmen. "Well," I remarked, "at last the old Brookshire Livery Stable is being torn down."

"It sure looks that way," replied Mr. Williams and then added, "It is the last symbol left that marks the end of an era."

And so it was, the last of its kind. At one time in Hendersonville there were fifteen livery stables.

The exact year it was built no one seems to recall. Older ones say about 1910, others 1908 and still others say earlier than that. I think so too because I was a good size boy in 1908 and 1910 and the Brookshire Stable building looked to me as if it had been there a long time. But most agree that the stable was built around the turn of the century when operating a livery stable was a lucrative and flourishing occupation in our mountains and buying, selling and trading horses and mules was big business.

The Brookshire Stable was built by Joe McCrary, a well known builder in Henderson County at the time. Mr. McCrary used the best lumber that could be sawed. He built it for a man by the name of John Burke, a lightning rod salesman from South Carolina who was investing his money in property here.

The livery stable was 100 feet long and 50 feet wide. There were box stalls in it and enough tye stalls to bed 30 head of horses at a time, a loft large enough to store tons of hay, corn and oats to feed the animals. As soon as the building was finished, John Burke leased it to Tom Jackson who was one of our leading citizens and an experienced livery stable operator.

After a few years it was operated in turn for short periods by Henry Lane, T. C. Wilkins and Tillman Brock. In 1914 J. B. Brookshire and V. C. V. (Vol) Shepherd bought the property and operated the business as a partnership. In 1916 Mr. Brookshire bought the interest of Vol Shepherd and from that time

Mr. Ernest Brookshire   (Photo by Barber)

forward the old red barn-like structure was a landmark known as Brookshire Stable.

Mr. Brookshire operated the stable until 1930. By that time the era of livery stables was past. Automobiles, garages and service stations were rapidly increasing in numbers. In 1930 Ernest and Otto Brookshire took over the running of the stables. It then became what is known as a sales stable, a place where horses and mules were bought, sold and traded.

Now that too is gone and the old place has been destroyed. Ernest Brookshire was the last of a long line of livestock traders. Some others were Coachworth Young, Mitch and Henry McMinn, Louis and Mark Anders, Furman Howard, Jim Dotson and his son Claude and Wallace Redden.

A few days after Roy Williams and I watched the destruction of Brookshire Stables, I dropped by to see Ernest Brookshire.

"Yes," he said, "I went to St. Louis in 1931 and bought my first carload of horses to ship here after I started my sales stable. After that trip I went to Texas and Oklahoma to get my horses. Work horses were what people wanted then but now thirty years later all they want are riding horses."

Ernest Brookshire paused as he looked around and then started talking again. "When I was a boy our stable was always busy. We put out a fancy family turnout," he told me. "Sometimes on weekends our one horse buggies would be booked two or three weeks ahead. Young men sparkin' their girls! Courtin' was getting serious when a young fellow took his girl ridin' in a livery stable rig."

"People back then could hire double rigs, carriages, surreys with fringes around the top. Young people only know what a surrey is these days from that song about 'A Surrey With the Fringe on Top,'" Ernest Brookshire concluded sadly.

The era that Ernest Brookshire and I were talking about was the days when traveling salesmen came to town on a train, carrying samples of the goods they were selling in suitcases. They were called drummers and a drummer always wore a black or brown derby hat. When a drummer hit town he would always go to a livery stable and engage a horse and buggy for the duration of his stay in the area to call on his customers. The standard risque jokes of the days before automobiles were always about a traveling salesman and a farmer's daughter.

Mr. Brookshire and I also talked about the great thrill young people had when they went on a straw ride on a moonlight night in the spring and summer. Sometimes the large flat-bedded wagons filled with hay or straw and loaded with boys and girls would require four and six horse teams to pull them over our rough country and dirt roads of that day.

We also talked about horse traders in the early part of the century. They were called horse jockeys and they went through the country side with strings of horses and mules gypsy-style, buying, selling and trading.

In a few days the old building was gone. When the last board was hauled away, Brookshire Livery Stable was only a memory in the minds of the old ones. The last reminder of a way of life in Hendersonville and Henderson County was gone forever.

CHAPTER 57

The Old Order Passes
(1968)

Hendersonville is often referred to as one of the most cosmopolitan towns for its size found most anywhere. Through the years Hendersonville and the surrounding area have increased in population due to the influx of industry and retired people who are coming here from all parts of the United States to make their homes. As a result, there has been a tremendous increase in permanent residents during the past fifteen or twenty years. There was a time that some of us remember when a body could walk down Main Street or go to the Post Office and know and call nearly everybody by their first names. That is no longer true. Social groups, clubs and civic organizations hold their meeting now in 1968 with their entire memberships made up of persons who have come here to live in recent years.

I was one among several at a gathering in December 1968 when the conversation turned to "Do you remember when?" or "If you remember when, you have lived here a long time." There are still a lot of us who can remember these things of the past; there are many who should remember but have forgotten with the passage of time.

Do you remember the last team of horses that pulled the firewagons before the Fire Department was motorized? It was a beautiful pair of shining blacks. It was a thrill to see those horses dashing down the street at a full

Main Street Hendersonville About the Turn of the Century
(Photo by Barber)

146

gallop with the driver strapped to the seat, leaning forward, straining on the reins and clanging the foot bell under the dash board. [1]

Do you remember when Main Street was unpaved and it was a sea of mud during a wet spell or ankle deep in dust in dry weather? There were stepping stones at nearly every corner to use when crossing the street. These were no longer necessary when Main Street was hard surfaced in 1910. The Blue Ridge Inn, later renamed the Plaza Hotel, stood on the corner of Main Street and Third Avenue West. Where Harold and Pat Flanagan have their printing shop on Third Avenue there was a livery stable as late as 1921 or 1922 and just off Main Street on Third Avenue East Frank Israel operated a livery stable. [2]

Do you remember when the biggest excitement in town was created when a team of horses or mules would become frightened and run away with whatever vehicle they were pulling? The team would dash down the street, followed by a crowd of men and boys and barking dogs trying to catch the run aways. In those days the bottom lands along the Southern Railroad tracks were used for pastures. People would pasture their horses and mules along the railroad when the animals were young so that they would become accustomed to the trains. When the horses or mules were broken for riding or driving they would no longer be frightened by trains. One of the highest recommendations in selling or trading a horse or mule was to guarantee that the animal would stand when a train went by.

The Candy Kitchen was across from the Depot. The small boys and girls with a penny or so would gaze at the candy displayed in the glass counters trying to decide what each would buy. If one still had a penny or two left, it was exciting to lay them on the track. The heavy engine and cars would mash them paper-thin and as large as a quarter. R. P. Freeman operated a general store on the corner of Seventh Avenue East and Locust Street where the farmers from the Ridge bought their overalls and work shoes. This was when Seventh Avenue was known as Depot Street.

And there are those still living here who can remember when nearly every family in Hendersonville kept a flock of chickens in the back yard. The City Council finally had to pass an ordinance forbidding keeping chickens in town because the summer visitors in our boarding houses and hotels complained that the roosters crowing and the cackling hens in the early morning daylight disturbed their sleep. Many families kept a cow for the family milk and butter; a pig or two to fatten for the winter's supply of lard, bacon, ham and sausage. Pigs and cattle were finally banned by law, over the violent protests from home owners. By this time health and sanitary laws were being enforced. People moved their pig pens to the bottom lands along Mud Creek.

Every morning and every afternoon people would be seen making a bee line towards the Mud Creek bottoms to feed their pigs and hogs. In the summer time the smell from the hog pens was horrible when the wind from the east blew the stench towards town.

[1] Vol. I "Vanished Landmarks"
[2] Vol. I "Days of Yore"

If you remember these things you are well past middle age. In fact you can consider yourself elderly and even on the verge of being old. And you are past the verge of being old if you can remember when a large stream of water flowed through the Plum Thicket and across the road where Five Points is today and there was a grist mill powered by this stream of water near where the V. F. W. Post is now.

You have lived a long time in Hendersonville if you can remember when there was no bridge across Mud Creek at the end of South Main Street. You drove your wagon, buggy, carriage or ox cart through the creek; small boys waded it barefoot and grownups on foot used stepping stones to cross it. In later years there was a wooden bridge and then a concrete one. The road to Flat Rock was referred to as the Causeway. You are an old timer if you can remember when Mr. and Mrs. John Francis operated a large livery stable where there is an automobile agency today. Across the railroad tracks from the livery stable was the West Hendersonville railroad station where several passenger trains on the Toxaway Branch of the railroad stopped every day to take on and let off passengers.[1]

There are those still living who can remember when Church Street came to a dead end at Eighth Avenue West and the High School was the remodeled, two story, white Noterman Building on the hill where Boyd Park is now. On the north corner of Seventh Avenue West and Main Street stood a long wooden building. Harry Hardy operated a sandwich and soft drink shop in the front of the building while Bobby Jones had a bicycle repair shop in the back. This was the place where the high school bunch gathered to gossip and exchange plans and news.

You are an old timer if you can remember when the athletic field was a baseball diamond and a football field in season and it was surrounded by a high board fence. At the south end of the athletic field on Ninth Avenue West stood a big wooden building, the first gymnasium with the first indoor basketball court. And where the present high school now stands there was a wild plum thicket where the winos of that day spent their wasted lives and where the high school students hid when they played hookey or where they sneaked to smoke forbidden cigarettes or chewed tobacco.[2]

You can really be classed as an old timer if you can remember when there were seven wooden bridges on the Chimney Rock Road from the lower end of Seventh Avenue East to where the WHKP and WKIT Broadcast House is now located. The road was next to impassable in the wintertime when it thawed after a hard freeze and the wagons were axle deep in the mud.

What an old timer you are if you can remember when the Confederate monument, now on the Court House lawn, stood in the middle of Main Street at First Avenue and the excitement caused that day when Major Theodore G. Barker was driving to town from Brookland, his summer home, and his horse dropped dead right by the monument. The monument was moved to its

[1] Vol. II "The Age of Steam"
[2] Vol. I "The Educators"

148

The Confederate Monument when it stood in the middle of Main Street with Skin Drake's store in the Background (Photo by Barber)

present position when automobiles began to become numerous and the monument became a traffic hazard.*

If you are not an old timer now, you will be if you live long enough and can tell your children and grandchildren that you remember when Main Street was a wide thoroughfare running through the middle of Hendersonville in a straight line.

* Vol. I "The War Between the States"

Hendersonville and Henderson County is growing by leaps and bounds and at a rapid pace not believed possible a few decades ago. This is progress, or at least what we think of as progress. Progress means that the old things must go to make way for the new. As a result, landmarks that have been familiar through the years are rapidly being torn down. As each one disappears, there is a tug at the heart strings and a feeling of nostalgia.

It all seemed to start when Skin Drake's Store was demolished. It was recognized as the first building in the city limits and was older than either the town or the county.[1] This was followed by the demolition of Judson College. This huge gray rock building had been in its time a college, a public school and finally a sanitarium. It disappeared to make way for a housing development.

Fassifern School for Girls has been torn down to make way for a modern supermarket.[2]

Gone is the Freeze mansion on the corner of Third Avenue West and Washington Street. For over half a century this magnificent house with its white columns was the home of Dr. R. P. Freeze and his family. It was one of the most striking houses in Hendersonville. In its place is the new Henderson County Public Library, built at a cost of half a million dollars. Across Third Avenue from the Freeze house was a hotel that catered to our summer visitors for many decades. This big three story wooden hotel was known by various names as the owner changed. In the last few years of its existence it was called the Jefferson.

The large grim sandstone house on Sixth Avenue West which was the home of the Flem Brooks family, has been demolished and in its place is a modern apartment house. The Brookland barns were built with hand-hewed virgin heart timber. The notched logs were pinned with locust pins and were as sound in 1968 as when they were hoisted in the years before the War Between the States. The Brookland barns on the edge of Highway 176 were also known as the Barker barns and were built by Edmond Molyneau, British Consul stationed in Savannah, to house his horses and cattle.

Blue Ridge School for Boys is closed for the first time since it was established in 1914. The buildings on Highway 64 East stand empty and silent, buildings that have echoed to the voices of boys from every state in the United States and many foreign countries. The school was established by Professor Joe Sandifer and his brother-in-law Professor A. G. Randolph. Its demolition is scheduled to start at once.[3]

Time marches on and with it disappear the landmarks that hold many happy memories for the old ones who knew them in the days of their youth.

[1] Vol. I "Vanished Landmarks
[2] Vol. II "Schools of Distinction"
[3] Vol. II "Schools of Distinction"

Part Nine
Big & Little Game

Part Nine

Big and Little Game

CHAPTER 58

A Possum Hunting Man
(1960)

"Kick me but don't kick my dog!" This old adage applies to mountain men of the Blue Ridge and particularly does it describe the feeling of men who hunt with hound dogs. There are three kinds of hunting in these mountains of ours that, once in a body's blood, stays there through life: fox hunting, coon hunting and possum hunting. All of these types of hunting are done at night.

At any and every crossroads country store since time immemorial talk will always eventually get around to hound dogs: red bones, blue ticks, Walkers and pot likkers. Each breed has its admirers. Then there are those who hold to red bone and blue tick crosses or red bone or blue tick crossed with Walkers or pot likkers. It is rare a body sees in these days a real pot likker, those long legged, big bodied black and tan hounds with sad faces and long drooping ears. There was a time when every rural mountain home had one or more of these dogs lazing around asleep in the shade.

The stories that mountain men can tell of the hunting abilities of these dogs sound fantastic to those who know nothing of the nocturnal delights of fox, coon and possum hunting.

Once he becomes a hunter, a mountain man will stay out as long as the stars shine and he can hear the mouth of his dog when it hits a hot trail on a crisp, cold, clear night.

Of all the hunters I have ever known, the most dedicated one was my old friend the late Silas Case, the father of Yap and Frank Case out Horse Shoe way. Silas Case, at age 90, was still a possum hunting, tobacco chewing mountain man. In all the years I knew him I never saw a time that he didn't have a chew in his mouth or he didn't have time to talk about how to grow tobacco or about the fun of possum hunting.

At the time of this incident, Maggie and I had a shaggy little dog named Susie Q. We never agreed as to her pedigree but we do agree that Susie Q. was as sharp as a briar. When she barked we could tell by her bark whether she was barking at a stray dog, a loose calf or cows, a person or whether the chickens, guineas or turkeys were in the yard.

On a cold January morning in 1960, Susie Q. woke me at 5:00 o'clock. I could tell by her tone that she was barking at a person. But who would be around at this time of the morning behind my house?

When I got to the kitchen window I could see a light slowly moving across my orchard on the hill across the branch. My first thought was who or what was a body doing out there at this time of morning when it was cold and black dark?

Then I suddenly remembered that my old friend Silas Case was visiting a friend for a few days on the adjoining farm. Silas Case, then 90 years old, had been possum hunting all night on nearby Corn Mountain with only his hound dog and a lantern for company. Dark as it was, it was 5:00 o'clock. That was breakfast time for him and he was coming in to eat. A possum hunting, hound dog loving mountain man, Silas Case hunted possums as long as he was able to walk and hear the music coming from his favorite hound's mouth as it opened on a hot trail or sent back the message that it had finally treed a possum.

CHAPTER 59

Rabbit Gums

In early days the fall of the year was the season to set rabbit gums. This was before rabbits were protected by stringent game laws and wild rabbits supplied a sizeable portion of the fresh meat eaten during the winter months. At that time it was not against the law to sell wild game in our stores and meat markets.

It is rarely done now but in the days of another generation practically every boy on a farm in Henderson County had a string of rabbit gums. They began to set rabbit gums after the first heavy frost had killed the vegetation. Many a mountain boy earned his first spending money selling the rabbits caught in his gums.

For those reading this who might not know, a rabbit gum is a simple trap made from a portion of a hollow log or made by nailing four boards together in the shape of a rectangular box. The opening to the trap or gum was a door held by a trigger. When the curious rabbit went into the gum the trigger was tripped, dropping the door, and the rabbit was caught. Rabbits were not the only animals caught. Many a boy on a cold, gloomy winter morning has been surprised to find a possum, small dog, cat or other animal in his gum instead of a rabbit. And it was a sad boy who found some morning a skunk in the trap instead of a rabbit.

As I mentioned, for a boy with a string of gums it meant money because the rabbits could not only be sold to the meat markets but also peddled around town to the individual housewives and boarding houses. When a boy caught a wild rabbit, skinned and dressed it for sale, the fur was always left on one of the hind feet. This was required so that the purchaser could know the animal being sold was actually a rabbit. At the beginning of one winter a rumor spread through town that some boys were killing and skinning cats for rabbits. The market for rabbits was completely wiped out until some wise person came up with the idea of leaving the fur on one hind foot for identification. The rabbit market immediately revived.

There was quite a technique to setting a string of rabbit gums. Several weeks before it was time to put them out, a farm boy would walk carefully over the territory he was going to trap. This was to locate the rabbit trails that criss-crossed through the woods and fields. It was along these trails that a successful trapper set his traps.

Every farm boy used his own favorite bait in the traps and in the one and two teacher schools recess was the time when boys argued about which bait was the best. Some held to apples. Others claimed that onions were better than apples. Some boys baited their gums with salt. Then there were those that argued that the best bait of all was a combination of cabbage leaves, onions and salt.

I can remember and so can some of you older readers possibly remember how these arguments were finally broken up. This was when the most successful trapper on the school playground would be appealed to.

"Heck! I don't use no bait at all! A fool rabbit will just poke his head in a gum to see what's in there! He's caught before he finds there ain't nothin'!"

The times when a mountain boy set rabbit gums are gone. In these days of consolidated schools and school buses and television, a boy misses something in life as he goes through his boyhood days and never sets and tends a string of rabbit gums, even if he did have to visit them every day before daylight on a cold windy snowy morning.

CHAPTER 60

The Beaver Invasion
(1958)

There are very few people who realize that we have beavers in Henderson County. There are even fewer people who know that beavers on the loose can be a problem in these modern days when agriculture is highly developed and intensified farming is practiced. But the farmers who cultivate the fertile bottom lands along Green River know what a problem beavers can be.

On these lands along the upper Green River Valley in Green River Township are produced the finest pole beans in the world. These same acres produce 100 or more bushels of corn per acre. This is the same area of the J. B. Beddingfield home. In 1958 he had recently been elected as one of our County

Commissioners. And it is this same area of Henderson County that offers some of the most beautiful scenery in the country. It is here the beavers made a sudden appearance creating a problem. How did they get here? Where did they come from? What are the problems created by them and what is the solution?

In the days before the white man came to these mountains of Western North Carolina, the broad plateau which is now Henderson County was the natural home of these fur bearing animals with the broad flat tails. The Indians relished the flesh of the beavers as food and valued the fur bearing pelts for their warmth when made into clothing or used for bedding.

Among the first pioneers to come into our mountains were many trappers and traders seeking beaver pelts that were in great demand in Europe. The beavers in Western North Carolina were soon wiped out. So valuable were beaver hides in pioneer days that they were used as standards of value and in many places as money.

The beavers have been nearly extinct for so long in our mountains that few people now living know that Henderson County was the natural home of those animals.

You can imagine my amazement in 1958 when I began to hear tales of beavers on Green River. That such a thing could be true in those days was unbelievable. The rumors became so persistent that I decided to find out if there was any truth to them. I drove past Tuxedo and stopped at the store operated by my friend the late Ulas Staton on Highway 25 on the side of Green River. Mr. Staton kept posted on everything that went on in that area. He and his son Paul were expert woodmen and trappers.

I sat by the pot bellied stove in the back of the store and asked him if what I had heard as rumors had any truth to it. He knew all about the beavers and had seen some of them. He told me where to go so I drove past Green River Baptist Church. Just this side of Cedar Springs Baptist Church, I stopped at the home of J. B. (Jiggs) Beddingfield.

"We sure have been having our problems," he said. "Get in the truck with me. I'll take you and show you."

He drove along a winding road and across the fields further up Green River. We stopped and walked down to the river. The day before he brought in a bulldozer to tear out a dam the beavers had recently built.

The beavers had built the dam so high that Green River was overflowing onto Mr. Beddingfield's fertile farming land. To make matters worse, the animals had cut down a large part of his field of corn, pulled the corn stalks into the river and used them with logs and mud to make the dam.

Where in the world did they come from? How did they get into Henderson County? Some one suggested that I talk to Frank Bell, owner and operator of Camp Mondamin. This was the first summer camp for young people to be established in the county.

Frank Bell and his brother Joe Bell, who operates Camp Arrowhead, are pioneers in camp operations in Henderson County and it's largely due to

Frank and Joe Bell that the county has become the summer camp metropolis of the southern states. Frank Bell was away at the time but I talked to Nathan Thompson and Kenny Ward, able assistants at Camp Mondamin. They told me how it all began.

All wildlife around the camp is protected so young people at camp can study wildlife at firsthand. Several years before my 1958 visit, Mr. Bell obtained two females and one male beaver from the N. C. Wildlife Commission. His idea was that these beavers would settle and build a dam on one of the camp streams. The campers could then see how this rare species actually lived and worked. A pen was built for them where Davis Creek runs into Bob's Creek. This pen was to hold the new arrivals until they became acclimated. In less than three days the beavers had escaped from the pen and disappeared. Six months later one of them was seen several miles up Green River from Camp Mondamin. Nothing had been heard or seen of beavers since that one sighting. It was taken for granted that all of them had been killed or had died.

Then suddenly unnumbered beavers began to build dams up and down the river flooding the lands and destroying the crops.

Something had to be done. Although beavers are protected as endangered species, they can be destroyed if they are destroying crops. Ulas Staton trapped several. A motorist killed one while it was crossing the Green River Road at night. It was hoped that Camp Mondamin could get several to stay on the camp lands where they could again become objects of interest.

But in these modern times of a thickly settled population and a highly developed agriculture, beavers on the loose can become a problem.

Today (1979) the beaver is once again almost extinct in Henderson County. A few still exist on remote sections of upper Green River tributaries.

CHAPTER 61

Isaac Lyda

Only a few of the very old ones still living remember the man. He is a legendary figure to the younger generation and although decades have passed he is still talked about in Western North Carolina when hunters gather to hunt and follow the trails of the wild things. At night when those people sit around the campfires and tell their stories of past hunts and the kills made on those hunts, the younger ones listen in awed silence as their elders tell about the deeds and exploits of Isaac Lyda. Isaac Lyda was a hunter among hunters. He was an outstanding bear hunter in a time and in a land when hunting bears was a test of a man's courage and stamina. Only the strongest could pass that test.

Isaac Lyda grew to manhood in Henderson County in a time when black bears roamed the area freely and in large numbers. Those big black bears were unafraid of man and were a menace to human life as well as to the life of a farmer's livestock and stands of honey bees. In the days when Isaac was a boy it was not uncommon for a settler and his family to come in from the patches of land being cleared only to find their cabin or smokehouse ransacked by the great hairy black creatures. Many a farmer in days that Isaac lived has rushed from his cabin in the dead of night, awakened by the squealing of pigs in the fattening pen or the frantic bleating of his sheep.

It was caused by a marauding bear seeking blood and fresh meat, to satisfy a craving caused by a summer diet of wild fruits and berries and a glut of honey from an over-turned bee hive.

Isaac Lyda was raised in what is now the Edneyville section of Henderson County. It is the area that is shadowed by Bear Wallow Mountain and the adjoining peaks known collectively as the Bear Wallow Range. The name was given to them by Williams Mills.* In the summertime the black bears gathered on the mountain tops to wallow in the mud to protect themselves from the tormenting insects and vermin that made their lives miserable.

Isaac Lyda started hunting as soon as he was big enough to shoulder his muzzle loader. He became a crack shot in an era when a man's life often depended on his marksmanship. He was happiest when he took to the trail with a pack of bear dogs that he raised and trained. As time went by his fame spread and it reached a peak when his muzzle loader misfired and he was charged by an enraged black bear on Bear Wallow Mountain. Before witnesses, he fought and killed that bear with only his hands and a hunting knife.

When the War Between the States erupted he donned a uniform, shouldered his rifle and marched off to fight for his state. He took part in many of the battles in northern Virginia and in the three-day Battle of Gettysburg. When the war was over he returned to his home near Edneyville and continued the hunting that he so much enjoyed.

As the game animals began to become scarce, Isaac Lyda decided to go west. He took his family and his pack of trained bear dogs to Idaho. Here the bears were larger and more plentiful. In Idaho he became as famous as a hunter as he had been in Henderson County. There in Idaho he not only hunted bear but also coyote, which were becoming a serious threat to the sheep raising industry.

Isaac Lyda and his sons Tom and John rendered their greatest service to sheep ranchers when they were called on to hunt and kill an enormous bear that had gone on a rampage and slaughtered more than a thousand sheep. With their pack of dogs the three men trailed the bear for days. Several dogs were killed and others were slashed and mauled severely. When the animal was finally killed it weighed more than 800 pounds.

Isaac Lyda and his sons died and were buried in Idaho. The fame of the man is still remembered and talked about in two states that are far apart.

* Vol. I "The Founders"

Isaac Lyda was a great uncle of the late Fred Lyda of Edneyville. Fred Lyda retired January 1, 1975, as a construction foreman with the N.C. Department of Transportation, after 47 years of service. He was a member of the Edneyville School Board for twelve years. His son Norman is chief engineer of WHKP and WKIT.

Part Ten
Explorer's Journal

Part Ten

Explorer's Journal

CHAPTER 62

The Ridge

That part of Henderson County which includes Upward, Dana, Edneyville and the area at the foot of the Bear Wallow Range is known as the Ridge section because the crest of the Blue Ridge Mountains runs through it. At one time it was regarded as the poorest area of the county economically and productively, but for nearly half a century all of this has been changed. It is now the heart of the apple growing area, the eastern part of Henderson County extending to the top of Sugar Loaf Mountain, 4000 feet above sea level. It is a nearly twenty million dollar industry.

Some friends of mine who have spent many summers here thought they knew our county very well until they started to explore the Ridge section on their own. They wound up lost on Tumble Bug Creek that flows into Little Hungry. Eventually they found their way home and were telling me of their adventure. I volunteered to show them through the Ridge; its beautiful fertile valleys and awe inspiring view, the apple orchards covering the hillsides and even the tops of the mountains.

I took them on the Sugar Loaf Road by the crossroads where the Blue Ridge Post Office was located until Rural Free Delivery of mail closed it. We drove through the Union Hill section and by the Broadus McCrain orchard which is one of the finest in that area. We went on across Lamb Mountain to Point Lookout and several miles farther to World's Edge. Those who have never been to World's Edge can't realize what they have missed. The road ends there and you feel as if it is exactly that, the edge of the world, as you look at the sheer drop of more than 1,000 feet. A body can gaze across North and South Carolina; six counties can be seen in the two states with Lake Adger sparkling like a diamond in the distance.

From World's Edge we came back by Gilliam Mountain Road, stopping where Dana Inn sits on the side of the mountain. From this place, sometimes called View Point, we could see in the distance below the broad plateau of Henderson County with Hendersonville in the center. On we went through Edneyville and from there through apple orchards on both sides of the road until we passed St. Paul's Episcopal Chapel and the Flack Hotel that was famous in the years before it was closed and later destroyed by fire. The Flack Hotel was famous for the square dances held there two or three times a week during the summer season for the entertainment of the guests and the local people. At St. Paul Cemetery is the grave of Jacob Lyda who, according to family tradition, lies buried in his red British uniform that he had worn at the Battle of Kings Mountain.* He afterwards wandered into this area to become one of its first settlers.

From here we drove to the top of Corn Mountain from which can be seen one of the prettiest panoramic views of our county. Corn Mountain lies just off the Howard Gap Road, between the Sugar Loaf Road and the Chimney Rock Road. This mountain is off the beaten path of travel and is not widely known but, if you once go to the top you will return many times. After this trip you will agree that the Ridge is the garden spot of Henderson County.

CHAPTER 63

Turnbritches Creek

I went to Edneyville and drove past Mount Moriah Church. I turned off on what is known as the Ball Mountain Road. In places the Ball Mountain Road overlooks the cove through which runs a clear, sparkling, sizeable stream of water, known to those who live in the area as Turnbritches Creek. It has been called this name as far back as the oldest one living can remember.

The story handed down through the generations has been told and retold. In the early days the cleared patches where the cabins of the early settlers were built were few and far between. The young men living on the ridges on each side of the creek would go courting the girls. These visits were always on foot and a young man thought nothing of walking five or six miles to call on his girl, spend a spell with her, walk back home in the dead of night, catch a few hours of sleep and be up ready for work before the break of day. And those work days back then were no eight hours either. It was from daylight to dark; hard, back-breaking work: plowing, grubbing stumbs and brush, clearing the land and tilling the soil.

The boys on the ridges, paying court back and forth and visiting the cabins in the coves and on the opposite ridges, would have to cross the creek on their visits. It was no problem when the weather was warm because the love-stricken young fellow would roll up his pants legs and wade across. But most of the crossing of the creek was done on foot logs and it takes some skill to cross a creek on a foot log, especially if the log has not been squared or is apt to be wet and slippery. It takes an expert to cross safely in the daytime, not to mention a night crossing.

The boys living in the valley along the creek resented the visiting back

* Vol. 1 "The Founders"

164

and forth of the ridge boys and would lay in wait after dark to rock the ridge boys on their way home. It is told that one night a ridge boy was crossing and was caught when he was in the middle of the log. It was dark and the rocks were falling thick and fast. The young fellow was badly frightened.

Something happened. The rest of what happened had best be left to the imagination. Or you can ask someone who lives in the area. But from that day to this the creek has been known as Turnbritches Creek. And there are those who call it by another name that I am too bashful to use.

CHAPTER 64

Sky Country

I drove up Ball Mountain Road that overlooks Turnbritches Creek. The road passes by Hog Rock Road where you can look down on the cascading water that is known as Stepp Falls. This cove, back in the days of Prohibition, was the scene of the biggest shooting battle between the revenuers or prohibition agents and the blockaders in the history of our county. Some of the blockaders were caught but the day long shoot-out gave them time to get their illegal run of whiskey hidden.

When I got to the top of Revis Ridge I stopped to enjoy the magnificent view. From Revis Ridge you can look back across to the mountain called Little Pisgah because it looks so much like the original Pisgah Mountain in the National Forest. The two mountains are in opposite ends of Henderson County. Little Pisgah is well known for the natural grasses that grow on it and the mountain has been used as grazing land for cattle since early days.

Between Revis Ridge and Little Pisgah you can see Fork Mountain where Bob Hill, a pioneer, started one of the first settlements in what is now Henderson County. You can also see the Bear Wallow Range from here and you can look over the entire valley of Reedy Patch through which flows Reedy Patch Creek.*

From Revis Ridge I could also see Sugar Loaf Valley and Sugar Loaf Creek. The Revis Ridge area was originally settled by the Collins family and the Williams family. As I slowly continued up the Ball Rock Road I could see across the fields what remained of the original house that was the home of Preacher Bob Gilbert. This man of God who has been dead these many years was a pioneer Baptist preacher who was instrumental in establishing Mountain Home Baptist Church. The old oak tree under which Bob Gilbert stood when he preached the gospel is still standing. More than a century ago he would gather his flock together while he stood under this oak to preach, until the church house was built.

* Vol. II "Name Lore"

The Mountain Home Church is on Point Lookout at the foot of Sugar Loaf Mountain. There by the church is a road that turns and winds by what is known as the Gottlieb place. Dr. Ruth Gottlieb lived here some 75 years ago in a rather pretentious house. Dr. Gottlieb was originally from Cincinnati, Ohio, and was one of the first women to get a medical doctor's degree to practice medicine in the United States.

Dr. Gottlieb was a friend of Mrs. Sharp who was a graduate registered pharmacist who helped establish the little school on Point Lookout that was called the Good Shepherd School. These two women did early missionary work for the Episcopal Church long years ago. I told about this pioneer .teacher and healer in Chapter 34 of this volume.

To the north of Sugar Loaf is Stone Mountain. To many people it appears to be part of Sugar Loaf but Stone Mountain is quite a mountain in itself. There is an abandoned logging road that winds through the gap between Stone Mountain and Sugar Loaf. In places along this old logging trail the wheels of my four wheel drive Jeep were only inches from a sheer drop of several thousand feet.

This trip will take most of the day. The magnificent scenery is well worth the trip but it is a journey that should be made slowly and only in a four wheel drive vehicle.

CHAPTER 65

Springtime On Green River
(1962)

The fields in the narrow valley are small but they are very fertile fields. Spring comes a little earlier in this valley than to some of the surrounding lands of higher elevation and so the fields of grass and small grains such as wheat and rye were a bright green that early March day that I drove through the valley.

Bob's Creek is in the lower edge of Henderson County not too far from the South Carolina line. It flows between Long Mountain and the Saluda Mountains. The fertile patches of land along Bob's Creek produce the finest and best flavored pole beans grown anywhere and they find a ready market. In this valley you find the many Levi families, the Wards, Shipmans and Joneses.

I passed the little white church on the hillside, the Bob's Creek Baptist Church, and parked my car near the homeplace of the late Jeff Jones. Dr. Levi Jones lived here. He was the father of Mont Jones, Postmaster for a long number of years until his death, of the Zirconia Post Office. Living along here at her father's homeplace was Miss Sarah Jones, 73 years old.

Dr. W. B. Howe

I was trying to locate a grave that was supposed to be in an isolated cemetery now abandoned. I followed the directions of Miss Jones and climbed up a winding mountain road. There were only fourteen graves on the hillside. All had stone markers but only two of them bore names. One told me that in this grave was the wife of J.P. Anders and the other marker only told us that a Levi infant rested here. So many of our old mountain cemeteries have grave after grave with no names; those who sleep in them known only to God.

I soon passed the dairy farm of Jennings Beddingfield, who in March 1962 was serving as one of the Commissioners of Henderson County. I crossed

Green River near Cedar Springs Church and took the Rock Creek Road. This is the area of Rock Creek, Dark Cove, Steam Hole Creek and Steam Hole Ridge, all isolated places you will read about in an upcoming chapter.

I stopped to talk to Sam Capps who lives on and tends the farm owned by W. B. W. Howe and before him by his father, the beloved Dr. W. B. Howe. In 1959, only three years before this, I had visited Mr. Capps after the freshet that had done more damage along Rock Creek than the flood of 1916. The freshet had washed out the fields and left others covered with debris, rocks and sand. Sam Capps had done an amazing job in the three years in reclaiming and restoring the land to productivity.

Nearly all the families along Rock Creek are Capps or Maybins or are related to those families by blood or marriage. Across the road from the Eli Capps homeplace stood the ruins of the picturesque old mill built more than a century ago by Alfred Capps, the first mill on Rock Creek to grind grain. At various times the mill had been operated by Eli, Sam and Jim Capps. Later Henry Briggs owned and operated it and some refer to it as Briggs Mill. Now abandoned, the mill is rapidly going to ruins through neglect. By the abandoned old mill, Rock Creek cascades more than 200 feet over a solid sheet of rock to plunge below into a blue-green natural pool. The continuous roar of the water gives a soothing feeling to one who stands on the river bank at the top of the falls.

CHAPTER 66

The Steam Holes

In Chapter 65 I told you that the Capps family is a large one in the Rock Creek area. The first one to come into that section was Aaron Capps. This was soon after the Revolutionary War. It was Aaron's son John who was father of Sam, Jim, Eli and Tom. Tom Capps' cabin was at the mouth of Dark Cove. The place is well named because if you stand on the ridge above the cove and look down, it looms as a dark, tree-covered mountain cove surrounded by Snaggy and Rich Mountains and High Cliff Ridge.

In the early days, cattle were grazed in the Dark Cove until a mysterious illness called the "Milk Sick" attacked them. What caused it nobody ever really knew although there were many theories. The strange thing about the disease was that the cows were not themselves affected by it but a person drinking the milk would get the "Milk Sick." The only cure for it was to drink brandy and honey. Jim Capps told me that the peculiar sickness was found where there was much walnut timber and that in pioneer days most of the timber in Dark Cove was walnut.

Jim Capps was taking me to the steam holes that were located on High Cliff Ridge above Dark Cove. The road ended at Tom Capps' cabin and we had to walk, climb and sweat up the mountain side.

Mr. Capps led the way along Steam Hole Creek, a clear stream of water that flowed for a mile or more over a bed of solid rock. When we reached Steam Hole Falls, the rest of our trip was straight up the mountain. There was no visible trail and we had to struggle up by pulling on the laurel bushes. At times the going was so steep that we had to crawl on our hands and knees. At one place we followed a narrow rock ledge, holding to bushes above us. A slip here and we would have plunged down a sheer cliff to the bottom 1,500 feet below. We were climbing the side of Steam Hole Ridge. I was plenty afraid, but Mr. Capps, 76 years old, took it all in stride. Suddenly standing on a rock ledge, he let out a shout. He had reached the top of Steam Hole Ridge and located the Steam Holes that gave the ridge its name.

The pioneers were told about the steam holes by the Indians who regarded them with a superstitious awe and avoided them. It was said that on a clear cold morning when the air is still, steam can be seen rising out of these holes and warm air can be felt. And from the days of the first settlers, it was claimed and verified by those still living that over an area of several hundred square yards surrounding these holes, neither ice nor sleet nor snow will stick to the ground. No matter how deep the snow piles up on the surrounding ground, it melts as fast as it falls around the Steam Holes.

Why is this? The Indians believed that at the bottom of these holes evil spirits dwelled and built their fires. Through the generations the white man has had many theories but the most logical one seems to be that the warmth coming out of the ground is carried by an underground flow of a warm stream.

On Steam Hole Ridge, we could look across Dark Cove to High Cliff Ridge in one direction and to Horse Pen Mountain and to Horse Pen Gap in another direction. Rock Creek, Dark Cove, Steam Hole Creek and Steam Hole Ridge and the Steam Holes themselves are a little known, isolated but beautiful, and interesting part of Henderson County.

CHAPTER 67

John Early's Cave

We stood near the top of the mountain at the entrance to the cave. The view was superb; several thousand feet below the entire Pacolet River Valley spread before us. It had taken two hours for my grandson Hank and me to reach the cave near the top of Warrior Mountain in Polk County from our car parked in this beautiful valley below.

When we started I looked up at Little Warrior Mountain with some misgiving. My grandson was a Boy Scout. It took only a short time before I realized that my Boy Scout hiking days were long years ago. There was nothing little about that steep mountain looming ahead of us. The only reason it is called Little Warrior is because its sister peak next to it is several hundred feet higher and is called Big Warrior.

We followed a little-used road for a while until it became a trail. Then as we began to climb the ever-steeper mountainside, the trail ended. From there on it was straight up the mountainside, puffing and stumbling. In places it was so steep one had to crawl on hands and knees; in other places pulling up with the help of bushes and saplings. Finally we reached the cave entrance.

More or less forgotten by all except a few of the old ones, the cave, in the years gone by, became famous for a long time and received much publicity not only in Polk County where it is located but in many areas of the United States.

John Early loved these mountains that he had roamed since boyhood days. When he was old enough he had a hankering to see other parts of the world so he enlisted in the United States Army. It was while on a tour of duty in the Philippine Islands that John Early noticed a rough scale on a small part of his body. When the scale started to spread he answered sick call. John Early had contracted the most dreaded disease, leprosy.

Although known since ancient times, leprosy was considered incurable. Colonies were established where those with the disease were sent to live out their lives in isolation. The United States Army had a leprosarium in Louisiana for the study of leprosy and to administer the most advanced treatment. It was here that John Early was sent to live in isolation with others who had the disease.

As time went by the soldier thought of his home and family in Polk County. He became homesick and the desire to see these mountains he loved so much became an overwhelming obsession. John Early slipped away from the leprosarium and headed for home. A search party was sent by the Army. John Early was found and returned to Louisiana. Through the years this was repeated time and time again. Each time it took longer to locate the homesick soldier.

We squeezed through a long narrow entrance to the cave, then along a steep, sloping corridor, at the end of which we descended a ladder. Some 200 feet along another narrow passageway the cave opened up. It was a large black hole, dripping with water and bats clinging to the ceiling. This was the cave and hiding place of John Early through the years. It was furnished to make it liveable and was just as it was when the homesick soldier last occupied the cave. Needless to say it would have been impossible to do this exploring except that Hank and I brought along several powerful flashlights, all with new batteries in them. My advice to would-be cave explorers: stay out of caves if you suffer from claustrophobia.

As the years passed treatment for leprosy improved. Modern study showed that the disease could be arrested and that with precaution it was not as easily spread as it was once thought to be. John Early was allowed to live out his last years once again happy and unharassed in these Blue Ridge Mountains of Polk County that he loved so well.

CHAPTER 68

Soapstone Gap
(1961)

I have never forgotten a story that my father told and retold when I was a small boy. It was the story of a great adventure when he was a boy growing up with his brothers and sisters in the Mills River Valley. Tom Osborne, first master farmer of Henderson County and, before his death, patriarch of the area was a young man at the time. Mr. Osborne took a yoke of oxen and two boys, one of whom was my father, and made a trip to what is known to the present day as Soapstone Gap. There they sawed a large slab of soapstone, loaded it on the ox drawn sled and brought it out of the mountains. It was a trip that lasted several days although the distance was not too many miles.

The slab was put in as a backstone lining the large open fireplace in the living room of my grandmother's home. Many were the roaring log fires kept blazing in that fireplace. So resistant was the soapstone to those fires that 75 years later when the FitzSimons home, known in later years as the Tom Osborne home, burned to the ground the old soapstone slab fireback was in as good condition as the day it had been loaded on the ox drawn sled at Soapstone Gap and hauled to the valley below.

I had always wanted to go to the Gap. It was the fall of 1961. I turned at the Mount Gilead Church and followed the McDowell Road to the Pennsylvania Turnpike. I stopped to get directions from Branch Bishop whose wife was the daughter of Ben West, the Confederate veteran who lost an eye in battle. After Ben West returned home at war's end, he worked the soapstone mine at the Gap until his death many years later. He was the last person to do this on a commercial scale; by then the demand for soapstone was declining.

When I left Branch Bishop's home I drove according to his directions and turned off the turnpike onto a narrow road. I could see the Gap ahead but I never reached it that day. The farther I went the worse the road became. Finally I could go no farther. I could not turn around on the narrow mountain road. I had to back the car for two miles to get back to the Pennsylvania Turnpike. My neck was stiff and sore for a week.

I was more successful a week later after I contacted Mr. and Mrs. Howard McElrath. Mr. McElrath said he would be glad to take me to the Gap which is in the center of his large boundary of land that adjoins the Pisgah

National Forest. He said he would take me in his jeep which was the only kind of power driven vehicle that could navigate the rough steep mountains and ravines we would have to cross to reach Soapstone Gap.

To fully comprehend that rugged, wild mountain area of Henderson County, I suggest that you go to Henry Sinclair's Office Supply Store on Main Street and get him to sell you the U.S. Dept. of Interior Geological Survey maps. This entire northwestern section of Henderson County is shown on the Skyland Quadrangle and the Dunsmore Mountain Quadrangle maps.

To get to where Howard McElrath lives, you drive out the North Mills River Road to the recreation area of Pisgah National Forest. This road more or less follows the North Fork of Mills River. Just past Seaman Whitaker's is a large old house on the right that is known as the Brittain Place. In the days before Rural Free Delivery the Pink Beds Post Office was located here. In 1961 the property was owned and lived in by the H. V. Owens family. Just below here Seniard Creek flows into the North Fork of Mills River and just past the Owens place a road turns to the right that takes you to where Mr. and Mrs. McElrath live.

Howard McElrath is a true mountain man, born and raised in a rugged area of Henderson County. He is an outdoors man who spends most of his time in the open. In 1961 he owned nearly 2,000 acres in this little known area of the county. His boundary of land is studded with clear, cold lakes and ponds stocked with our native fish. Log cabins, some of them more than a century old and built by the first settlers to come into this area, dot his land.

These cabins are leased or rented to hunting parties during the fall and winter hunting season and to fishermen during the fishing season. Mr. McElrath has thirty miles of crude roads through his wilderness paradise; roads that can be traveled only on foot, horseback or by jeep.

Mrs. McElrath, who was Miss Jessie Walden from Madison County before her marriage, invited me into their modern home which was built on a hill; Seniard Creek rushing past in front of the house and Seniard Mountain rising to a height of 3,000 feet behind it. The creek and the mountain take their name from a first settler who came into the area. Nobody knows how long ago because there are none of that name now in the immediate area.

I sat in the big kitchen talking to Mrs. McElrath while waiting for her husband. She asked me to guess what she was cooking in the large pot. The aroma was most appetizing. Bear meat, she told me, and the bear had been killed almost in their backyard. She said she boiled the bear meat in several waters. She then cut the fat off of it and baked the meat in pure pineapple juice.

When Mr. McElrath reached the house, he suggested that we get his uncle, George Mullinax, to go with us as he could tell me much about the early history. George Mullinax was then past his four score years. He was born nearby and had lived his entire life in the vicinity. Shortly after the war his father, a Confederate veteran, had brought his family through the mountain gaps in a one horse wagon and settled on the South Fork of Mills River. Soon after the family had settled the horse died, which was a real tragedy. To help get a new start in life, his mother made baskets out of white oak splints to sell; his father walked eight miles to and from his job where he worked for Solomon Whitaker and Billy Cairnes, two well established early settlers at the time.

Our first stop was at a 100 year-old log cabin where Sugar Creek made a beautiful pool. As we continued towards the headwaters of Seniard Creek we passed the spot where Jule Allen, the pioneer, built the first lath mill, turned by water power. For a number of years Mr. Allen made spinning wheels and chairs on this lath.

We finally reached the headwaters of Seniard Creek where Isom Stuart built his log cabin and set up the first blacksmith shop in that part of Henderson County. Isom Stuart came through Corn Cob Gap so long ago that in 1861 his sons were old enough to enlist in the Confederate Army. As the jeep climbed slowly along Corn Cob Branch, we started up the steep mountain side to Corn Cob Gap, crossed Middle Ridge to the headwaters of Sitton Creek and came to a stop on Soapstone Gap.

Soapstone Gap rises to a height of 2,700 feet. It is a solid mountain of soapstone. The place was well known to the Indians before the white man arrived. Bands of Indians came to carve their arrowheads, their crude pots and their peace pipes which were smoked on ceremonial occasions. Remnants of these things are still found in and around the Gap.

Mr. McElrath and Mr. Mullinax told me that the stone cut from one side of the Gap is soft soapstone while on the other side of the Gap it is hard soapstone. Here in this Gap Adam Moore and Riley Whitaker, early settlers, and later Ben West, Confederate veteran, sawed and cut soapstone to supply the valley settlers with firebrick, firebacks and bricks for bed warmers and travelers, and slabs for grave headstones.

We crossed the Gap and started down the opposite side following Soapstone Branch. A jeep on rough, steep roads and trails is not exactly as restful and soothing as a featherbed and I was getting well "shook up." But the interesting things I was being told and the awe inspiring scenery helped to keep my mind off my poor old aching bones.

As we drove down the far side of Soapstone Gap, George Mullinax pointed out where he and Howard McElrath and Howard's father, W. C. McElrath, were one day splitting a huge chestnut tree that had fallen. The trunk of the tree was hollow and when it was split open, bones were found in it. On examination the bones were found to be human. In Volume II of "From the Banks of the Oklawaha" I told of the mysterious disappearance in 1910 of the old Confederate veteran, John Hunter. Was John Hunter murdered and his body stuffed in the hollow trunk of the huge chestnut tree? No one knows to this day but there were those still living in 1961 who believed those bones were the remains of that same John Hunter.*

We soon stopped at an old cabin. This was the home place of Riley Whitaker, an early settler. The entire chimney was made of soapstone cut from the Gap. Soft soapstone is best for chimneys, explained Mr. Mullinax;

* Vol II "Mysteries"

hard soapstone is best for grave markers. He should know because in a lifetime of more than 80 tears he built many chimneys and carved out many grave headstones. It was in this old Whitaker cabin that Judge Jim Shipman boarded in 1891 when he was a young school teacher, before he studied law.

From here we drove across the steep high ridges, through the ravines and coves to the old graveyard on the mountainside behind the McElrath home. Here at one time stood the one teacher school known as Shanghai. Nobody knows how a little schoolhouse in the wilderness of Henderson County got the name of a Chinese city half way around the world from these mountains.

Hamilton Osborne taught in this isolated little school before he marched off to war to fight and die with the Confederate Army. The old Shanghai School was used on Sundays as a place of worship. W. C. McElrath gave the plot of ground for the cemetery. It is no longer used but a score or more of the pioneer settlers sleep peacefully here.

Here lies Isom Stuart, born in 1804, who came here as a young man and set up his blacksmith shop on the headwaters of Seniard Creek. Here buried is his son Melvin who left a trust fund, the income from which is used to keep the little burying ground in immaculate condition.

On one headstone is the name Yankee Rose. Rose is a man of some mystery. Nobody has ever known from where he came or his given name. Legend tells that he quietly came here soon after the end of the Civil War in the uniform of a Union soldier. He lived for many years among his Confederate neighbors and went to his grave known only as Yankee Rose.

The ancient Shanghai school and church house is now gone. Where the building stood on the bank of a little mountain stream is now a cold, clear pond stocked with fish. And here ended my trip through a little known but beautiful part of Henderson County. I expressed appreciation to Howard McElrath and George Mullinax for the wonderful journey they had made possible.

CHAPTER 69

Corbin Mountain
(1961)

It was a beautiful, clear and unseasonably warm day in January 1961 that I made my first trip to the fire tower on top of Corbin Mountain in the southern part of Henderson County. Many people who have lived here a lifetime have never heard of this mountain, half of which is in Henderson County, N.C. and half in Greenville County, S.C.

I wanted Ulas Staton to go with me because he knew that part of the county, so when I didn't find him at his store on Highway 25 I drove to his home. A genuine mountain man, descended from pioneer stock, Ulas Staton hunted and trapped over the Green River area for more than sixty years. I found him in the yard with several other men, rocking on their heels and dickering over a pile of furs. Many Henderson County men and boys still trap during the winter season for muskrat, mink and other small fur-bearing animals. One pelt on the stack of furs had every one puzzled. It was from a rather large, black, long haired animal. Even Mr. Staton shook his head. "I have trapped these mountains for over sixty years but I have never seen anything like that," he said.

The fur trading finished, Mr. Staton said he would be glad to go to Corbin Mountain with me.

"Just thought I would close the store," he said, "and do a little trapping while I could. Once you get it in your blood this trapping gets a holt on a body," he told me as we drove off towards the Elks Boys Camp where we turned left on the road that dead ends at the home of Mr. and Mrs. Pearson Stanton, on top of the mountain and at the foot of the fire look-out tower that serves both Henderson County, N.C. and Greenville County, S.C.

The road up Corbin Mountain has a good solid road bed but it is narrow and one of the steepest mountain roads that I have ever driven an automobile on. In places it runs along narrow ledges where the slightest skid would plunge the car down the sheer sides of mountainous ravines. The mile and a half to the top was made all the way in low gear. When we reached the fire tower I figured from the topography map that we had gone up over a 1,000 feet in altitude during the mile and a half drive up that steep narrow road and had crossed back and forth from North to South Carolina four times.

As Ulas Staton and I got out of the car, a window opened in the glass-enclosed room at the top of the fire tower. A lady leaned out, waved and called down to us to come on up. As we started to climb the steep, winding stairway, Ulas explained to me that the lady on duty was Mrs. Pearson Stanton; that she and her husband took turns watching for forest fires and that he had known them for a lifetime.

Mrs. Stanton proved to be a charming person, attractive and vivacious with sparkling gray eyes and a merry twinkle. She had an infectious, rippling laugh and was brimming over with enthusiasm for her work. I told her why I had come. "Just go ahead and ask me all you want to know," she laughed, "and I will tell you what I can." She proved to be full of knowledge and an excellent conversationalist. Mrs. Stanton told me she was Grace Pruitt before her marriage, the daughter of Mr. and Mrs. Allen Pruitt and the granddaughter of Noah Pruitt who was a pioneer settler in the area. She pointed out Pruitt Mountain below us in South Carolina, named for one of her ancestors.

Corbin Mountain is 3,028 feet high and the tower we were in is forty feet high so we were 3,068 feet above sea level. Actually we were on top of the world and looking down on it because we were at the highest place in the entire area.

The view was awe inspiring because a body could look in all directions as far as the eye could see. Mrs. Stanton pointed out the beautiful Green River Valley, Bob's Creek in Henderson County and Terry's Creek in South Carolina. Across from Corbin Mountain is Posey Mountain where Confederate fortifications can still be seen. They were thrown up in the spring of 1865 to stop the Yankee General Sherman's Army if it tried to invade North Carolina through John Guest Gap between Corbin Mountain and Posey Mountain.*

Way down below us could be seen the Greenville watershed lake and far in the distance was Caesar's Head and Cedar Mountain. Far to the northern end of Henderson County could be seen the fire tower on Bear Wallow Mountain.

Mr. and Mrs. Stanton live here on top of the mountain in the only house in the entire area although years ago all the land was cultivated by the mountain farmers. The cleared land was all abandoned half a century or more ago and has now been reclaimed by the forest wilderness. From the tower Ulas Staton pointed out the spot where he had killed his last wild turkey and also the side of the mountain where during a night coon hunt he had stumbled into a den of pole cats. It was a sad and smelly experience; before he could back out of the den he was half blinded with eyes and nose stinging from the perfume released by the mama skunk.

The fire tower is equipped with telephone service and by radio and telephone with all the other fire towers in Henderson, Polk and Greenville Counties. In the center of the glass enclosed tower is a contraption that is called an Alidade. It is a fixed circle marked in all 360 degrees of the compass. On a pivot in the center of the circle is an instrument, on one end of which is an upright flange that has a small peep hole. On the opposite end is a perpendicular opening with a thread in the center. When the tower attendant sees smoke, the observer looks through the peep hole, swings the pivot until the string is on the center of the smoke. The degree reading is then marked on a wall with a pin. Mrs. Stanton then calls on the radio or telephone the nearest fire tower to the smoke just spotted. This observer then makes a circumference degree reading. Where the lines from the two readings cross is the location of the suspected new forest fire. This information is then radioed to the Fire Warden of that county who dispatches fire fighters to the scene.

The top of Corbin Mountain is also a popular picnic place. Near the foot of the tower are four picnic tables and four grills for outdoor cooking. As Mr. Staton and I were leaving we thanked Mrs. Stanton for being so nice to us.

"Come back and bring your wives," she said. Then she laughed, a twinkle came into her eyes. "I believe you are a little nervous about that drive down the mountain." I told her I sure was and that I was going down all the way in low gear and riding the brake at the same time.

* Vol. II "The Confederacy"

CHAPTER 70

Big and Little Willow
(1961)

It is a beautiful part of Henderson County, that area drained by Big Willow Creek and Little Willow Creek, both of which flow into the French Broad River. The Willow section of our county was given the name by the first people to settle in the area because of the giant willow trees that lined the banks of both of those streams of water.

One day in the autumn of 1961, I took a trip through the Willow area, guided by Carl Cantrell of Etowah who was descended from those pioneers and raised in the area. It was a trip through fertile river bottom lands, through picturesque rolling pasture land criss-crossed by clear, sparkling streams of water. And we traveled a number of miles over sparsely settled, wild mountain country, sometimes at altitudes of 3,000 feet or more above sea level.

Pisgah Mountain could be seen rising majestically in the distance through the soft haze of the Indian summer morning. The fall coloring painted the hillsides with an unbelievable beauty.

There is a road near Etowah that runs across from the Brickyard to the Boylston Spring Road near where Watt Gash at one time operated a dairy farm.

I wanted to see the so called Soap Pot on the French Broad River. Few except those that live in the area know where it is or have ever heard of it although the earliest settlers gave it that name. Standing on the bank of the river after a short walk through the woods, we could see in the middle of the river a large circular area as calm as water in a bucket. This calm spot of water was surrounded on all sides by the swift, swirling current of the river water. Old ones will tell that no matter how high the flood waters of the river rise or how swift the currents on each side rush, the Soap Pot is always calm.

The river is black and foreboding now but the old ones say that in the early days the waters of the river were so clear that the bottom could be seen in the deepest parts, but where the Soap Pot was calm, it looked as if it were rimmed by a high stone basin resembling the large black iron pots in which the pioneers boiled and made the only soap they had. Thus they began to call that part of the French Broad River the Soap Pot. To make the name even more appropriate, the swift current on all sides of the Soap Pot is continuously covered with a foam whipped up by the rushing water that looks like the bubbles on a pot when making soap.

When we left the banks of the French Broad, Carl Cantrell and I took the road that ran through Sky Brook Farm. A large flock of sheep was grazing in fertile bottom land. Sheep are rarely seen now but in our grandparents' day every farm had a flock of sheep and every home owned a spinning wheel. Before the railroads came, home-raised wool was the only source of clothing and our grandmothers carded the wool, spun the fiber and wove it into cloth.

The bridge across from the T. T. Whiteside home on the French Broad River was washed away in the 1916 flood and was never replaced. We passed the farm where George Holmes, the Englishman who was the leader in the Bowman's Bluff settlement, lived. The area is rich in early history. The George Holmes farm was once owned by the late Dr. Cummings but in 1961 was owned by J. Cason Ives.

All of this large acreage of fertile land around the area of Bowman's Bluff was in colonial days owned by Elijah Williamson who was a soldier of the Continental Army led by George Washington. He came here soon after the war ended and tradition tells us that he purchased the Bowman's Bluff property from an Indian chief. The purchase price was said to be a gun, a pony and a bridle. But the early records show that the land was a grant for service during the war.

The road that goes through the Sky Brook Farm and by Bowman's Bluff takes you to Beulah Baptist Church which was established in 1815. The hill above Beulah Church was once the site of Gethsemane, the little Church of England built by the English settlers under the leadership of George Holmes. Gethsemane was built in 1886 and consecrated by the Bishop of the Episcopal Church in 1887.

For nearly twenty years the services of the Church of England were conducted in this little church by the beloved Rev. Mr. Wainwright. In 1907 church services were discontinued because the English families had over the years gradually moved away. The site of this little church is overgrown with bushes and briars but Carl Cantrell and I pushed through the undergrowth and found remnants of the church house foundation. In 1923 the church was dismantled, hauled to Upward and rebuilt. It was a house of worship there for a number of years after it was renamed the St. John Episcopal Church of Upward. Today the church no longer exists.

Many of the graves at Beulah Church were headed by soapstone markers. Side by side were two graves with their hand carved inscriptions. One of them read: "Mary Blythe, born 1788, Died 1811." The other one: "William Blythe, died 1813, age about 34." Here they have peacefully slept through the years in our beautiful Blue Ridge Mountains.

At Beulah Church we followed the road to where it crosses Big Willow Creek near where the creek flows into the French Broad River. This is the back road to Kanuga; it winds through picturesque rolling fields and hill land. The mail boxes along this road bear the family names Cantrell, Drake, Blythe, Revis, Mace, Huggins, Sentell — all of them descendants of pioneers who settled the Big and Little Willow areas. All of this area lies in Crab Creek Township of Henderson County.

In 1961 Linell Huggins operated a store on Big Willow Creek. Here the old Indian trail crossed the creek. This trail ran east and west from the Smoky Mountains into what is now the state of Georgia and had been used by unnumbered generations of Indian warriors on the warpath and by hunting and trading parties. This same trail had been followed by the pioneers coming into the area.

Carl Cantrell and I stood where the Indian trail crossed the creek. We could see where it came down the mountain through the gap between Echo Mountain and Hebron. We could also see where the trail went through Wild Cat Gap, the low place between Wild Cat Mountain and Brushy Knob. Here, where the trail crossed Big Willow, the first Blythe to come into the area built a mill to grind his neighbors' corn. It was known as a "corn cracker" or pound mill because the corn was made into meal and grits by a hammer pounding the grain as it was lifted and let fall by the action of the water. Later, mill stones were brought by ship from England and hauled into the mountains on an ox cart. A water wheel was built to turn them. Traces of the mill race and the large rocks over which the water poured to turn the mill wheel are all that is left.

Legend and tradition handed down for nearly two centuries say that the mill was unlucky. It had been in operation only a few months when one evening the miller was late coming home for supper. His wife sent one of the children to see what was keeping his father.

The little boy came running back in tears and terrified. He sobbed out that his father was in the mill yard lying on his face. When neighbors gathered they found the miller sprawled on the ground with an arrow buried to the shaft between his shoulders.

Soon weird tales began to be told of strange sounds heard in the night in and around the mill. Figures were seen which disappeared if one was bold enough to try to approach. Customers became superstitious about taking their grain to be ground. The old mill was abandoned. But even to this day there are those who believe that the spot is still haunted and ghosts can still be seen flitting around the old mill site.

Continuing on our trip, Carl Cantrell and I passed the site of the Sentell mill which is now a recreation picnic park on Big Willow Creek. We crossed Hant Branch and Lewis Evans Mountain and passed the neat farm of Mr. and Mrs. C. G. Thornton on the Evans Road. The Thorntons have one of the few apple orchards in Crab Creek Township.

Soon we came to and stopped at the spring known as the Shepherd Spring. In the days before drilled wells and electric pumps, this spring was famous over a wide area because of the boldness of its flow and for the cold, sweet mountain water that gushed out of the hillside. The old ones said that the water was colder and sweeter than the waters from other springs, in an area where mountain springs were plentiful.

A story has been handed down about a farmer on the way home one summer day after tending his patch of ground. He was hot, thirsty and tired and stopped here to quench his thirst. The water was so cold and refreshing that he sat by the spring and continued to drink gourd after gourd of water. When he failed to return home those who went to search for him found him sitting by the spring with a gourd full of water in his hand but he was dead. The coroner of that day ruled that death was caused by drinking too much of too cold spring water too fast.

The spring has been in the Shepherd family for several generations. Nimrod Shepherd had a grant for a large part of the surrounding area. On the hill above the spring he built his log cabin. It was in this cabin that Jesse Shepherd was born. A young man when North Carolina became part of the Confederacy, he walked across the mountain to the mustering ground near Asheville to enlist in the Confederate Army. At the Battle of Chancellorsville he was struck in the head by an enemy minnieball which imbedded in his skull. For the remaining years of a long life he carried the bullet in his head. The young Confederate veteran returned home after the war and became a successful businessman and farmer. His descendants of several generations are still active and successful in business, civic and political activities of Hendersonville and Henderson County. The rock work around the spring was put there over 75 years ago by his sons.

CHAPTER 71

The Playford Lands
(1962)

Grassy Creek and Grassy Mountain, Jim Creek, the Flat Woods, Long Rock and Long Rock Branch, Briery Creek; all are names in a part of Henderson County that few people know or have ever heard of or ever visited. These places are in one of the most remote sections of our county. They are well known to older people who in the years gone by enjoyed fishing and hunting when Grassy Creek and the Flat Woods abounded with fish and game. This area was the last place wild turkeys were hunted. Deer were plentiful and although the land now is privately owned, they still can be found. In recent years hunting has not been allowed but before hunting and fishing were forbidden it was a coon hunter's paradise and a fox hunter's dream.

Julian Blythe in his younger days was an outdoor man and he knew the Grassy Creek area like you and I know our own back yards. He was the son of F. M. Blythe who spent much time hunting and fishing. As a boy, Julian followed his father with a rod and a gun tramping through the mountains and flat woods of Grassy Creek. In later years when more than 5,000 acres of the region was owned by Harry Playford, Mr. Blythe was caretaker and game warden. For several years he patrolled the land on foot, horseback and in a jeep.

In 1962 Julian Blythe took me through the area he knows so well. Just after we passed Frank Edney's place on the Crab Creek Road, we turned on the C.C.C. Road at the foot of Pinnacle Mountain. We crossed Dismal Creek and reached the point where Dismal Creek and Shoal Creek cascade down the mountainside in a series of water falls. At the old Anders home place the C.C.C Road joins the Shoal Creek Road. We continued until we reached the heart of the Flat Woods. The Flat Woods are so called because on top of the mountain for several miles in every direction the land is level.

Here in the Flat Woods in the early days, wild game including deer was in abundance because of the nutritious native grass growing over the entire flat mountain top. During the Depression of the early 1930s, a long lasting, severe drought dried up the grazing lands of Texas and adjoining cattle grazing states. The cattlemen did not have the means to purchase feed and their cattle were dying from starvation. The United States Government bought the starving cattle and shipped them to areas where grass was available. Several car loads came to Henderson County.

Wild Texas cattle were accustomed to being driven and handled from horseback. A man on foot was a mortal enemy and a thing to be destroyed. Many still living remember the confusion and difficulties that took place from the time the Texas cattle were unloaded from the railroad cattle cars at the Depot and herded all the way to the Flat Lands by men and boys on foot. Many a tree was hastily climbed when a confused, wild-eyed, half-starved Texas steer took after one of the herders on foot.

At the hunting lodge that Playford had built we stopped to talk to the Hargus family, the only people living in this wilderness area where the road climbed and twisted across Rocky Ridge. We crossed Jim Creek. The reason for its name has been lost in the passage of time. It was here that we came to the camps for boys, one of them operated in 1962 by J. Y. Perry, Jr. and one by his father. This area is known as Sky Valley.

Sky Valley is on the headwaters of Grassy Creek and it was here at the headwaters that Vardy McBee built a grist mill to grind the grain of what few neighbors were in the vicinity. There is no longer anyone left to grind grain for and all traces of the old mill are gone. After leaving the McBee mill site, the road starts climbing.

We were going along Chestnut Ridge. The mountain was covered with the skeletons of the dead chestnut trees which were wiped out by the blight that hit the chestnut timber in the early years of the century.

At Long Rock we stopped to look at the deep, circular pot holes made there by the Indians with their signal fires. We drove for miles along the top of Sandy Flat and passed a long-abandoned farm, the only sign that we had seen that told at one time there had been human habitation.

At last the road started winding its way down the mountain until we came to Blue Ridge Baptist Church at Green River Gap. Here at this church the dividing line between Henderson County and Transylvania County passes through the middle of the church. On Sunday some of the worshipers sat in Henderson County, while others were sitting in Transylvania.

In the little cemetery were the graves of George E. Howard, a veteran of World War I and Julian Brossart of World War II. Other graves bore head stones with hand carved names. Here lie the Joneses, Markhams, Warrens, Summeys and Burnses, all pioneer settlers in this once wild region.

At the county line we got on the hard surfaced road and soon came to Reasonover Creek and Reasonover Lake. The legend is that the Reasonovers were early settlers. One day one of the Reasonover boys was sitting on the creek bank with his girl friend. They were suddenly both struck and killed by a bolt of lightning. The creek has been known by that name since that time.

Julian Blythe and I came back to Hendersonville through Buck Forest which is now owned by DuPont and is the site of a large manufacturing plant. Here in Buck Forest in the horse and buggy days stood the Buck Forest Hotel. It was a famous stopping place for tourists and for hunting parties when game was plentiful. The road wound around until we came to beautiful Cascade Lake. On to the Crab Creek Road and back home. It was a long rough trip but it was well worth the time and effort.

CHAPTER 72

A Church In The Wildwood

In April 1972, Claude Morrison and I made a visit to Green River Cove, the upper part of which is in Henderson County and the lower part in Polk County. Our objective was to visit Mountain Valley Baptist Church which was the place of worship for several generations of the people of Green River Cove before the flood of 1916. This flood caused the people to abandon the Cove because of the damage done to the fertile farm land of the area.

Situated on a side of a hill above the road, the small wooden church resembled a one teacher school building more than it did a church. The land for the church was given by the Newman family and, standing there in the church yard, we could look across the road and see the remains of the Newman home, barns and out buildings, standing empty and ghost-like.

Claude Morrison and I were surprised that there were no indications of a grave yard anywhere near the church which is at least a century or more old. A Mrs. Bradley, who was a member of one of the few families still living in the Cove, explained that in the days when Baptists worshiped at the church there were many people farming in the Cove. The roads were in such bad condition that each family in the Cove had its own grave yard on each homeplace.

This Mountain Valley Baptist Church in Green River Cove in Polk County must not be confused with a church in Henderson County. The Mountain Valley Baptist Church in Henderson County is in an area known as Mountain Valley on the headwaters of Green River.

Mountain Valley Baptist Church – Green River Cove

A few days after Claude Morrison and I visited the Green River Cove, I paid a visit to Mrs. Rass Hollifield. In the spring of 1972 when I talked to her she was in her middle eighties. Mrs. Hollifield then lived at Dana. Before her marriage she was Lillie Bishop, daughter of Jasper and Ella Bishop. In her early married years she lived in the Cove and was a member of Mountain Valley Church. Mr. and Mrs. Hollifield were living in the Cove when the 1916 flood hit. People began to leave the area and worship at the church stopped.

Thomas Pace was Postmaster of Fish Top Post Office and also clerk of the Mountain Valley Church. When the old church was closed and deserted, Mr. Pace notified all members to come get their church letters so that their memberships could be transferred to other churches. All the members came except Mrs. Hollifield who to this day still has her letter in the Mountain Valley Church.

Soon after this a few who were left in the Cove started to tearing down the now abandoned church house. Whaley Bradley, a member of a pioneer Cove family, stopped it. He told the men that Lillie Hollifield still had her letter in the church and the church could not be destroyed as long as Mrs. Hollifield lived and kept her letter of membership there.

For a number of years the old church house stood deserted. Then itinerate preachers riding through the Cove began to hold Sunday services and wandering singing teachers would stop for a week or two to teach music or to hold all day singings in the old building. In 1972 the place was once again a place of worship. Preaching was held every second and fourth Sundays of the month, with plans being made for expansion.

All of this has been made possible because Lillie Bishop Hollifield failed to get her church letter of transfer from Tom Pace who kept the church records nearly three quarters of a century ago.

CHAPTER 73

Manteo To Murphy

The most eastern town in North Carolina is Manteo, a village on an island by the same name in Albermarle Sound. Manteo and the island are separated from the Atlantic Ocean by a narrow reef. The most western town in our state is the city of Murphy, approximately 150 miles west of Hendersonville and only a few miles from the borders of Tennessee and Georgia. It is more than 400 miles from Manteo across the state to Murphy and so originated the expression "from Manteo to Murphy" which means to cover the whole state of North Carolina.

I had been to Manteo but never to Murphy, so Maggie and I decided to take a trip there so we could say we had covered the entire state, that we had actually been from Manteo to Murphy. We took Highway 64 West through Brevard, Rosman and Toxaway. Lake Toxaway and the Toxaway Hotel were the playgrounds of the tycoons of a period when wealth was flaunted by luxurious private railroad pullman cars. These private cars came to Hendersonville by the hundreds to be switched to the Brevard Railroad which began at the Hendersonville Depot and terminated at Lake Toxaway.[1]

The Toxaway Dam was wrecked by the flood of 1916 and later that year it washed out and caused considerable damage to life and property as the waters of the lake rushed through the mountains to the flatlands below.[2] Toxaway declined as a resort area and the luxurious hotel was finally demolished in 1948. In late years the lake has been restored.

We continued on through Cashiers Valley. Here is located High Hampton, the summer home of General Wade Hampton, Confederate cavalry leader and after the war Governor of South Carolina and United States Senator. At Cowee Gap, where the Blue Ridge and Cowee Mountains meet, we were at 4,200 feet elevation. The view was breathtaking.

From Cowee Gap we proceeded on 64 West to Highlands and then to Franklin. At Franklin we saw where DeSoto crossed the Little Tennessee

[1] Vol. II "The Age of Steam"
[2] Vol. I "Fateful Years"

River with his band of Spaniards in 1540. DeSoto was searching for gold and his exploration finally ended on the banks of the Mississippi River where he was killed in battle with the Indians. His followers weighted his body with stone and sank it in the river to keep it from being mutilated by the Indians.

At Haysville, we saw the location of Fort Hembree where the Cherokee Indians were forcibly gathered by the United States Army for their removal to Indian Territory in Oklahoma. This was one of the most disgraceful episodes of our country's history.

We arrived at Murphy early in the afternoon. It is a lovely little town located in a prosperous agricultural area.

In 1567 Juan Pardo passed through this area leading a band of Spaniards on an exploring expedition on orders from Pedro Mendendez de Airles who was Governor of Florida at the time. It was here in 1715 that Major George Chicken led the English military expedition against the Cherokee Indians.

We spent a pleasant night in Murphy and started back to Hendersonville the next morning. On the return trip we went through Andrews, Topton and Bryson City. The trip through the narrow Natahala Gorge on Highway 19 will long be remembered; the road runs for miles along the banks of the clear, sparkling, rushing waters of the Natahala River.

From Bryson City we cut across to Dillsboro, Sylva and Cullowhee.

Cullowhee is the location of Western Carolina Teachers College which later became Western Carolina University. Many Henderson County young men and women get their higher education here.

Never have we been on a trip where the scenery and views were as continuously magnificent and awe-inspiring with so much variety. It is a trip well worth taking.

Part Eleven
Stories
For a Winter Night

Part Eleven
Stories For A Winter Night

CHAPTER 74

The Orr Farm Mystery

Tom Orr and his wife Milda Guice Orr live on their farm on the Howard Gap Road about midway between the Sugar Loaf Road and the Dana Road. Both Mr. and Mrs. Orr are descended from pioneer settlers of Henderson County who came into these mountains in the 18th Century. The Howard Gap Road that borders their farm is possibly the oldest road in the county. Centuries ago it was an animal trail made by migrating herds of bison, elk and deer, grass eating animals going back and forth to their seasonal grazing grounds.

Mr. & Mrs. Tom Orr driving old Haley

When the Indians came into our area, they followed the animal trails on their hunting and trading expeditions back and forth from the Smoky Mountains to the coastal flat lands. Captain Howard defeated the Cherokees at the gap of the mountains high above Tryon and opened our mountains to the white settlers.* So these early settlers naturally followed the Indian path through the gateway that became known as Howard's Gap.

Before the railroads came, it was over the Howard Gap Road that the people of Kentucky and Tennessee drove their herds of cattle, hogs, sheep, horses, mules and even turkeys to markets along the South Carolina and Georgia coast.

In fact, Mrs. Orr's great, great grandfather, George Allen, lived on the Howard Gap Road just south of where the road crosses the old highway going from Hendersonville to Bat Cave. There he operated a large log inn and stock pen. This was a stopping place for the drovers with their livestock on the long trip south. It was this same George Allen who in 1816 gave two and a half acres of land on which to build the first Ebenezer Baptist Church house.

The mystery started to unfold when Ronald Lamb, son in law of Mr. and Mrs. Orr, was leveling and clearing a tract of land on the Orr farm. Near a small stream flowing at the foot of the hill, the bulldozer suddenly uncovered some masonry. Further digging by hand revealed two brick and stone lined kilns, buried under several feet of top soil that erosion had washed down from the hill above.

Some of the bricks that were uncovered were glazed with various colors. It is thought that this was caused by the intense heat they had been subjected to in the manufacturing process. The brick lined kiln ran back into the hill some thirty or more feet. In moving more dirt, they uncovered large fragments of pottery and several unbroken and perfectly shaped clay pipes, the type that were smoked here in the mountains generations ago by both Indians and early settlers.

After much more careful digging, a stone arch was uncovered. It proved to be the actual furnace to what must have been a pottery kiln. This furnace was intact and remains of the ashes of the last fire that heated the kiln were still there. Mr. and Mrs. Orr picked up nearly a gallon of small wedge shaped artifacts of various sizes. These wedges were identified as chinks or spacers used in ancient times in building arches of brick or stone.

By now a second kiln had been uncovered, a twin to the first one. The news of the findings had spread and aroused great interest. Many were the theories advanced about these kilns. They had to be ancient because erosion had covered them so deep. Were the kilns operated by the earliest white people in the area or did the kilns go further back in time? Was the potter's wheel known to the Cherokee before the white man came?

Then someone said that the perfectly shaped and sized chinks or spacers traced back to the Aztec Indians of Mexico and at one time had been a

* Vol. I "Twilight for the Indians"

Mr. & Mrs. Tom Orr discuss artifacts found in the ruins of old kiln with the author (center)

forgotten and lost art. Of the many who came to see the discovery for the next few days, each one had a theory. Each speculation was interesting.

Inquiring and research continued. The most plausible theory? When the first settlers came to this area they established pottery kilns where the clay was suitable. The subsoil on the Orr farm was red clay and suitable. These early kilns were always on a traveled road and along side a stream for ease of mixing the mud.

Several of the older people who had lived their entire lives in this area recalled a story told them by their grandparents but now mostly forgotten. Long years ago, in the days of the American Revolution when the Howard Gap Road was the only semblance of a travel route through here, two white men, the first in the area, built the kilns and started making clay pipes, pottery and brick for trade with the Indians and others who might travel the road. After a time the two men quarreled. Some said it was a quarrel over the love of an Indian maiden; others thought it was over the division of the profits from the kiln and still others said it was only a brawl following a drunken spree. One partner cut the other's throat while he slept and the murderer fled the country.

Who these men were has long been forgotten. What is the true story and how and when these kilns came into existence will possibly never be known.

But for years to come, the mysterious discoveries on the farm of Mr. and Mrs. Tom Orr on the Howard Gap Road will make interesting conversation around the hearth fires. It is in this manner that our mountain legends are made.

CHAPTER 75

Soapstone

In Chapter 68 I told you about a trip to Soapstone Gap. Soapstone is known by many names and its characteristics made it important in the lives of people even before the dawn of civilization. It is a mineral and a stone but a soft stone with a greasy, soapy feeling that gives it the name that it is commonly called by here in the mountains where it had an important place in the lives of the Indians as well as the pioneer settlers. It is also known by other names such as talc, French chalk, steatite and in some parts of the mountains it is called pot stone because the early settlers did not have tin, iron or copper cooking utensils so plentiful in our kitchens today. In those early days the Indians and the first settlers made these things out of soapstone.

There have been excavated in Crete and Rhodesia engraved soapstone that dated back more than 3,000 years B.C. that can be easily read. The early Egyptians made scarabs and other amulets out of it and the early Assyrians carved out of soapstone the early seals and signets that are uncovered in the excavations made by our present day archeologists.

Soapstone is found in a variety of colors: greenish, blue, brown, white, grey and redish.

There is hard soapstone and soft but whether it is classified as either hard or soft, it is still easily cut with a knife. This has made it a favorite material with those who enjoy carving. It can also be cut with an ax or a cross-cut saw. It can resist heat and no matter how hot it is heated, it never cracks or crumbles even when water or other liquids are poured or spilled on it in its hottest stage. When once heated it retains that heat for a long time.

Soapstone has its uses even today in the highly developed, complicated industry of our modern scientific age. When finely ground, it is used in the manufacture of some types of paper, in dressing leather and in the manufacturing of certain kinds of paint and lubricants. The talcum powder that we use on our faces and bodies contains soapstone as do the highly perfumed soaps found in our bathrooms. But it was the ease with which it could be cut and carved and its resistance to heat and its ability to hold that heat that made soapstone so indispensable to the Indians and our pioneer ancestors. Long before the white man came to our mountains the Indians knew about soapstone. Because it resisted heat the Indians used it to fashion crude pots and other cooking utensils.

The more primitive tribes fashioned arrowheads and tomahawks out of the easily carved softstone and their peace pipes and other ceremonial pipes were always made from it.

In a generation gone by, cornerstones and entire basestones of early churches were hewed from soapstone. Boys of the present generation have never had the thrill of carving their initials on the soapstone, between the time

Sunday school turned out and before the morning church services started. In pioneer days when it could be found, the chimneys of the log cabins were built out of it or at least the fireback was made of soapstone brick or better still the fireback was a solid slab of soapstone.

There are a few houses still occupied in the Mills River Valley built before the Civil War that still have their open fireplaces with soapstone firebacks and the hearthstone and even the mantle shelves made of the same material. The hearthstones were very important because much of the cooking was done in front of the fire on the hearth and a hearth made of soapstone needed no grease to keep a cornpone from sticking.

There are old ones still living who declare that a cornpone is not fit to eat or a griddle cake either if they are not made from water ground meal and cooked on a soapstone hearth or griddle.

In the big old farm houses or log cabins in earlier days, before stoves or central heat came to the mountains, every family had several soapstone bricks. These were heated in front of the hearth fire, wrapped in flannel and taken to bed to keep the feet warm through the long winter night. Because the soapstone brick retained heat, they would still be warm when it was time to get up. These same bricks were heated, wrapped and put in wagons or buggies to keep the feet warm when driving a long distance on cold, snowy winter days.

Because soapstone was so easily carved and shaped and inscriptions cut on a slab of it with a knife, our ancestors used it for headstones to mark the last resting place of loved ones. Many of the headstones in the older cemeteries of Henderson County are made of it and I have visited some of these cemeteries and seen inscriptions that were cut 150 years and more ago and can be easily read to this day because these headstones made from soapstone do not weather with time or exposure to the elements.

CHAPTER 76

Quilting

Quilting is a craft and it is one of the earliest known to man. When it started and who was the first woman to make a quilt nobody knows because it all started so long ago. It grew out of the necessity to meet a basic human need and that need then was the same as it is today, to keep warm through the long, cold winter nights.

The craft or art of making quilts started in ancient Persia, India or Egypt. We know that the Crusaders discovered quilts when they first invaded the Middle East in the 11th and 12th Centuries when they marched across Europe to deliver the Holy Land from the hands of the Infidels. Those knights of the

Crusades returning home wore quilted material beneath their metal armor. That is how the craft of quilting was introduced into Europe and the British Isles.

Some ingenious knight, or possibly a serf of superior intelligence, soon devised the quilting frame and the art of quilting spread rapidly. At first the women of English, Ireland, Scotland and Wales made them for both clothing and bed covering. So popular did the art become that in centuries now long past even queens and ladies of the highest nobility indulged in it for pleasure and recreation.

In the castles of the nobility in England and in cottages and farm houses of the common people, the wife became the keeper of the quilting frames and the designer of the quilting patterns. When the days work was done, the quilting frame was set up and in the long English twilight and by the flames of the hearth fires, mothers taught the young girls of the household. So from the very early days it became known as a fireside craft. And as those same girls learned the art they dreamed of the days when they would have homes and be wives and mothers. Early in life the young ones would start their quilts to put in their hope chests for the time when they would become brides.

It was natural that when the colonists came to America to make new homes the women brought with them the family quilts and patterns and knowledge to make them. Woe betide the pioneer girl who could not make a quilt! Her chance to get a husband was slim. A few of the very old ones in our mountains can still recall a popular saying in earlier times and I quote it as it was told to me: "At your quilting, maids, don't dally. Quilt quick if you should marry. A maid who is quiltless at twenty one never shall greet her bridal sun."

The life led by the early settlers in the mountains of Western North Carolina, Tennessee, Kentucky and Pennsylvania was harsh. There was little recreation but lots of hard work. The cabins were far apart which did not allow visiting for purely social reasons. When neighbors did gather it must be for a purpose. But groups of women from widely separated farms did gather to work around the quilting frame. These quilting parties were usually held when the crops had been "laid by" or in the winter after the crops had been harvested.

These quilting parties became very popular. While nimble fingers plied the needles and pieced the old patterns, the women, talking in quiet tones (and sometimes not so quiet), exchanged gossip and happenings; what babies were born, who had died and who had married. Generally while the women quilted and gossiped, the men came to lend a hand at tasks on the outside.

Those were the happy times of simple homely pleasures. And the quilting parties with the accompanying log raising and corn shuckings was courting time for timid, bashful swains and for those not so timid and bashful. It was the time to walk their girls home.

We all know the ballad written by Stephen Foster. "Twas from Aunt Dinah's quilting party I was seeing Nellie home."

And then I heard of the Quilting Woman of Henderson County.

CHAPTER 77

The Quilting Woman
(1962)

I knocked on the front door of the little house on the side of the hill at the end of the driveway. The cheerful, gray haired lady who opened the door greeted me cordially and invited me to come in, after I told her who I was and why I had knocked on her door. She was Mrs. Stella Ratliff, wife of Alonzie Ratliff. I told her I had come to see her to learn about quilting and to find out why she was known as "the Quilting Woman of Henderson County." Before I ended my visit I had learned much that I understood and a whole lot more that I did not understand. I had entered a woman's world. I was asking for information about an art or craft that was as old as civilization and which had started soon after a woman had woven the first garment of cloth, fashioned by the first needle from the sharp bone of some animal.

Mr. and Mrs. Ratliff were both born and raised in the mountains of Pike County, Kentucky. Mr. Ratliff worked in the coal mines of Pike County until they came to Henderson County 31 years before my visit which was in April 1962. In the early 1930s Mrs. Ratliff was a very sick person whom the doctors had given up. The magic of our Blue Ridge Mountain climate had wrought wonders and on that day in 1962 she was a spry, active, robust picture of health and energy. At the time of my visit she and Mr. Ratliff had been married 47 years and had raised seven children.

She grew up on a mountain farm in Pike County. Her father raised his own sheep and the family made their own clothes. When she was only a small child her mother taught her to hand card the wool and to spin it on a spinning wheel. Those spinning wheels are only occasionally seen now in an antique shop or found tucked away in some attic. When the wool had been spun into thread she was taught to weave it into cloth from which the clothes for the entire family were made. Store bought cloth and clothes were rare things in our Appalachian Mountains whether those mountains were in Kentucky, Tennessee or Western North Carolina.

In the large front room of her home was her quilting frame suspended from the ceiling. She explained that the quilting frame could be lowered when the evenings were long and she had time to quilt. During the day it could be pulled back out of the way of other household activities.

Mrs. Ratliff's mother started to teach her to quilt when she was only 12 years old. She came from a quilting family because the mother had been taught by her mother. The handcraft had been handed down from mother to daughter through generations that extended far back into time, even as the patterns pieced into the quilts had been passed from generation to generation.

As time went by Mrs. Ratliff gave more and more of her time to quilting. With her ability, her fine, even hand stitching and needle work, her fame grew

The Quilting Woman, Mrs. Alonzie (Stella) Ratliff

and spread until she was known far and wide as "the Quilting Woman." When she left Pike County, Kentucky and came to Henderson County, her reputation and title followed her.

Mrs. Ratliff explained to me that quilts were made from scraps of material and how wool or cotton called batting was quilted in to give warmth. The base of all quilting is a square and she explained how the squares are pieced into patterns and how the patterns are designed and take the names from the everyday things one sees in nature.

Mrs. Ratliff's quilting frame had been made by John Perry for his mother when he was a young boy. Mrs. Perry had inherited the quilting frame from her mother-in-law after she married John. Mrs. Perry gave the frame to Mrs. Ratliff because Mrs. Perry thought that Mrs. Ratliff was the only person she knew in these modern days who would value the old frame, care for it, use it properly as it should be.

Mrs. Ratliff, "the Quilting Woman," showed me some of her quilts. Even as ignorant as I was, I could appreciate the skill and the art reflected in them and I could comprehend the patience necessary to make one. There were 600 to 900 pieces in each quilt she showed me, scraps left over from old dresses, shirts, sheets, blankets. These scraps were carefully selected and saved until enough were accumulated to make a quilt.

Mrs. Ratliff explained the patterns to me as she showed each quilt. There was one with a single eight-point pattern and one that was called "steps" or "a trip around the world." One pattern was called the "flower garden" and another the "wind mill." The "sunflower" pattern was one of the oldest patterns. As a child I had slept under a "crazy quilt" and on this visit I learned why it was called by such a name.

There is no set pattern but the scraps are pieced together "every which a way until it is a crazy looking thing." The patterns and hundreds of others have been handed down and exchanged at quilting parties for generations.

Such parties are rarely held now in these days of automobiles, radio and television. But quilting is still done as a craft in many farm homes in Henderson County where a quilting frame is a prized possession. When I left the home of Mrs. Ratliff, I realized that I had visited and talked with an artist and a craftsman.

CHAPTER 78

The Rocky Bluff Irish Potato
(1964)

Only a very few old ones still living have ever heard of the variety of Irish potato that is called the Rocky Bluff potato. Those very few old ones who can recall the name live in the western edge of our county in the area around Etowah, Blantyre and Bowman's Bluff. Yet the Rocky Bluff potato is still planted by one family from seed potatoes that have been in the family for more than 100 years, the seed handed down from one generation to another. Each year enough potatoes are saved from the previous year's crop to plant the next year. A century is a long time and the quality and vitality of the Rocky Bluff potato has to be good and strong to last that long.

My friend, the late C. E. Ledbetter was a gentle man and he was a gentleman; quiet, unassuming and efficient in his work. At an age when most men have been retired from active work for a number of years, C. E. Ledbetter, 84 years old, was still active and doing the work that most men many years younger would consider hard labor.

Mr. Ledbetter was born and raised on Ivy Knob, a small mountain near Etowah that rises north of the old Brickyard. Mr. Ledbetter was the son of Ephram and Isabella Hollingsworth Ledbetter. His grandfather, Isaac Ledbetter, came to what is now Henderson County in pioneer days, the first Ledbetter in the area. Isaac Ledbetter, in those far away days, owned a land grant in the vicinity of where Blantyre is today. His grant was for a square mile which is 640 acres.

Mr. Ledbetter first remembered the Rocky Bluff potato as a small boy helping drop the potato eyes in the furrows at spring planting when he would follow the bull tongue plow pulled by a steer opening up the furrows. In the fall of the year he would help harvest the Rocky Bluff potato and help his father hole them up to feed the family during the cold winter months and some for seed to plant the next year.

Who originated the strain and named it Rocky Bluff nobody now remembers but the name was the same as the area where it was first planted. The Bowman's Bluff area was called Rock Bluff by the first settlers who came before Mary Bowman, on horseback, plunged into the French Broad River and stamped the name Bowman's Bluff permanently on the section.*

Mr. Ledbetter said that it is a good potato, yields well, is disease free, keeps well and there never has been a better flavored one. Mr. Ledbetter should know; during his 84 years he has eaten a lot of Irish potatoes of many varieties but most of them have been Rocky Bluffs.

In 1964 Mr. and Mrs. Ledbetter lived on Sixth Avenue West in their cottage across from Oakdale cemetery. Mr. Ledbetter had been working in the cemetery for over 25 years and for the past 17 years he was custodian and superintendent. He took pride in his work but the neat, well groomed appearance of Oakdale tells this far better than words. He knew the location of graves and family burial lots. His courtesy was known to our home people as well as our visitors and tourists. No matter the time of day or how busy he was, he was always willing to stop his work to answer questions, help a stranger locate the grave of a long departed loved one, or to point out a grave of historical significance.

* Vol. I "Tall Tales"

In April 1964 when I stopped by to talk to Mr. Ledbetter and to get the story of the Rocky Bluff potato, he gave me a poke of seed potatoes, Rocky Bluffs that have been planted for over a century in his family.

I planted them in my garden. There were enough of them, even when I had cut them properly with several eyes to each piece of potato, to plant a long row. I will tend them and cultivate them carefully as is due such venerable seed handed down through the generations of the C. E. Ledbetter family.

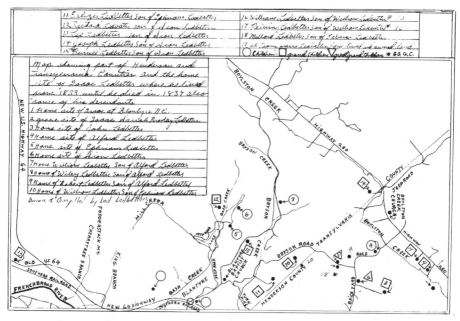

Map Showing Homesites of Ledbetter Families

Part Twelve
In the Public Service

Mr. Brownlow Jackson

Capt. M.C. Toms

Part Twelve

In The Public Service

CHAPTER 79

The Henderson County Public Library
(1964)

He came here from Cleveland, Ohio in the early 1900s on the advice of his doctor because he was a sick man. His doctor told him that his only chance to regain his health was in the mountains of Western North Carolina. He purchased a large boundary of land in Transylvania County on the edge of Henderson and built a palatial home. When he left Western North Carolina several years after regaining his health, Sylvester Everette went home with a heart full of love, appreciation and admiration for the people who had been so nice to him and for the climate that had restored his health.

Colonel Sylvester Everette had made many friends while residing on his farm and one of his closest was Charles French Toms, a civic leader of Hendersonville. When Col. Everette decided to go back to Ohio he went to Charles French Toms and told him he felt under obligation to our community and asked what he could do to repay that obligation. Mr. Toms told Col. Everette that the city of Hendersonville needed a public library more than any other thing and asked the Colonel to use his influence with his business associate, Andrew Carnegie. Mr. Carnegie had recently endowed the Carnegie Foundation which was establishing free libraries all over the United States. Col. Everette said he would certainly do that and if Mr. Carnegie would not do so he would give the city the library.

When Col. Everette went to Pittsburg to discuss the matter with Carnegie he was told that the inflexible rules of the Carnegie Foundation limited grants for free libraries to cities of more than 10,000 population but Carnegie agreed to personally give $10,000 to build a library in Hendersonville, provided the city would secure a suitable lot to build it on and that the city would appropriate tax funds for operating the library. Charles French Toms persuaded his father, Captain M. C. Toms,* to give a lot to the city for that purpose and then persuaded the City Council to accept the terms laid down by Mr. Carnegie.

This lot given by Capt. Toms was on the southeast corner of King Street and Fourth Avenue East. In 1911, when Captain Toms gave this property to the city, it was a quiet residential area and was considered an ideal location for

* Vol. II "The Builders"

Hendersonville's First Library   (Photo by Barber)

a library. In June 1911, the City Council accepted the lot from Capt. Toms and the gift of money from Mr. Carnegie. The Council appointed as the first trustees of the library Capt. M. C. Toms, Postmaster Brownlow Jackson and City Commissioner W. C. Rector.

These trustees were authorized to take bids for erecting the building and the contract to build the library was let in 1912 to W. P. Bayne. Life was more leisurely then than it is now and the building was not completed until December 1913. In January 1914, the equipment and furnishings were installed but it would be several months before the library was opened to the public. Finally on a rainy day in September 1914, the doors were opened and the people turned out in large numbers to visit the new library and to bring books as gifts.

Mrs. Norma Sandifer was the first librarian. In later years her daughter, Mrs. Sarah Sandifer Oates, served for a long period of time as a member and secretary of the Library Board of Trustees. Mrs. Sandifer was followed by Miss Ann Sample who served as librarian for 35 years. Miss Sample retired in the fall of 1956. She devoted her life to the library and the fact that we have such an outstanding institution today is due to her love and devotion. It was a struggle in those early days to keep the library functioning because of a limited operating budget and a small number of personnel. The dedicated guidance of

Ann Sample kept the library open and functioning. To show appreciation for her long years of service, the Board of Trustees named the reference room the Ann Sample Reference Room. On September 18, 1957, a plaque was unveiled on the entrance to the room with appropriate ceremonies honoring Ann Sample.

During the early years the services of the library were free to the residents of the town but county residents were required to pay a monthly fee to take out reading material. In 1951 the county joined the city in financial support and the free services of the library became county-wide. This enabled the library to qualify for financial aid from the N.C. Library Commission. This same year free bookmobile service for the rural areas was added.

A real crisis arose in 1956. Under the law at that time, only non-ad valorem tax money could be used by a county to support a library. In the fall of 1955, the people voted out the sale of wine and beer in the county which meant that the county could not appropriate its share of library support money for the fiscal year of 1956-1957. This also meant we would lose state aid. The Library Board was faced with only one choice. The Hendersonville Public Library would have to be closed.

It was the darkest time in the history of our library because there seemed to be no solution. Help came from an unexpected source. The Junior Chamber of Commerce Jaycees came to the rescue. The Library Commission

Interior of Hendersonville's First Library   (Photo by Barber)

in Raleigh said that if the Junior Chamber of Commerce raised $2,500 and the county would accept it, the state aid would be continued. This was done and it meant that the library would function until June 30, 1957. The Library Board and the City and County Commissioners met with State Senator Lee Whitmire and Representative J. T. Randall, both of whom represented Henderson County in 1957 in the State Legislature. These men agreed to introduce a bill in the Legislature to authorize the Commissioners to levy an ad valorem tax for library support. The bill was passed. The future of the library was assured.

Through the years the direct responsibility of the library fell on the Library Board of Trustees. During the period the library was financed by the city, the board was appointed by the City Commissioners. These were the difficult years and much praise and credit for keeping our library in operation is due to the people who served from 1914 to 1951. Some of these were Mrs. George Moland, Mrs. O. A. Meyer, Mrs. Kate Durham, Ben Foster, John T. Wilkins and Mrs. Lila Ripley Barnwell.

Under Article 8, Chapter 160 of the General Statutes of North Carolina, our library on July 1, 1957, was established as a free public library and all assets were transferred from the City of Hendersonville to Henderson County. The name Hendersonville Public Library, which it had borne for so many years, was changed to the name it bears today, The Henderson County Public Library.

I well remember a cold night in January 1956. I was chairman of the Board of Trustees at the time. Mrs. Henry J. Channon had come to Hendersonville to live the previous year. Her husband was an executive of General Electric. Mr. and Mrs. Channon had moved here from Massachusetts. On that January evening Mrs. Channon called me by phone and asked me if I

Henderson County Library, 1979

thought the Library Board would object if she tried to organize a Hendersonville Chapter of Friends of the Library.

In March 1956, the Friends of the Library was officially organized. Mrs. Channon was elected president with 32 charter members. The chapter has grown through the years and has contributed much to the growth and progress of the library. These contributions have consisted of money and untold hours of work helping the regular library staff.

This brief sketch of the history of our library covers only the period of years from its founding to 1964.

CHAPTER 80

The Lions Club Patrol

By the middle 1950s, drag racing on our highways had become a public menace and was taking a shocking toll of lives in our state and in Henderson County, not to mention the wrecked automobiles and the large number of people who were being injured and crippled for life. The worst part about drag racing on the highways is that so often the dead victims are innocent, law abiding motorists who are observing traffic regulations but are innocently involved in head-on collisions with drag racing maniacs roaring abreast at tremendous speeds on the public roads.

Drag racing on highways can be stopped if a community wants it stopped. An example of this occurred in Henderson County in 1956. The N.C. Highway Patrol was getting very strict on racers in several adjoining counties. At the same time the Haywood Road, running through the Mills River Valley, had been straightened, widened and reinforced.

Drag racers in the adjoining counties decided to move their activities to the Mills River Valley. The first night they raced there two cars wrecked but luckily no one was killed or injured. Within less than 24 hours, S. R. (Bob) Cathey, prominent citizen of the Mills River community, Clerk of Court of Henderson County and at that time president of the Mills River Lions Club called a special meeting of the club.

At this meeting it was agreed that members of the Lions Club would take turns patrolling the roads in the community at night. In cooperation with the Highway Patrol and the Henderson County Sheriff's Department, it was planned that whenever two or more cars were congregated the Lions Club members on patrol would immediately notify the two law enforcement agencies. The Lions Club members also agreed to testify in court against offenders.

Several nights after this eight or ten cars were spotted. They had planned to have a gigantic drag race but it was quickly broken up. The Lions Club members on patrol notified the law enforcement agencies. This happened one more time. There was no more drag racing in the Mills River community. It was stopped before it began because an alert civic organization backed by community support was ready and willing to assume its responsibility as a group of law abiding citizens.

CHAPTER 81

The Henderson County Rescue Squad

During the last part of February and the first three weeks of March 1960, Henderson County experienced unprecedented severe cold weather which was accompanied by a series of heavy snows, one piling on top of the other. There was much suffering in the mountainous rural areas due to lack of food and fuel where people were isolated by the snow and sleet. A number of emergency cases needed immediate medical attention yet doctors and ambulances found it impossible to reach them because the roads became impassable in the deep snow and our limited removal equipment was unable to cope with it. Mrs. Alice Reese, executive secretary of the local chapter of the Red Cross, the volunteer fire departments of Valley Hill, Blue Ridge, Fletcher and Green River rendered tremendous service during this emergency period.

In June 1958, a group of energetic, unselfish and patriotic young men of Hendersonville and Henderson County gathered and organized the Hendersonville Rescue Squad. This was the first rescue squad organized in Western North Carolina. Their charter stated that the object of the organization was to serve at any time upon proper request any mission of mercy and to aid and assist in case of disaster or accident where human life was endangered where such was within the capacity and mission of the squad.

The charter further stated that the organization was essentially a first aid and rescue squad to aid and assist the city and county officials in times of emergency. I am sure that most of my readers have seen the white uniformed men directing traffic, assisting at fires and various accidents and wrecks on the highway. These people are members of the Rescue Squad.

In the spring of 1960 the Hendersonville Rescue Squad was composed of 36 members, all of them young men of the finest type of citizens with a high degree of honor, integrity and sense of civic and public duty. The officers at that time were: Ed Hunnicut, captain; Glenn Marlow, adjutant; Broadus Harden, personnel officer; Ralph W. Jones, Jr., training officer; Joe Orr, communications officer; Robert Gillespie, equipment officer; Howard Cagle and J. T. Edenfield, sergeants. The board of directors at that time were Woodrow Bentley, Neal Grissom, James Bartlett and Ed Edney.

When the big snows of 1960 started with the unprecedented cold weather, the Rescue Squad was on the alert 24 hours a day and went on 54 emergency missions of mercy which required approximately 1,000 man hours.

Those man hours were given freely and took the men giving them away from the work whereby they earned their living.

Many of these rescue missions during the period of disastrous weather required long hours of hard, back-breaking work under bitter cold conditions and often during the dark of the night. There was the case of a man with a heart condition and a woman needing insulin. The rescue team had to fight its way up the steep, winding, narrow Davis Mountain Road to reach these people. On Jeter Mountain in the Crab Creek area, an 80 year old woman had been marooned so long that she had completely run out of both food and fuel. It took the Rescue Squad team convoy of 4 wheel-drive vehicles ten hours to reach her. The narrow road was 24 inches deep in snow and sleet with drifts in places that were three feet deep.

The most dramatic rescue was its 54th mission. The rescue team left the City Hall at 9:30 p.m. during a driving sleet storm. Mrs. John Chastain who lived near Horse Shoe was seriously ill with a heart ailment. It was imperative that she be moved to the hospital.

The rescue team, followed by Shepherd's ambulance, fought their way over the snow and ice covered country road to within a half mile of the Chastain home. The men had to walk the half mile to the home and put the lady on an Arctic sled. While the sled was being pulled by some of the men to the ambulance, other squad members had to administer oxygen to the patient several times. When they reached the ambulance, the rescue squad radioed ahead to Dr. Nick Fortescue who was waiting at the hospital when the ambulance arrived.

To operate efficiently in all cases of disaster, a tremendous amount of all kinds of equipment is necessary. Much of this equipment was paid for by the members themselves who were always giving their time freely. Some of the necessary equipment was paid for by generous citizens who realized and appreciated what the Rescue Squad was doing. Our town and county was fortunate in having such an organization during the winter crises of 1960 and will continue to be fortunate in having them during the years ahead.

Part Thirteen
Men with Dreams

Part Thirteen

Men With Dreams

CHAPTER 82

The First Sewing Machine

In Chapter 30 I told you about Burgin Whitaker who served in the Civil War with Edney's Greys and who lost four brothers in that terrible conflict. When the war ended he came home to Laurel Creek.

After Burgin finished his log cabin and filled it with the crude furniture fashioned by his skillful hands, he felt that something was lacking. A pretty, buxom mountain girl caught the young man's fancy and finally his heart. After a spell of courting, he got up nerve enough to ask Lizzie Freeman to marry him. Burgin and Lizzie were united in holy wedlock and Burgin Whitaker brought his charming bride to the new log cabin. They settled down to make a living and to raise a family.

Time went by and Lizzie made a good wife. She was full of energy and worked hard. She not only kept house and raise the children but helped with the farm work as well as all worthwhile mountain women did in those days. There were no store-bought clothes to be had and so she made all the clothes for her family to wear. She became as skillful with thread and needle as her husband was with his tools. But sewing all the clothes by hand for an ever growing family was a slow process.

Lizzie began to hear talk about a machine that had been invented that a body used to sew clothes, a machine that sewed many, many times faster than by hand. She thought what a wonderful thing it would be if she had such a machine that talk told was so easy to operate. A sewing machine! She even dreamed about it at night although she had never seen one nor could she imagine how such a marvelous thing looked.

Then one day a man wearing a black derby hat drove a horse and buggy in the yard of the cabin on Laurel Creek. He was the forerunner of the traveling salesman and in those days was referred to as a "drummer." This drummer was going through the rural areas selling that wonder of wonders, sewing machines, and he had one strapped on the back of the buggy to show folks how easy it was to operate.

Her heart sank when the drummer told Lizzie and her husband that the sewing machine cost all of $40. That was a lot of money in our mountains in those years just after the War Between the States and cash was scarce and hard to come by. There were no banks in Henderson County where a person could borrow money but her husband knew a man who would lend it. He went to him and gave him a mortgage on twenty acres that lay across the creek from the log cabin home. And that is how Lizzie Freeman Whitaker came to be the first woman in all of the Edneyville area to own a sewing machine.

When the word spread people came from miles around; the old and the young, the rich and the poor, to see that marvelous sewing machine. They came from Bear Wallow, Bat Cave, Point Lookout and even from the little village of Hendersonville to see Lizzie sew on that machine. When the time came for her husband to pay the mortgage on the twenty acres of land that he had given to raise the $40, he could not raise the money so he lost the land. But Lizzie had her sewing machine and she used it throughout her life. When she died, family tradition tells, it was traded to Jerry Stepp who operated one of the first funeral homes in the county. Lizzie Freeman Whitaker's sewing machine, the first one in the area, helped to pay for her burial.

CHAPTER 83

The First Washing Machine

It was a big day in Hendersonville that morning in April 1911. *The French Broad Hustler* was our only newspaper at that time and it was published only weekly. But the *Hustler* announced the great day that April with large headlines on the front page. The paper stated that a patent had been issued by the United States Patent Office to G. W. Connor of Hendersonville for his new invention, a washing machine. M. L. Shipman was editior of the *Hustler* at the time and he claimed that the marvelous machine would revolutionize the traditional Monday wash day for overworked housewives and washer women over the entire United States.

So great was the interest in the new invention that a public demonstration of the machine was held on Main Street. Such a sensation was created by this unheard of thing that the demonstration was attended by a large crowd headed by R. H. Staton, Mayor of our town, and City Commissioners J. Mack Rhodes, J. W. McIntyre and J. D. Davis.

What became of the sensational invention and G. W. Connor, the inventor?

In 1961 I remembered that my friend Luther Wilson, a retired miller, was in some way connected with Mr. Connor. When I visited Luther Wilson at his home on the Tracy Grove Road, he told me that G. W. Connor was his brother-in-law. So new and revolutionary was such a machine that Mr. Connor was unable to raise the money to finance the manufacturing of the washing machine and it was never put on the market.

A few years later Mr. Connor built and operated a large hotel on Bearwallow Mountain call the Bonnie Bell Inn that catered to the summer tourists. When this type of rural hotel proved no longer profitable, Mr. Connor moved to South Carolina where he died around the middle of the century. Like so many inventors, he was a man who was way ahead of his time.

CHAPTER 84

S. S. Stabler and The Rev. J. L. Mauney

There are only a few left who remember the Henderson County cheese factory and Mountain Maid Ice Cream. In the late teens and early 1920s, dairy farming in Henderson County was beginning to grow. A realization was beginning to dawn on the farmers that this was an ideal area for producing milk, with its mild summers and not too severe winters. Grass grew lush in Henderson County where the average rainfall is sixty inches or more and well distributed throughout the twelve months of the year.

There were no distributing plants for dairy products such as we have now in Coble Dairies and Biltmore Dairy. The market for milk was limited. S. S. Stabler had come here as County Agricultural Extension Agent in 1921. He soon realized that a market must be found if the dairy industry was to grow. He believed that the manufacturing of cheese was the answer. Under Stabler's leadership, the farmers of Mills River and Horse Shoe organized a cooperative for the making and marketing of cheese. Stock was sold and a building erected.

June 8, 1923 was a big day at Horse Shoe and one to be long remembered. The cheese factory was completed and ready to operate. An all-day celebration and picnic was held with hundreds of farmers and their families attending. Many prominent people in agriculture and politics from all parts of the state were present. A new day in the agricultural economy of Henderson County was dawning. Cheese making was demonstrated. A cattle judging contest was held. There was a band concert and lots of speeches. Oh, it was a great day!

E. V. Fowler was plant manager and Parmer McCrary, who had taken a course in cheese making, was in charge of the manufacturing. Farmers were paid 15¢ a gallon for their milk delivered in 5 and 10 gallon cans at the plant. Later the price was raised. In less than six months, 100 pounds of cheese a day was being produced and all of it was being sold on the local market.

So successful was the plant at Horse Shoe that meetings were held at Dana, Edneyville and Upward in efforts to establish other cheese making plants but the one at Horse Shoe was the only plant that ever materialized.

The cooperative cheese factory at Horse Shoe functioned for several years and served its purpose in offering a market for milk when the dairy industry was in its infancy in Henderson County. Then the land boom of the middle 1920s came to Western North Carolina. The demand for whole milk in Hendersonville and surrounding towns increased. The prices paid for the milk delivered in the cities was more than the cheese plant could pay so eventually the changing economic conditions forced the Horse Shoe Cheese Cooperative to liquidate.

But that was not the end of cheese manufacturing in Henderson County. The Rev. Mr. J. L. Mauney was minister of the Lutheran Church here and was pastor of a comparatively small congregation. One of the outstanding achievements of the Rev. Mr. Mauney during this period was increasing the number of members in his church to such an extent that the capacity of the Lutheran Church building then in use was too small to accommodate them. During his pastorate and under his leadership the present Lutheran Church on the corner of Seventh Avenue West and Church Street was built (1979).

In the early 1920s, during the same period that the Horse Shoe cheese factory was operating, Rev. Mauney established a plant for the manufacturing of ice cream made from milk and cream produced in Henderson County.

This building was on King Street behind a building on Second Avenue East and Main Street. Newton Lanning, who in later years worked for Francis and Wright and still later operated a coin machine laundry, was associated with Rev. Mauney in his ice cream which was manufactured and marketed here and in the surrounding territory under the name Mountain Maid Ice Cream.

When the cheese factory at Horse Shoe closed, Rev. Mauney purchased the cheese manufacturing machinery at Horse Shoe and installed it in the building where he produced his Mountain Maid Ice Cream. He started now to also make cheese. This cheese was delicious, made an instant success and was marketed under the name Mountain Maid Cup Cheese. The Mountain Maid plant operated for several years.

Again economic conditions and the Great Depression made cheese manufacturing unprofitable. The huge nation wide companies such as Kraft absorbed the cheese market. The Mountain Maid Ice Cream Company was sold to the Garrison interests who made and distributed ice cream products in several states under the name Blue Bird Ice Cream. And so ended the manufacturing of cheese and ice cream out of milk and cream produced exclusively from Henderson County dairy herds.

CHAPTER 85

The Henoco Club

Not many Hendersonville residents remember the Henoco Club. It has been a long time since Henoco existed. During the years that the club functioned it served its purpose. You could call the Henoco Club a kind of super chamber of commerce, a high powered boosters club.

In 1921 Hendersonville was strictly a summer tourist town and the people of Hendersonville and Henderson County lured the tourists in a big way. The Henoco Club was organized by W. A. Smith, a prominent attorney here, and by Sam Hodges and Jake Wells, both leading entrepreneurs who built the Hodgewell Hotel which stood on the corner of Fourth Avenue and Church Street.*

The sole reason for the Henoco Club was to sell Hendersonville and Henderson County as the place to spend the summer season. The name was derived from the first two letters in Hendersonville and the first two letters in North Carolina. In the spring of 1921 the Henoco Club made a pilgrimage to Florida and adjoining states to urge the people to escape the heat and mosquitoes of their summer season and to come to the beautiful Blue Ridge Mountains where delightful cool breezes soothed the fevered brows and where mosquitoes did not exist; where the water was cold, sweet and pure; where even on the hottest summer night a body would find it necessary to sleep under a blanket.

The members of the Henoco Club were no pikers and when they undertook a project they went at it in a big way and saw that project to a successful conclusion in a royal manner. That February afternoon in 1921 the people of Hendersonville turned out and were at the Depot because everybody supported the Henoco Club and on a winter afternoon in 1921 there was not much else to do but go to the Southern Railroad Station on Seventh Avenue and take part in anything that gave promise of some excitement and entertainment. All of Hendersonville was there that day to see the Henoco Club pilgrimage off on its trip to Florida.

When the chartered Pullman car was hooked on to the Florida-bound passenger train the large crowd cheered long and loud with a tumult that was only exceeded in enthusiasm by the commotion that went up a few minutes later when the passenger train started to pull out.

There were 28 members of the Henoco Club in that gaily decorated Pullman car. Sam Hodges had already gone ahead to map the visits to all the larger cities of Florida and to arrange for the club's activities.

On both sides of the railroad car were large banners which told the world the who, what and why of the Henoco Club. Bright colored pennants waving from the car windows invited people to spend the summer in Hendersonville.

* Vol. I ''The Roaring Twenties''

Broad green silk ribbons with "Hendersonville, N.C." written on them were worn across the chest of each of the 28 members.

Sixty thousand pieces of literature were taken along, describing the virtues and attractions of our area. This literature was handed out at every station along the way, along with cards listing all the hotels and boarding houses in our town and county.

At Daytona Beach, the club attended a Billy Sunday tent meeting in a body, to hear and see the world famous, evangelist of that period. The celebrated preacher recognized the Henoco Club and had them stand while he told the huge congregation about Hendersonville.

In Miami they were received by the great orator, William Jennings Bryan, in front of an overflow audience. The Henoco Club returned by way of Atlanta and was entertained there by Colonel Woodward, head of the Georgia Military Academy. In Atlanta another Pullman car full of Henoco Club members joined the first Pullman.

The Henoco did big things in a big way in those days long ago. That summer of 1921 Hendersonville had one of its best tourist seasons because of the pilgrimage. The only surviving member of the Henoco Club who made that grand tour of 1921 is E. J. (Erv) Anders.

CHAPTER 86

The First Consumer Installment Loan

It was in the early spring of 1930 and the young man was trying to borrow $600 and pay the loan back at the rate of $50 a month over a period of twelve months. He first went to Ed Brooks, vice president of the Citizens National Bank on the corner of Main Street and Fourth Avenue East. When the young man explained his idea to Mr. Brooks, the vice president was both amazed and horrified. He stated his objection to such a loan emphatically, although he admitted that the young man's character, credit rating and collateral was acceptable.

The idea of a loan for a year, repayable in twelve equal installments, was unheard of and the application was turned down immediately, flatly and in a rather haughty manner.

So across the street the young man went to Mack Rhodes who was vice president of the First Bank and Trust Company. The reaction of Mr. Rhodes was the same. But he accompanied his prompt refusal of such an unheard type of loan with a fatherly lecture as to why such a loan could not be made.

The American Bank and Trust Company was located on Fourth Avenue West, next to the present Federal Building. The site is today a large parking lot which Northwestern Bank donated to the city.

The late Emmett Lott was cashier and loan officer and Harvey Reagen was the teller. They were both much younger men than the officers of the other banks. Weary by now, the would be borrower explained his idea: the loan to be paid back in twelve equal monthly payments.

Mr. Lott and Mr. Reagen were both skeptical but instead of rejecting the proposal at once, Mr. Lott said he would take the matter up with his board of directors. "Come back in a few days," he said. When the young man returned several days later, Mr. Lott said that while such a thing had never been done before, his bank would make the loan as an experiment. He had, ready to be signed, twelve notes. Each one was made for $50 plus the interest and each note was dated to be due the first day of each succeeding month.

This was the first time a monthly installment loan had been made by a bank in Hendersonville, Henderson County or the surrounding area. This was the beginning of the present day method of financing, so successful all over the United States. It is now known as a personal monthly installment loan or monthly installment consumer loan. Today a borrower signs only one note and the interest is added to the loan or deducted as the borrower desires.

But that first monthly installment loan made in 1930 by the American Bank and Trust Company of Hendersonville was like all bank loans, a lot harder to pay back than it was to get.

CHAPTER 87

The Peter Guice Bridge

The shadows were beginning to lengthen that hot, sultry early fall day as the herd of cattle crossed the long wooden bridge over the raging river and moved slowly up the steep road that led to the top of the mountain. The air was filled with dust and a jumble of raucous noises. The bawling of the bone-weary cattle mingled with the shouts of the drovers and the continuous cracking of their blacksnake rawhide whips. The men on foot and horseback were having all they could do to keep the tired cattle moving.

The pace suddenly quickened as the leading animals sensed that the top of the mountain had been reached. The bars to the entrance of the cattle pens were slammed in place. Men were hard at work forking feed to the cattle and the persistent bellowing of the animals had quieted. Soon the drovers were filling their empty stomachs in the bar room and at the tables of the inn and tavern across the way. Darkness had settled and now all was still around the compound as man and beast sank into a weary sleep.

When the Guice family first came into the area and acquired land on both sides of Green River and the Howard Gap Road is not exactly known. But it is known that it was after the Revolution and that the family was among the first

One of the first bridges over Green River on Howard Gap Rd. at present site of Peter Guice Bridge   (Photo by Barber)

in that area which was to become parts of Polk and Henderson Counties. Peter Guice was born November 10, 1788, and the family had been in the area for several years before his birth.

The Howard Gap Road became the main thoroughfare between the earlier settled western areas of our country and the Carolina and Georgia coast lands. The movement of horses, cattle, hogs, sheep and even turkeys from Kentucky and Tennessee to the coastal markets was ever increasing. The stagecoach and other methods of travel east and west had to follow this Howard Gap Road.*

* Vol. I "Twilight for the Indians"

By the time Peter Guice reached maturity, the family inn had been developed. The stock pens had gradually increased in numbers. Now there was a pounding mill to crack grain to feed the droves of animals stopping overnight on their way to market, a grist mill for grinding grain into meal and flour, a blacksmith shop and finally a shingle mill each in turn was added. Peter Guice was by now a man of importance and enterprise.

It is not known when Peter Guice got the idea to build a bridge across Green River where the Howard Gap Road crosses but it was around 1820 that the bridge was built to avoid the loss of animals fording the raging waters of the river. About the same time, January 21, 1821, a son was born to Peter Guice. Through the years Peter Guice raised six boys and two girls. His son Joe had a family of two boys and six girls. The Guice family was on the way to becoming one of the largest families in Henderson and adjoining counties.

Sometime along the way an unrecorded flood washed out the toll bridge built by Peter but his son Joe rebuilt it and maintained it until the flood of 1916 destroyed the second bridge. Methods of travel and transportation were changing. New and better highways were being constructed. Highway 176 replaced the Howard Gap Road. Then I-26 was platted and surveyed. It was found that the natural place to cross Green River was exactly where Peter Guice had built the first bridge ever to span that river here in the mountains. This bridge which was 220 feet high and cost $3,758,028 was opened to traffic in 1972.

On April 9, 1976, at the rest area of the south bound lane of I-26, this magnificent new bridge was dedicated. It was built on the exact spot but much higher than the first one built by Peter Guice or the second one built by his son

The Peter Guice Bridge, 1979

Joe. The new bridge was named most appropriately the Peter Guice Memorial Bridge and a plaque was unveiled.

The dedicatory address was made by Jacob F. Alexander, Secretary of the North Carolina Board of Transportation. One of the highlights of the dedication and naming of the bridge was the history of the Peter Guice family. This was given by Mrs. Beulah Ward Hess, a fifth generation direct descendant of Peter Guice.

The Peter Guice Memorial Bridge is recognized as a magnificent structure. Spanning the Green River Gorge 220 feet below, it stands as an example of modern engineering, architectural and constructural skill. Few stop to think that when Peter Guice built the first bridge across Green River and when his son Joe E. Guice replaced it with a second bridge, those two pioneers had only a few yoke of oxen, axes, adzs, crude blocks and tackles to work with. Their engineering and construction skill in building the first two bridges across the Green River Gorge was equal to or even greater than the skill of the present day builders.

Peter Guice, his son Joe and others of the Guice family rest in peace in the older section of the cemetery of the Friendship Baptist Church which is near Saluda and not too far from the location of the Guice bridges that spanned Green River.

Part Fourteen
Some Famous Native & Adopted Sons

Some Famous Native And Adopted Sons

CHAPTER 88

Three Presidents

It is a startling sight to one who enters the lobby of the Hendersonville City Hall for the first time. The first thing that catches a body's eye is the life size bronze statue of a man on horseback and two men seated, one by the front legs of the horse and the other by the horse's hind legs. This statue dominates the lobby of the first floor, yet few who see it know what the statue represents, why it is in the City Hall or what the statue's significance is.

The man on horseback is General Andrew Jackson, hero of the Battle of New Orleans and President of the United States from 1829 to 1837. The men seated are James Knox Polk, President of our country from 1845 to 1849, and Andrew Johnson, President from 1865 to 1869. All three of the men are natives of North Carolina yet no memorials had been erected for any of them by the state of North Carolina until 1943. That year a commission was appointed to study the matter. On October 19, 1948, an original statue was unveiled with much ceremony on Capitol Square in Raleigh, a memorial to these three great North Carolinians.

Notables from all parts of the United States were present that day in Raleigh and the main speaker at the ceremony was President Harry S. Truman. The sculptor was Charles Keck, an internationally known native of New York City. The statue unveiled that day in Raleigh was cast in bronze by the Gorham Company of Providence, Rhode Isand and the stone foundation was made by Benish Brothers of Brooklyn, N.Y.

The statue in our City Hall is the plaster model made for casting the original bronze statue which was unveiled in Raleigh on October 19, 1948. Mrs. P. F. Patton, authoress and historian of Hendersonville, was then a member of the N. C. Department of Archives and History. She knew that this plaster cast would be available to some city or county in the state. It is through her influence that this replica of the original statue was brought to Hendersonville and placed in our City Hall. Sam Seigle and Herman Kimmell, summer residents of our county, paid the cost of transporting and assembling the plaster model.

In the fall of 1949 the model, as you see it today, was unveiled and presented to Hendersonville and Henderson County. Dr. Christopher Crittenden, Director of the Department of Archives and History, made the presentation.

If you are interested in more detailed information, you can find it in our library in a book titled "Presidents that North Carolina Gave the Nation." If you have lived here a long time and have not seen this statue, or if you have recently come here to live, you should visit the lobby of our City Hall and see this life size statue of the three native North Carolinians who became Presidents of the United States.

Three Presidents From North Carolina
Jackson – Polk – Johnson

CHAPTER 89

Bill Nye

Calvary Episcopal Church on the outskirts of Fletcher is sometimes referred to as the Westminster Abbey of the South. At the entrance to the church yard is an ivy clad monument with the inscription: "In Loving Memory of Edgar Wilson Nye - Billy Nye - American Humorist and Friend - Born in Shirley, Maine August 25, 1850 - Died at Buck Shoals near this spot, February 22, 1896. A member of Calvary Episcopal Church for many years. His body is interred in yonder church yard."

After reading this inscription I went in search of his grave "in yonder church yard" and I found it in the middle of the cemetery under a large oak tree. The grave is marked by a large block of native granite on which is a bronze plaque inscribed: "Bill Nye 1850-1896 - American Humorist - Jeremiah 31:13: 'I will turn their mourning into joy and will comfort them and make them rejoice from their sorrow.' "

Christened Edgar Wilson Nye, he is better known in the literary world as Bill Nye, journalist, humorist, writer and lecturer. Bill Nye was born in Shirley, Maine, the son of Franklin and Elizabeth Loring Nye.

His parents were of New England farming stock. Theirs was a hard life, trying to scratch a living from the soil during the short growing season of that far northern New England state. In 1852, when the boy was only two years old, Franklin and Elizabeth Nye went west and settled a farm on the St. Croix River in northern Wisconsin in an attempt to improve their financial position.

When the family moved to Wisconsin it was still a wild area but the Nye boy managed to attend school, as he himself once wrote, "between the Indian massacres." He studied law and graduated at the nearby Falls River Academy. This was in 1876 and he immediately went to the new settlement of Laramie City in Wyoming Territory. There he was admitted to the practice of law in what was still a wild, Indian-inhabited, frontier area. There was little work for a young lawyer in 1876, but there was a crying need for a justice of the peace and a school teacher in that fast growing settlement of Laramie City.

So Edgar Wilson Nye started to teach school and also became justice of the peace and before he left the Wyoming Territory he had also served as Superintendent of Schools, a member of the City Council and Postmaster of Laramie. During these years he also began to write and contribute to the newspapers of the Territory under the name Bill Nye and that is the name by which he is known in American literature. Among the newspapers he contributed to were *The Cheyenne Sun* and *The Denver Tribune*.

In 1881 Bill Nye established his own newspaper, *The Laramie Boomerang*. Soon he and his newspaper were nationally known and his reputation as a humorist was well established. But the hardships of that wild frontier territory were too much for him. His health failed and he came back east. In 1885 he became a staff writer for *The New York World*. There Bill Nye and his writing became even more famous. In 1886 he teamed with the great poet of that period, James Whitcomb Riley. Together the two men made a lecture tour of the United States and from that time on he was in constant demand.

In 1881 he published his book, "Bill Nye and Boomerang." In 1882 he published "Forty Liars and other Lies," in 1886 "Nye and Riley's Railroad Guide" and in 1894 "Bill Nye's History of the United States." His last book was published in 1896, the year of his death. It was titled, "Bill Nye's History of England from the Druids to the Reign of Edward the Eighth."

Bill Nye ranks in American Literature with Mark Twain and Artemus Ward, a brilliant trio of middle and late 19th Century men of American letters. In 1891 Bill Nye came to Western North Carolina for his health. He bought a tract of land in Henderson County on the French Broad River and there he built his home. He named it Buck Shoals and he lived there until his death in 1896.

In Fletcher there is an historical marker that tells you that Bill Nye's home is 3½ miles west of that point. The house is a large rambling structure of Victorian architecture so popular in that period. It has not been lived in for a long number of years and the last time I was there it was much in need of repairs. It was visited every year by many people from all parts of the United States.

A few years ago a literary group wanted to purchase the old home and restore it as an historical landmark, a shrine in memory of Bill Nye, but the owner refused to sell it. Soon the ravages of time will destroy the old landmark and all that will be left to remind us that a great American man of letters spent the last years of life in Henderson County will be the monument and the grave in the cemetery of Calvary Episcopal Church.

CHAPTER 90

DuBose Heyward

He was born into an aristocratic family in Charleston, S.C., but spent his childhood in genteel poverty. In the years of his early manhood his constant companions were the black dock hands of the harbor waterfront. He was unsuccessful in his early business adventures yet he became internationally known and recognized and in the latter part of his life his success not only brought him fame but financial independence. Much of his renown and fortune came to him while he lived in Henderson County where he did much of his work. But only a few of the elderly still living here remember it all.

DuBose Heyward was born August 31, 1885, descended from a long line of distinguished colonial and Revolutionary ancestors; one of whom was Thomas Heyward, a signer of the Declaration of Independence and a close personal friend of George Washington.

Not too long after his birth, the family suffered a series of financial reverses. As a result the boy had to quit school when he was only 14 years old. In those days there were no compulsory school attendance laws; neither were there any child labor laws which kept a boy or girl from working until a certain age was reached. Young Heyward went to work in a hardware store to help support the family. When he had put in a few years, he went to work on the Charleston Harbor waterfront ship docks; the hours of labor were from dawn to dusk.

His only companions for days at a time were the black stevedores who loaded and unloaded the ships tied up in Charleston Harbor. As a result he became intimately acquainted with the low country Negro, many of them known then and now as the Gullah Negro. It was while working on the Charleston wharves that he absorbed the knowledge and atmosphere that later made him a famous man. When he left the docks he then started to sell insurance.

At the end of the First World War a young man from the North came to teach at the Citadel, the famed South Carolina Military College at Charleston. This young man was Hervey Allen who became a famous author in later years and is possibly best known for his novel, "Anthony Adverse." It was while DuBose Heyward was selling insurance that he met Hervey Allen. They became close, intimate friends. In 1922 the two men collaborated in writing and publishing a volume of poetry of the Carolina coastal area and of the mountains of Western North Carolina. The book of poems was an immediate success. Heyward had found his field and he was launched on a career that would lead to fame and fortune.

In the meantime, he met Miss Dorothy Hartrell Kuhns, a charming and talented young lady from the Midwest. Miss Kuhns was a playwright and a successful dramatist in her own right. In 1923 Heyward and Miss Kuhns were married. During his courtship and after his marriage, Heyward was writing his first novel. This was "Porgy." It was an interpolation of Negro life in Charleston; Porgy the black beggar with no legs drove on his rounds pulled by a rancid old billy goat whose odor did not remind one of French perfume. It was also about Porgy's woman, Bess. The novel made Catfish Row in Charleston famous all over the world. "Porgy" was published in 1925 and immediately became a best seller.

This book and the others that followed it made DuBose Heyward world famous and he became financially independent, a contrast to the genteel poverty of his early life. The midwestern girl that he married in 1923 saw the dramatic possibilities of Porgy. She and her husband collaborated in preparing the stage version of the novel which was produced and presented in New York by the New York Theatre Guild in 1927. As a play "Porgy" became as successful a Broadway production as the book.

In 1929 the novel "Mamby's Daughters" was published, another portrayal of Gullah Negro life. This was followed in 1932 by "Peter Sheley," a story of the fall of Fort Sumter, "Lost Morning" in 1936 and "Star Spangled Virgin" in 1939. Much of the writing of these novels were doen by DuBose Heyward at his home, Dawn Hill, in Henderson County.

CHAPTER 91

DuBose Heyward and George Gershwin
(1959)

DuBose Heyward was now living in Henderson County at his home, Dawn Hill, and it was while living here that real international fame came to him in 1935 and the years that followed. Those years made two men immortal: George Gershwin and DuBose Heyward. The dramatic play "Porgy" was such an outstanding success that George Gershwin believed a musical based on "Porgy" would be even a greater success.

Libretto is the text or words of an opera or any extended choral composition. Gershwin came to Dawn Hill, Heyward's home in Henderson County, to confer with him about the libretto. The result, after several years of hard work by both men, was the musical play that all of us know as "Porgy and Bess." Gershwin wrote the musical score and DuBose Heyward wrote and adapted the libretto. The finished production was first presented in 1935 and it has since become an immortal popular musical classic.

"Porgy and Bess" has been produced all over the world and each year its popularity has grown. In 1959 an all American black cast completed a tour of Russia where it was received with ovations.

In 1940, while here in Henderson County, DuBose Heyward, only 55 years old, had an attack of what he thought was acute indigestion. He went to Tryon to be treated by his friend and relative, Dr. Allen Jervey. While undergoing a physical check-up to diagnose his trouble, DuBose Heyward collapsed and died from a heart attack on June 16, 1940.

There are quite a few people still living here who knew DuBose Heyward personally and intimately although few who have come to live here in later years realize that much of his life was spent here and that much of his writing was done at Dawn Hill. And fewer still are those who know that George Gershwin wrote most of the musical score for "Porgy and Bess" while living at Heyward's home.

If you are interested, drive out the Kanuga Road until you come to Faith Tabernacle that replaced the well known log church on the corner of the Kanuga Road and Price Road. Turn right on Price Road and drive to where

Old Kanuga Road crosses Price Road. There at the crossroads is a beautiful grove of majestic white pine trees covering several acres of land. Here turn left on the old Kanuga Road. There is a marker with the road name; a few hundred feet along this road is a red cottage in rustic surroundings.

This red cottage was built by Heyward in the early 1920s and lived in while he was having his permanent home, Dawn Hill, constructed in the white pine grove.

The entrance to Dawn Hill is on the Price Road. Standing beside the big house and slightly behind it is a one room building. This one room building is the studio where Heyward did most of his writing and where he and Gershwin collaborated in producing the musical "Porgy and Bess." In 1959 Dawn Hill was lived in and owned by a Mr. and Mrs. Colton. Mr. Colton, as a small boy, lived on his father's estate in Germany. An adjoining neighbor was Otto Von Bismarck, the Iron Chancellor who united the many German principalities into the German Empire before World War I.

Miss Jean Drake knew the Heyward family because DuBose, his grand-mother, mother and sister Jennie spent the summers from the time he was a teenage boy at White Pines Cottage, the L. E. Rackley place. The Rackley place adjoined the property where Jean Drake was raised. She told me she was a guest at the White Pines Cottage when Heyward celebrated his 21st birthday. She said he liked to walk, to ride horseback and was highly regarded by all the people in the community.

Every summer when he first arrived he always went around the neigh-borhood visiting and every autumn before he left he would visit the neighbors to tell them goodby. This was before he lived here permanently and before he became famous and wealthy.

John Drake, a brother of Miss Jean Drake, was a former deputy sheriff of Henderson County and law enforcement and security officer at Ecusta. I talked to Mr. Drake about DuBose Heyward. He told me that he was always impressed by Heyward's friendliness and his interest in our area and our people. Mr. Drake built the swimming pool for Heyward at Dawn Hill.

In 1959, Mr. and Mrs. Charles F. Matthew had lived in the Valley Hill section of Henderson County for twenty years in a large 22-room house just off the Willow Road. When Heyward stopped working on the waterfront in Charleston, he and Mr. Matthew were partners in the insurance business. In later years Heyward sold Dawn Hill. He and Mr. Matthew together bought the large home where I went to talk to Mr. and Mrs. Matthew. They showed me several autographed first editions of several of Heyward's books that he had given them as presents. They also knew Hervey Allen and George Gershwin.

They told me that Gershwin had spent much time on Folley Island and other nearby islands to get the proper atmosphere and background before coming to Hendersonville to write the musical score to "Porgy and Bess." When Gershwin played some of the score before it was published, Mrs. Matthew said that she was astonished how quickly he had gotten the feel of the low country Negro music. Gershwin explained to her that he was a Jew, a member of a suppressed race since the children of Israel had been enslaved by the Egyptians. The pathos, the sadness and the groping for freedom that runs throughout the opera of "Porgy and Bess" is the same that runs through the songs, the spirituals and music of all suppressed and persecuted peoples since the beginning of time, he explained.

While staying with the Matthew family in Valley Hill, DuBose Heyward had a severe attack of what he thought was acute indigestion. It was Mrs. Matthew who drove him to Tryon to see Dr. Allen Jervey and she was there when the famous man collapsed and died while being examined on June 16, 1940.

CHAPTER 92

Champ Osteen

When he died on December 14, 1962, only the elderly still living here remembered James Champlin Osteen because Champ Osteen was an old man by then and he had lived in South Carolina most of his life. Champ Osteen was born in 1876 in Henderson County near Blantyre, the son of Richard and Mary Shipman Osteen.

James Champlin Osteen was the first person born in Henderson County to become a major league baseball player. His family moved to Greenville, S. C. when he was six or seven years old and he also became the first person from Greenville to make the major leagues. Champ Osteen had a long and brilliant career as a professional baseball player in the days before World War I when million dollar bonus babies were unheard of and a player had to fight his way up through the ranks by sheer determination, hustle and ability.

Because he had all of the above qualifications combined with boundless energy, grit and a fighting spirit, Champ started at the bottom and went to the top of his profession. Professional baseball was a rough, tough game at the start of his career around the turn of the century, when he started playing semi-professional baseball in the textile league of South Carolina.

He soon attracted the attention of the baseball scouts. His first professional experience was with the Wilmington, N. C. team in the days when the outfielders often had to share their territory with a cow or two staked out to graze.

In 1901 he was traded to Newport News, Virginia whose franchise was soon transferred to Charlotte, N. C. Champ Osteen's proudest boast was that he played shortstop on the Charlotte team when it won 25 straight games. He was on his way up because in 1903 he was the shortstop with the Washington, D.C. Senators. This was his first major league experience. The next season he was with the New York Highlanders in the American League managed by Clark Griffin. This team is known today as the New York Yankees.

Griffin sold Osteen to the Cleveland Indians but Champ refused to report and so in 1906 he came back to Greenville and coached the Furman University baseball team that year. He was back in the major leagues in 1908 when he played shortstop with St. Louis Cardinals. His major league career as a player ended in 1910 but not his professional baseball career because in 1911 he managed the Dallas, Texas team and the Charlotte, N. C. team in 1912 and 1913. He finished his diamond career in 1914 as manager in Columbia, S. C. in the old South Atlantic League known to baseball players and fans as the Sally League.

He returned to live in Greenville and was an employee of that city until his retirement in 1957. Champ Osteen's career paralleled those of many other great ballplayers. He knew them all and either played with them or against them: Hans Wagner, Ty Cobb, the Georgia Peach, the great pitcher Christy Mathewson, Shoeless Joe Jackson and John McGraw. There was also Mordecai Brown, famous as "Three Fingered Brown" because he had only three fingers on his pitching hand. Brown was one of the greatest in his day and he kept a bottle of whiskey in the dugout and took a swig each inning before he went to the pitcher's mound. Brown always bragged that he was a better pitcher drunk than the best of them when they were sober. Champ Osteen knew them all, the great and the near great.

Many of Champ Osteen's relatives live here: Mrs. Margaret Osteen Taylor and Mrs. Annie Thacker Stewart are nieces. The late Judge Jim Shipman, Mrs. Kitty Lane, Mrs. R. P. Freeman, Mrs. Kate Durham, Mrs. Mamie Whitmire are first cousins of Champ Osteen.

Although the greater part of his life was spent in other places, Champ Osteen loved these mountains and at every opportunity he visited his relatives here as long as his health permitted.

James Champlin Osteen passed away on December 14, 1962, one of the last of "the Old Guard" of professional major league baseball players when the game was a hard, rough, tough fight in the early years of the century.

Part Fifteen
In the Name of the Law!

In The Name of the Law!

CHAPTER 93

The Ax Murder of Charlie Silver

It happened a long time ago. To be exact, it happened in 1831. This is the true story of a young mountain man and a pretty young mountain girl, a story of love and romance, of jealousy and revenge that ended in cold blooded, premeditated murder.

She was small, blond, blue-eyed, the daughter of a pioneer farmer. Her father was possibly the most properous man in that sparsely settled area and his daughter, though only sixteen, had many young men who came a courtin'. More would have come except they were bashful and timid.

The boy who caught her fancy was tall and broad shouldered and he could sing the mountain ballads, pick a banjo and play a fiddle in a way that a body's feet could not keep still. He wandered about with a nonchalant, devil-may-care manner. The boy had a way with the women and could have had the pick of the countryside. Older parents shook their heads when Charles Silver's name was mentioned. He was shiftless, they said, and the girl that married him would rue the day.

When Charlie Silver was a little boy and Frankie a mere child, they had eyes for each other and as they grew their attachment became stronger.

Frankie's father finally forbade her to see Charlie Silver and told her if she had ideas of marrying him she would be disinherited. This only made the young people more eager to meet and, as has always happened and always will, there were many times that they managed to meet.

On one of these secret meetings, the young couple sneaked down the ways a piece and were married. True to his word, the father went into a rage when he found out; he ordered his daughter to take her clothes and leave his home. Charlie took Frankie to his cabin up on the ridge to live. They were happy in their new life and together they worked hard and talked of their dreams for the future.

When Charlie Silver took his bride to the little old cabin way up on the side of the mountain, all was fine for a while. Together they cleared patches of land and Frankie helped her husband to plant, hoe and harvest the crops. Charlie fished and hunted to add variety to their food and to supplement what they raised. Game was plentiful then in our Blue Ridge Mountains.

The years went by and then Charlie Silver began to slip away. A day at a time at first and then for longer periods. All the work was now left to Frankie.

The lonely life on the mountainside, the years of hard work in the open fields, the hot sun in the summer and the cold winds in the winter began to have their affect on Frankie. Now she was becoming a tough, dried up old woman way before her time. Gone was the peaches and cream complexion, the plump figure and the quick ready smile, the blue eyes twinkling and sparkling like dew drops in the early morning sun.

To add to her growing discontent, she could see in the valley below her father's fields all neat and fertile and she recalled the warnings of the old ones in the courting days: "The girl that marries Charlie Silver will rue the day she does." Alone in the now ramshackled log cabin high on the mountain ridge, Frankie began to brood and worry. Now when her husband would return home after several days absence she would nag and pick at him, demanding information of his whereabouts, and she began to accuse him of all the things that her wild imagination had thought of while he was gone. Love now turned to bitter hatred and each time he came home she hated him more and more.

The breaking point came the time that her husband had been away for more than a week. He came in late one night after his wife had gone to bed. Roughly and rudely he made her get out of bed, get dressed and cook him something to eat. When he had filled his stomach he stretched out on the floor in front of the open hearth fire. Soon the cabin was filled with his loud, raucous, rumbling snores.

Late in the night, as Charlie Silver lay snoring in front of the fire, his stomach filled with fried bacon and corn pone, Frankie cowered in bed. Her hatred for the man she had once loved began to overpower her sanity. Every few minutes, she began to slip out of bed, tip toe in her bare feet across the cabin floor to stand looking down at the man asleep at her feet. How repulsive he was! How she hated him!

Then in the flickering light of the fire her eyes caught sight of the ax in the nearby corner. She was a wild woman now, completely beserk. Small, wizened and tough, all reason now gone, her hair in wild tangles, she grabbed the ax and brought it down with all her might on her husband's head, not once but time and time again. Then she ran to her bed and for a time she lay shaking under the ragged quilts. Gradually in the darkness the awful truth of her actions began to seep into her mind.

At first there was a feeling of exultation because she was now free from the man she had come to hate. This was followed by the realization that she must get rid of the body. The fire had died down when once more she crossed the cabin floor to look down on the horrible sight at her feet. Suddenly there flashed in her head what she would do to hide her crime for all time; there crept slowly across her face and in her eyes a look of shrewd cunning. She must act quickly before some distant neighbor happened by.

She stirred the dying fire and then some splinters of hot pine and many dry logs were heaped on the glowing embers. While the flames leaped high, Frankie Silver went to the shelf by the side of the mantle where the knives used to butcher the hogs in the winter were kept sharp and polished. Bending over her husband, she pulled off his clothes and threw them on the blazing fire. She set to work methodically butchering the body as she had learned to butcher hogs on her father's farm and when she married Charlie Silver.

As she cut the parts of his body into smaller portions, she threw them piece by piece into the roaring fire.

On through the rest of the night and into the early morning hours she continued her gruesome, ghastly task until only the crushed head was left. She could not bring herself to burn her husband's head. There it lay on the hearth, bloody and crushed, the death-glazed eyes staring at her. It was all that remained of Charles Silver and the evidence of his murder. Suddenly reaching down she grasped the head by the blood-matted hair, walked out into the early morning light, crossed the yard to the edge of the woods and dropped the head into the hollow stump of what remained of a once huge sourwood tree.

CHAPTER 94

The Quiltin' Party

Frankie Silver was rid of her husband but now reaction set in. Her conscience began to bother her; not about what she had done but whether her foul deed and the horrible way she had cut him into small pieces and burned them would be found out. She became increasingly afraid alone there in the cabin high on the mountainside. She began to shut herself in the cabin and would sit and brood day and night and as time went by her feeling of guilt mounted. She let the fire die and was afraid to light another one. She no longer cooked her meals but ate what little food she had cold and raw.

Early one morning, days later, just at dawn, there was a loud knock on the cabin door. It frightened the woman. The knocking continued. Frankie Silver slowly, slowly crept to the door, unhooked the chain and jerked the door open. On the doorstep stood a small barefoot boy.

"I am Bertie McGuire's boy," he stammered. "Ma's having a all day quiltin' and would be proud to have you come." The McGuires were the closest neighbors, even if they did live quite a ways below on the only road through the valley. When Frankie arrived at Mrs. McGuire's there already were several women at the quilting frame.

They greeted her in a friendly fashion and began to include her in the conversation.

Frankie told them she hadn't been feeling well lately and they all agreed that she did look poorly. Each in turn began to tell about their aches and pains and latest sick spells. The women sewed and gossiped. Frankie sewed and listened. Bertie McGuire left the quilting frame to cut some bacon and fry it over the hearth fire. The fat meat fried on as the pan got hotter, the smell of the frying meat filled the cabin, and then the smoke. The panful of meat was taken outside. The door of the cabin was opened and all the guests began flapping their aprons to free the place of smoke.

When they finished, they found Frankie sitting by the hearthfire moaning and holding her head in her hands. She said that the stench of the frying hog meat had made her sick. All the time, swaying back and forth, she was thinking of her husband and how she had cut him up and thrown him, sliver by sliver, into the fire. Was this then the vengeance of the Lord? How could she go home now and pass right by the sourwood stump where she had hidden Charlie's head?

The tormented woman began to cry and scream, at times breaking into hysterical laughter. Those at the quilting party were amazed at what was taking place and couldn't understand what it was all about. When they managed to calm the hysterical woman, they washed her face and neck in the cold mountain water, combed and tied her hair. Then and there, Frankie Silver told them in detail the story of her crime. They walked with her to her cabin and left her alone.

What Frankie Silver told at the quiltin' party spread through the mountains in the days that followed. Into every cove and on every ridge where there was a cabin her story was told and retold. Then one day there was another knock on her door. This time it was the law. The nearest jail and court house in 1831 was at Morganton.

She was tried for the murder of her husband before Superior Court Judge Ruffin. The crime was committed in December 1831. She was found guilty and sentenced to be hanged in June 1832. The sentence was carried out on July 12, 1833, before a large crowd. Her mountain neighbors poured into Morganton that day to see Frankie pay for her sin. She was the first white woman to be hanged in North Carolina.

This true story is still told in isolated mountain cabins to this day and it is preserved in the court records. It has also been handed down in a mountain ballad called "The Quiltin' Party" that was composed at the time of the trial and sung by a now forgotten balladeer.

CHAPTER 95

The Great Jewel Robbery

All the month of August 1909, the population of Hendersonville was more than double. The excursion trains from the deep South had been arriving daily, crowded with visitors seeking relief from the low country summer heat.

Every boarding house, hotel and spare room in town was filled to capacity. W.H. Maxwell was Chief of Police. There was only one night police officer to patrol our crowded town but that one policeman had always been sufficient; our townspeople and summer visitors were law abiding citizens.

The streets of Hendersonville were poorly lighted at night with only a street light here and there. Most of the street lights were on the corners of the avenues where they crossed Main Street. Some of the lights were coal oil street lamps and some were carbon electric lights. None gave much light; night street lighting was in a period of transition from the oil lamps to the new carbon electric lights that were being installed to use the electricity now being generated by Bob Oats in the rock building power house on the corner of Seventh Avenue East and Main Street.* The lack of street lighting made little difference because in 1909 there was no night life as we know it in this day and time. People went to bed early even in the summertime.

On this August night in 1909 in the hour just past midnight, two young men walked briskly up the alley that ran behind the stores which faced the west side of Main Street. Each man carried a medium sized black leather satchel that was popular in those days for a short train trip. These black leather bags or satchels were carried by family doctors when visiting their patients.

When they reached their destination the two men turned up a large wooden packing case kept by the back door for the store's trash. The men helped each other up on the packing case. Each took a tool from the black satchels and went to work as quietly as possible to force open the transom over the back door. Each in turn managed to squeeze through, opened the back door from the inside, re-entered and proceeded to fill their satchels.

Later that morning the two men walked down Seventh Avenue towards the railroad station to catch the early passenger train going south. They attracted no attention on their walk to the Depot, when they arrived there or when they boarded the train. There were dozens and dozens of people doing the same thing and carrying the same kind of satchels. This was the last that was seen of these two men in Hendersonville. Just two more of thousands of tourists that were here that August of 1909.

Soon that morning the sensation of the month spread through Hendersonville and in the afternoon edition of *The Hendersonville Daily Herald* there were big black headlines: "Boldest Burglary ever committed in Hendersonville. W. H. Hawkins and Son, Jewelers, Ransacked." W. H. Hawkins and Son was the only jewelry store in Hendersonville at that time. It was a very select place that carried only high quality merchandise. W. H. Hawkins and his son were leading citizens here not only in business but in civic affairs also. Hendersonville was proud of the two men, their families and their store.

The newspaper went on to say that the store had been robbed during the night and Chief of Police W. H. Maxwell said that entrance had been gained through a transom over the back door. Six valuable diamonds were stolen as

* Vol. I "The Marvels of a New Age"

well as more than a thousand dollars of choice jewelry and a number of watches. A few days after the robbery, 175 valuable watches were recovered from a pawn shop in Spartanburg.

No clue was ever found as to who the robbers were. Everything except the 175 watches was a total loss; in those days nobody here had ever heard of or thought of such a thing as burglary insurance.

The W. H. Hawkins and Son jewelry store robbery was the sensation of that summer of 1909 and was discussed for years afterwards.

CHAPTER 96

The Bad Man

Today nobody goes to the railroad station in Hendersonville to see the trains. The only trains are freights and there is little of interest in a diesel freight train. But there was a time when several passenger trains stopped at the Hendersonville railroad station every day. There were many coaches in each train and they were always full of passengers because in the early years of this century traveling by railroad trains pulled by steam locomotives was the only fast method to go from one place to another. That was before the sky was filled with flying machines and before hard surfaced roads wound through our mountains like black or gray ribbons, crowded with speeding automobiles.

The center of activity in Hendersonville then and in every mountain town was at the railroad station at train time. Everybody met the passenger trains and the Depot was the place to get the latest news, to hear the spiciest gossip, to talk to friends and neighbors. And, very often, unusual things seemed to happen at the Depot.

There was a flurry of excitement at the Hendersonville station that winter afternoon in 1910 and the man who caused it all was Bob Moore. Who Bob Moore was or what became of him after he created the uproar nobody knows or cares now. Nobody here had ever heard of him before that afternoon when the train came in and as far as I know nobody has heard of him since.

But for a brief time that cold winter day Bob Moore was the man of the hour. He claimed to be a bad man and he was from Asheville. It was published on the front page of *The Hendersonville Daily Herald* in the next afternoon edition for our parents and grandparents to read about.

To quote the newspaper: "Bob Moore, a bad man from Asheville, rode all the way from Spartanburg to Hendersonville on one of the Southern Railroad passenger trains yesterday. He refused to get off the train or pay his fare. The train's conductor telegraphed ahead to the Hendersonville police for help when the train arrived at Saluda. Deputy Sheriff Connor of the

Henderson County Sheriff's Dept. was waiting at the Hendersonville station when the train pulled in. It was necessary for the deputy sheriff to be quite rude to the bad man and to use force to take him off the train. Once on the ground Moore asked permission to put on his overcoat. It was given him but as the train pulled from the depot, Moore caught the last coach and swung aboard.

Deputy Connor, however, was equal to the occasion because he caught the bad man's coat tails and swung after him although the train was gaining speed. The deputy pulled the signal cord and the engineer stopped. Connor alighted with the bad man who is now an honored guest of Sheriff Blackwell in the County jail.''

CHAPTER 97

A Blind Tiger

Do you know what a ''Blind Tiger'' was? If the words were used today, only an old one would know what they mean. It is a nomenclature that is strictly Southern and was in common used before World War I. So when in April 1911 Hendersonville's only newspaper announced in big black headlines that ''two Blind Tigers had been raided in the middle of Hendersonville's business district'' everyone understood it.

Chief of Police Maxwell and Officer Garren raided the Central Cafe which in 1911 was on Third Avenue and the Dixie Cafe on Main Street. These officers confiscated a large amount of beer and wine and 292 bottles of whiskey, all of which was illegal because Hendersonville and Henderson County was ''dry'' territory at that time.

The editor of *The French Broad Hustler* wrote that ''such places are a stench and an abomination to all decent and law abiding citizens.'' The pride of the law abiding citizens was eased to some extent when it was disclosed at the trial of the Blind Tigers that all of them were men from Asheville ''who were trying to corrupt the morals of our community.''

A Blind Tiger was a place where any alcoholic beverage was sold illegally. A later generation called such a place a ''Speak Easy.'' A Blind Tiger was also a person who sold such illegal beverages. What our grandfathers and grandmothers called a Blind Tiger, the present generation calls a ''bootlegger,'' a term imported into our mountains after World War I from the western states. A ''bootlegger'' in that part of our country was a cowboy who carried whiskey in bottles hidden in his riding boots onto an Indian reservation, which was illegal.

CHAPTER 98

Gun Play In Druid Hills
(1970)

If you refer to the place that sells gasoline and oil for automobiles as a filling station, you at once identify yourself as belonging to the older generation. They were called filling stations in the first years of the century but they are now referred to as service stations. That is because of the many and varied services offered to motor vehicle owners other than just filling the gasoline tank.

The Times-News of July 10, 1929, carried a news item with the headline: "Druid Hills Filling Station Shot Up." It all happened early that morning of July 10 around 4:00 a.m., when honest folks are still in bed except farmers and other people who milk cows and even they are just trying to get their eyes open. The newspaper account continues: "The Howard Smith Filling Station operator saw a man at the pumps ready to help himself. Mr. Smith took no chances and opened fire from within the station, shooting through the plate glass window. Sheriff Will Garren was called. The Sheriff reported that when he arrived it looked as if the filling station had been used as a machine gun base. Sheriff Garren also reported that Mr. Smith shot straight but a little high so the would-be stealer of gas escaped."

Filling stations were not as plentiful around Hendersonville then as they are now so it is possible that those living here in 1929 remember that fifty years ago there was a service station where the entrance to Coble Dairy is now. Howard Smith is a well known, successful businessman who lives at Horse Shoe. I asked him if he remembered the attempted robbery. He laughed and told me that a short time before this he and his station were involved in a much more serious hold up.

He was alone in his place one night. About 10:00 o'clock four tough looking men drove up in a tan colored Buick. Two of the men came inside the station and asked for a package of cigarettes. He was suspicious so he threw his money bag under the counter and at the same time turned to get his 32 caliber Colt revolver. One of the men hit Howard Smith on the side of the head, cutting him severely, and took his revolver.

About then, young Brownlow Jackson and his date drove up. The two men outside covered them with guns. In all, the holdup bandits got $68 in cash, took a diamond ring off the finger of Brownlow Jackson's date, took Brownlow's car keys and the keys to the service station and drove off.

When the robbery and the description of the robbers was reported, it turned out that the four men, along with four others, were being sought by the F.B.I. They were notorious gangsters from Chicago and New Orleans. After holding up Mr. Smith and Mr. Jackson, they shot a policeman in Asheville and escaped. Several days later the men were caught breaking into the Charlotte Post Office. Howard Smith and Brownlow Jackson were witnesses when the men were tried in Federal Court in Asheville. They identified the four men who had held them up here and the four gangsters went to Federal prison.

Part Sixteen

Sketches

The Thomas Wolfe Angel

Part Sixteen

Sketches

CHAPTER 99

George Carson

He sold newspapers on Main Street in the summertime in Hendersonville in the early days of 1900 when I was only a boy. He has been dead since 1926 and yet to me he was a person I shall never forget. The reason I have never forgotten George Carson was his continuous and habitual cheerfulness and his never-failing energy. Standing on the corner on Fourth Avenue and Main Street or Fifth and Main, by the bench where he kept his daily papers from all the larger towns of the South, he would all day long and well into the evening hours call, "Papers of all kinds. Get your hometown papers here." And the summer visitors strolling up and down Main Street would stop to buy and to gossip with George Carson.

George Carson was in his middle or late thirties when I first knew him. He was born in 1872 in Rutherford County. He had an intelligent and sharp mind but a broken body. His head and torso was the fully developed body of a large strong man in every way but his legs were those of a small child and his feet were tiny. He was 3½ feet tall and most of that height was from his waist to the top of his head.

Every year along about the first week in June George Carson would appear on Main Street and everyone living here knew that the tourist season was in full swing. All day long he would greet his friends who lived here, his arriving tourist friends from previous years and he would sell his papers that were brought here by railroad passenger trains. The papers would be thrown off the mail and baggage car at the Depot and brought to George's bench by one of the horse drawn buses or hacks. In the fall of the year shortly after Labor Day when you strolled down Main Street and you didn't see George Carson and his stack of papers you knew that the tourist season was over.

He was raised in Rutherford County but he made his living selling his newspapers in Hendersonville in the summertime and in Charlotte during the long winter months. As he grew older his bodily afflictions became more than he could bear. He was forced to stop trying to make a living selling his newspapers and entered the Rutherford County Home, "the Poor House" it was called in those days.

Then one day he received a letter from a law firm in a western state. The news in it was that George Carson was heir to a small fortune. A brother,

Taylor Carson, had gone to Nevada as a young man. He had not kept in contact with his family in Rutherford. Only his brother George was still living. In Nevada, Taylor Carson had become a prospector and had grown wealthy in the mining business. The letter from the law firm said that Taylor Carson had recently died. He had never married and had left all of his wealth to his brother George.

George Carson was then able, on the advice of his doctor, to go to Hot Springs where his health was restored for a while. But the time came when the tiny feet and the childlike legs could carry the man sized body no more. He died in 1926 at the early age of 54 years.

When his will was opened and read, it was so typical of his cheerful outlook in life. Half of the fortune that he inherited from his brother in Nevada was left to the caretakers of the Rutherford County Home, the husband and wife who had done so much to make his invalid years bearable, happy and easy.

He left a large sum in trust for his friends, the less fortunate inmates of the County Home. This money in trust was to be spent to supply them cigars, cigarettes, tobacco, candy, chewing gum, fruit, music and spending money for personal toilet articles, things for happiness and pleasure that so many of them had never had.

With a clear mind but a broken body George Carson spread cheer and happiness while he lived and he left the same for others less fortunate than he when he passed on.

CHAPTER 100

Samantha Bumgarner

A ballad is defined as a romantic song having the same melody for each stanza. A ballad is also defined as a short narrative poem which recounts a legendary of traditional event and is passed orally from one generation to another. In plain mountain language, a ballad is verse set to music which tells a story about some strange or tragic happening and there is general romance and love involved. Our earliest type of folk songs handed down through countless generations are ballads.

Ballads and their composition have been popular among the native mountain people of Western North Carolina and Eastern Tennessee since the first settlers came into the area. These people who were English, Scotch, Irish and Welsh brought their folk songs and ballads with them from the old countries and continued to sing them until new ballads were composed and handed down which told of things that took place here in our mountains. The traditional mountain ballads are always sung to the accompaniment of banjo, guitar or fiddle.

The greatest composer and singer of mountain ballads of Western North Carolina was Samantha Bumgarner. Her fame was not limited to this area because she was known wherever ballads were sung over the entire United States and in many foreign countries. She was affectionately called Aunt Samanthy by all her family and friends; the last "a" in her name was pronounced as if it were "y" as is done in our mountains with most words ending with an "a".

Aunt Samantha Bumgarner, the nearly 90 year old Fiddlin Balladeer of our mountains, died Saturday, December 24, 1960 at her home near Sylva. There was little notice of her death in the newspapers or over the radio or TV; much too little for a woman who was so famous and who in her field was the greatest. Her death attracted such little public attention probably because it happened on Christmas Eve and so was overshadowed by the rush and bustle of the Christmas season.

She was born Samantha Biddix and inherited her talent from her father Has Biddix who was a "banjo pickin' and fiddlin' mountain man from way back." She taught herself to play the banjo and fiddle by sneaking them out when her father was away from home.

Composing words to the folk songs just came naturally. She was the main attraction every year at the annual Asheville Mountain Dance and Folk Festival. She missed the festival for the first time the summer of 1960, a few months before her death, because of her age and health.

Samantha Biddix Bumgarner is gone to her great reward. Her banjo and fiddle are laid away but the ballads and folk songs that she composed, sang and accompanied will continue to be popular and passed on from generation to generation.

CHAPTER 101

Four Graves In Oakdale

In Chapter 78 I told about C. E. Ledbetter and the Rocky Bluff Irish Potato. Mr. Ledbetter was then care taker of the Oakdale Cemetery. When he finished telling me about the Rocky Bluff potato, he told me that there were a number of graves in Oakdale that had interesting stories and histories connected with them. We left his front porch and crossed Sixth Avenue. He began to point to different graves and tell me what he knew about each one.

He pointed out the grave of Laura Vance Nelson, who was the first person to be buried in Oakdale in 1886 when the land was first set aside and being cleared for a municipal burying ground. She was the daughter of the Rev. Mr. D. B. Nelson and his wife, Sarah Y. Nelson who rest nearby. Daniel B. Nelson was a widely known teacher and Baptist minister who did much to make Judson College a success. For a number of years, beginning in 1875, he was pastor of the First Baptist Church on the corner of Fourth Avenue West and Washington Street. A number of his descendants still live in Henderson County.[1]

Mr. Ledbetter led me to a grave with an unusual marker. The stone was carved out of solid native granite and represented a part of a trunk of a chestnut oak tree. Portions of the limbs were broken off and vines were carved growing on the tree trunk.

On one side of the rock tree trunk, at the very top, was inscribed: "Lewis Tunstall, born at Amelia Court House, Virginia, December 8, 1852; Died June 17, 1890." Near the bottom of the tombstone was carved a railroad engine and tender of the type used long ago and now only seen in railroad museums. Carved on the engine was the number 391. It was an unusual kind of grave marker. To add to my curiosity, the foot of the granite slab was chiseled to represent a railroad crosstie stuck upright in the ground.

Lewis Tunstall was only 38 years old when he died in 1890. He was a railroad engineer on an engine pulling a train from Hendersonville to Spartanburg. At that time there were no safety switches on the Saluda Grade. The brakes on the train that Lewis Tunstall was taking down the mountain gave way. The train, out of control, jumped the tracks; the engine hit a huge chestnut oak tree and Lewis Tunstall was instantly killed. His family erected the marker which was symbolic of tragedy. But Lewis Tunstall did not die in vain. After the train wreck the railroad built a series of safety switches on the mountain between Saluda and Melrose that are used to this day and have prevented many train wrecks and saved an untold number of lives.[2]

There was the grave of Watt M. Bryson and across the road was the grave of George Mills, 1844-1926, Henderson County Home Guards, Confederate States of America. Around these two graves, one of them a grave of a white man and one of them the grave of a black man, is woven an astonishing and amazing story of two brave men and a story of devotion and loyalty.[3]

There in Oakdale is also the grave of Lela Davidson Hansell who has become known after death as the Sunshine Lady of Oakdale.[4] Nearby is a life size figure made famous as the angel in Thomas Wolfe's novel, "Look Homeward Angel."

[1] Vol. I "Some 19th Century Names to Remember"
[2] Vol. II "The Age of Steam"
[3] Vol. I "The War Between the States"
[4] Vol. I "Portraits"

CHAPTER 102

Letters To Santa Claus

In 1910 a little boy wrote a letter to Santa Claus and the letter was sent to *The Hendersonville Daily Herald* which published it on the front page.

"Dear Santa Claus, I want you to bring me a rifle, a bat and ball and glove and a goat and some candy, some fruit, nuts and apples. I also want you to bring me a football and a bob tail dog."

Did Santa Claus bring little Robley Carson a goat and a bob tail dog? This I don't know but I do know that the little boy asking for a bat, a ball, a glove and a football in 1910 was already pointing to the future. Ten years later Robley Carson was one of Western North Carolina's outstanding athletes, playing football and baseball at Hendersonville High School and then at Blue Ridge School for Boys. Robley Carson who wrote that letter in 1910 was in 1979 a gray haired bachelor who lived with his sisters in Hendersonville after a life career in the hardware business, known to his friends through the years as Bob Carson.

Aiken Pace   (Photo compliments of Pace Family)

The Miller Brothers
L to R standing: *Theodore E. Miller, Winfield (Win) D. Miller*
L to R sitting: *Hubert (Bert) E. Miller, Norman W. Miller, Jr.*

"Dear Santa Claus, Please bring me a doll and a doll bed. You are a nice man but I have not seen you. Bring me a doll carriage, some candies, some bananas, some oranges and doll shoes. I am bad sometimes and I am good sometimes. I love to go to school and I like my teacher. I get my lessons everyday. Your friend, Ruth Leverette."

Sometimes good and sometimes bad little Ruth Leverette who loved to go to school and liked her teacher was 8 years old when she wrote to Santa Claus in 1910. In 1960 she was Mrs. George T. Deeland and lived in Athens, Georgia.

And who were the little boys and girls writing to Santa Claus from Hendersonville in 1935?

"Dear Santa Claus, We want you to bring us a pair of long handle bars, a pair of gloves and an air rifle. We will hang a large stocking up on Christmas Eve. Signed, Bert Miller and Aiken Pace."

Two inseparable little boys in 1935, Bert Miller and Aiken Pace are still close friends. Bert Miller and his brothers, Norman, Jr., and Winfield, oper-

Frank Todd, Age 4½   (Photo compliments of Todd Family)

ate Miller's Laundry and Aiken Pace is today (1979) a popular and well known pharmacist.

"Dear Santa Claus, I am a little boy 13 years old. I don't want much for Christmas, just a radio, a bicycle, a pony and saddle and a car. If you have any left over you might bring me a sweetheart. I love you. Frank Todd".

I wonder what Santa Claus thought when he read that letter from a little boy who didn't want much. I don't think Santa had a sweetheart left over that Christmas of 1935 but I do know that some years later Frank had a sweetheart because he married Betty Ann Drysdale. Today Frank is a lawyer, active in the management of Moland-Drysdale Corporation, largest manufacturer of brick in Western North Carolina. Now in 1979 he is also Mayor of Hendersonville.

In these modern days boys and girls write letters to Santa Claus and the letters are sent in care of the local radio stations, read on the air and lost to oblivion. In early days the Christmas letters were sent to the local newspaper which published them. These letters to Santa Claus were saved for posterity to read in the permanent files kept by every newspaper.

Part Seventeen

Wheels
1888 – 1962

258

Wheels, 1888-1962

CHAPTER 103

Run Away!

Traffic accidents happened in the old days long before the automobile came to our mountains and when there was an accident involving serious injury there was no county or city ambulance service or emergency medical service or rescue squad to summon to rush the injured ones to the hospital.

In 1888 it had been nine years since the first railroad train had pulled into the Depot at Hendersonville where the tracks ended. But it was only a short time before the tracks were extended to Asheville. Most of the traffic on the tracks between here and Asheville had been gravel trains hauling ballast from the huge rock quarry at Balfour to stabilize the new track bed.

The Buncombe Turnpike, which was the dirt road or the highway from Hendersonville to Asheville, closely followed the railroad tracks as far as Biltmore. In fact, a traveler by horseback, wagon, or buggy crossed and recrossed the railroad track between Hendersonville and Biltmore nine times. It was quite a trip. The trains roared down the railroad tracks, black smoke pouring from the engine stack and leaving a long trail behind, the engine whistle blowing for the many road crossings.

All of this was a frightful thing to the mules and horses pulling the wagons, carriages and buggies traveling the Buncombe Turnpike. Even the stolid, plodding yokes of oxen which were used to move heavy loads would often panic when a train passed where the road and the train tracks were very close.

In 1888 and for several years before and after that date until he moved his office to Asheville, young D. M. Hodges was a prominent and popular young lawyer in Hendersonville. One Saturday morning in 1888 he and a companion drove a buggy to Fletcher on business. That afternoon on the way home, as young Hodges and his friend were driving on a part of the turnpike which ran along an embankment parallel to the railroad track, one of the gravel trains came huffing and puffing along. The horse, frantic and terrified, became unmanageable and dashed headlong down the road.

Young Hodges, fearing that the buggy would either turn over or crash through a bridge ahead, decided to jump. When he did so his left leg was broken below the knee; both bones were fractured so severely that one of them pushed through the flesh and skin of the leg.

The driver finally succeeded in controlling the frightened horse. He turned and drove back to D. M. Hodges, lying helpless on the ground.

The horse was tied securely to a nearby tree. A freight train that came along just at that time was flagged to a stop and with the help of the train crew the injured young lawyer was lifted to the caboose and brought to the Depot in Hendersonville. From there he was taken home in a wagon. Dr. C. Few was called and proper medical attention was given to the seriously and painfully injured man.

That is the manner in which many of our traffic accidents happened in our mountains nearly a century ago and that is one way aid was finally attained.

CHAPTER 104

Hacking

"Hacking was big business in Hendersonville and Henderson County in the days when everybody traveled by passenger trains, and the busiest time of the year was during the summertime when the excursion trains ran."

So said the late Smiley McCall one day as we were talking about changes over the years. At the time, Smiley McCall was owner and operator of the Depot Salvage Company which he had started in a small building across from the railroad station and had expanded until it occupied the entire block on Seventh Avenue East from Grove Street to the railroad tracks. Mr. McCall knew about the business of hacking; as a young man he drove a hack for N. D. Hollingsworth livery stable at Flat Rock.

Only the older folks now know the meaning of the word "hack." It was a four wheeled covered vehicle with two or more seats, pulled by one or two horses. A hack was the taxi cab of the days before automobiles. Hacking, before World War I, was not only big business but a highly competitive one. The cream of the customer crop for the hack operators were the passengers that came on the excursion trains during the four months of the summer. Many of the same people came year after year on the excursion trains and they had their favorite hack drivers whom they patronized every summer.

Long forgotten is the Sunset Inn on the Highland Lake Road operated by a Mrs. McCullough, a favorite of the summer visitors.

Glover Orr ran a large livery stable and operated hacks before World War I. When automobiles came to the mountains, Mr. Orr started one of the first taxi cab services in town.

Oak Hill, a large boarding house in the Valley Hill section, was operated by Mrs. Charles E. Moore. Will Turner's livery stable was on Maple Street where Ernest Roper's Superior Laundry is now. Earle Jackson drove a hack

Smiley McCall

for Turner's stable. His hack drew most of its patronage from the Wheeler Hotel that stood on the hill where Bruce Drysdale School is today.[1]

Rufe Anders and his hack worked the depot at Highland Lake and Flat Rock and the boarding houses in the same areas.[2] Alonzo Shipman was connected with Kanuga Lake Inn long before it became a conference center for the Episcopal Church. Mr. McCall said that of all those early hack drivers, Alonzo Shipman was the most successful. When the automobile began to take the place of horse drawn vehicles, Mr. Shipman switched to automobiles for transportation of people.

From a start with one automobile for public transportation, Mr. Shipman eventually developed Queen City Trailways, an interstate bus system.

King of all the hack drivers here during the early 20th Century was B. Gregory who drove the hacks for the Kentucky Home.[2] The Kentucky Home Hotel was the first hotel here to operate a horse drawn bus to take its guests to and from the railroad station. B. Gregory also drove this bus. He was a tall, dignified, and rather handsome man. He wore a Kentucky Home Hotel uniform bright with gold braid. He was the envy of every boy in town. It was a rare day that the bus was not filled with passengers bound for the hotel, attracted by the magnetic speel and personality of B. Gregory.

These names and places that Smiley McCall and I talked about and personally knew and about whom I have written in this chapter will all be remembered by older ones living here now who were young residents here in that last colorful era of horse drawn transportation.

Smiley McCall in the Era Following Hacking
(Photo compliments of McCall Family)

[1] Vol. I "Vanished Landmarks"
[2] Vol. II "The Inns of Yesteryear"

Smiley McCall in Modern Dray
(Photo compliments of McCall Family)

CHAPTER 105

The Dray Business

In the days now gone, an essential service in Hendersonville and most all towns before the advent of motor trucks was the dray business. The man who operated a dray was an important person in our community. A dray was a wagon pulled by horses or mules and was used to haul anything that had to be moved from one place to another. The word is rarely used now except by the older generation; after the First World War automobiles and trucks became common. The motor trucks took the place of horse drawn wagons. Moving and hauling began to be called the transfer business.

I now remember three men who were prominent in the dray business here in the early 1900s. They were Patton Arledge, John Livingston and Sam Corn. I have told about Sam Corn in Volume I of "From the Banks of the Oklawaha." The thing that I remember best about Mr. Livingston was the magnificent pair of mules that pulled his dray wagon and how high the trunks were stacked on the dray that he drove from the railroad station to the hotels and boarding houses in town.

Patton Arledge was the father of Isaac Arledge, well known businessman and for many years a prominent bondsman here. Patton Arledge over the years had a number of horses that he used to pull his dray. I remember best a beautiful chestnut sorrel horse that I was envious of. Mr. Arledge always hauled the merchandise from the freight depot and express office to the merchants of the town.

Drays & Hacks Ready to Go on Main Street (Photo by Barber)

One business that he transported all of the merchandise for was Justus Drug Store. He and Dr. Justus had been friends for many years. The drug store is still in the same building on the corner of Main Street and Third Avenue West that it occupied in the days that Mr. Arledge hauled freight there for Dr. Justus. It was a well known fact around town that he rendered a bill to Dr. Justus but once a year; it was always paid promptly without question.*

As far as I remember, Mr. Arledge was the last of the old time draymen in business here who used his horse and wagon up to the time of his death. A dray was classified as a 1-horse dray, 2-horse dray or 4-horse dray according to the number of horses required to pull the loaded wagon.

A 6-Horse Dray (Photo by Barber)

* Vol. II "The Builders"

CHAPTER 106
The Jitney Bus

You never hear the word now because it has been a long time since it has been an active word in the United States English language. But just before, during and a few years after the First World War, it was in common usage. The word was "jit" and when you asked a friend to lend you a jit, you were trying to borrow a nickel and in those days a nickel was worth much more than it is now. A body could buy a cigar in those days for a jit and a jit would get a body a cup of coffee, a Coca-cola, a slice of pie, a large candy bar and many other things. There has been many a filling and satisfying lunch eaten on the old Jockey Lot that consisted of a nickel can of sardines and a box of Uneeda soda crackers that also cost only a jit. [1]

During those same years that the word jit was popular and in common usage, Henry Ford introduced the assembly line for the mass production of his Model T Ford automobile and he had put the price within the reach of the average working man. Taxicabs as we know them now had not come into existence yet but an enterprising man who owned a Model T Ford would take a stand on a street corner in Hendersonville, load his Model T Ford touring car to capacity and take you within a reasonable distance of your destination for the price to each passenger of a nickel.

And so the Model T Ford quickly became popularly known as a jitney bus and then as a jitney. And so for years, until Henry Ford sounded the death knell of the Model T by manufacturing the Model A Ford, when you were asked what make of automobile you owned, you said "I own a jitney." Everyone knew what you meant.

When the Dummy Line that ran from the corner of Fifth Avenue West and Main Street to Laurel Park and Crystal Spring was discontinued [2] Hendersonville saw the first jitney buses. This was a small fleet of Model T touring cars (glass enclosed automobiles had not come into existence yet) that operated on a 15-minute schedule between Hendersonville and Laurel Park during the summer of 1918. For a jit, a body could ride to Laurel Park crowded into a jitney. They were very popular and did a rushing business during the summer season for several years. The increasing number of privately owned automobiles finally made the jitney line to Laurel Park unprofitable. They were discontinued about 1920.

[1] Vol. I "Vanished Landmarks"
[2] Vol. I "The Marvels Of A New Age"

CHAPTER 107

Demons of the Road

Before the 55 mile an hour speed limit, you could get on I-26 and drive from Hendersonville to Charleston, S.C. in four and a half hours and there were some who bragged that they had driven the distance in less time than that. Even a cautious driver could make the trip in five hours. But it was not always like this.

Only the oldest ones who were living here in 1914 can remember when there was no bridge across Mud Creek at the end of South Main Street, and the present Greenville Highway from the lower end of Main Street through Flat Rock was known as the Causeway. There was not a hard surface road in Henderson County and for that matter not a single stretch of even a mile in length of hard surface road between here and Charleston.

There were few automobiles here either in 1914 and what few we had were the Model T Fords which are collectors' items today. But in the summertime a few of the more wealthy visitors would bring heavier, more expensive and more powerful automobiles with them. But even these were divided into two types: roadsters and touring cars. The closed hard tops of today had not yet been developed.

Only the elderly who were living here in 1914 remember John Maybank, wealthy cotton broker from Charleston, his brother Dr. Joseph Maybank, and their close friend and associate Frank Hanckel. All of these men had summer homes here. The John Maybank house, gray granite with large white columns, still stands but is little noticed now because it is hidden by the surrounding giant white pines. It is on the high hill just off the road to Flat Rock overlooking Hendersonville.

Dr. Maybank's summer home was still occupied in 1965 by members of the family at Highland Lake but the Hanckel home was torn down several years ago to make way for the large, white Collison mansion.

These three men made history in 1914 and their achievement was talked about, told and retold for several years both here in Hendersonville and Henderson County, in Charleston, in the towns between here and Charleston and at every cross roads country store. What did these three men do?

They drove an automobile from Hendersonville to Charleston in the unbelievable time of 17 hours. *The Charleston News and Courier,* on the front page of that sacred voice of South Carolina, gave the following account under big headlines.

"From Hendersonville to Charleston, 265 miles, is the record made on Wednesday by John F. Maybank, Mr. Frank S. Hanckel and Dr. Joseph Maybank in John Maybank's automobile. The actual driving time of the touring car was only 15 hours which is a record. The party left the mountain town at 5:00 a.m. and arrived in Charleston at 10:00 p.m., having stopped in

Newberry for an hour and in Orangeburg for an hour. The average running time was 19 miles an hour which in consideration of the sorry condition of some stretches of the road was very fast."

This newspaper account did not mention how many tires they had changed and patched, nor did the account tell how dusty and dirty the travelers were after riding all that distance on dusty dirt roads or how exhausted they were at the finish of their record-making trip: 17 hours from Hendersonville to Charleston, averaging 19 miles an hour.

CHAPTER 108
Beginning of the End
(1962)

The Charleston News and Courier headlined it: "End of an Era is Recorded." Few people here noticed a dispatch datelined Columbia, S.C. which was carried on the inside page of *The Asheville Citizen* one morning in October 1962. This story was headlined: "Carolina Special Ends Part of Run."

Many who did notice the news item passed it by but to the old ones living here in October 1962 it caused a nostalgic sadness. In the days now gone the Carolina Special was the luxury train of the Southern Railroad. It connected the Carolina coast and our mountains with all points in the Middle West. This passenger train was the pride and joy of railroad men and the traveling public.

In 1883 a railroad was built from Charleston, S.C. to Hamburg, S.C. It was the longest such road in our country at that time even though the length of the railroad track was only 30 miles . The track ran through Branchville, S.C. which became the first railroad junction in the United States when a railroad track was built to run from Charleston to Columbia, tapping the Charleston-Hamburg line at Branchville. This was in 1842.

By November 1859, the track had been extended to Spartanburg. In 1861 the Civil War stopped work on the railroad so that it was not until 1877 that the tracks reached Tryon. One of the greatest days in the history of Hendersonville was July 4, 1879 when the first train, belching and spewing black smoke and cinders from the engine smoke stack, came to a brake-screeching halt at the new little station on the end of Depot Street, now Seventh Avenue East.*
It was not until 1886 that the railroad bed was finished to Asheville, thus linking the Carolina coast with the middle western states and fulfilling a dream of a generation of railroad people.

The isolation of our mountain area was over. Flat Rock and Hendersonville in truth became the tourist center and recreation area of the southeast. In

* Vol I "The Marvels Of A New Age"

the early days of passenger service to Charleston, Columbia and Hendersonville were served by so called local trains, passenger trains that stopped at every village, cross road and pig track. A train trip was dirty and tiresome but still a great improvement over stagecoach travel.

In 1912 our town and county were thrilled by the announcement of the Southern Railroad that a new and fast train would run daily in both directions between Charleston, S.C. and Cincinnati, Ohio. It would be a special, a luxury fast train. Trains number 27 and 28 to railroad men, the Carolina Special to the traveling public. There would be day coach service but the Carolina Special would also carry through Pullman service, a dining car and an observation car.

In its prime days the Carolina Special stopped after leaving Columbia only at Union, Spartanburg and Tryon. It paused at Melrose long enough to hook to a helper engine to get up the Saluda Grade and at Saluda long enough to unhitch the helper. Then on to Hendersonville and Asheville.*

I still think that one of the most exciting things I remember in the days of my youth was to stand at the Depot and see the Carolina Special roar around the curve from Flat Rock, whistle blowing, bell ringing, leaving a long trail of black smoke behind to grind to a stop at the station.

For the first time in 83 years we will have no through trains from Charleston to Hendersonville because now the Carolina Special, a special in name only, will run only between Columbia and Hendersonville. People just don't travel by train any more and it will be only a short time until we will have no passenger train service. And so an era will end.

* Vol. II "The Age Of Steam"

Part Eighteen
My Old Friend

My Old Friend

CHAPTER 109

Good Friday
(1972)

It has been my custom, for so many years that I can hardly remember for how long back, that I pay a Good Friday visit to my old friend who lives alone on the side of the mountain. The old man and I were much younger when I started doing this. In fact in my young days when I first started visiting on the mountain I would walk all the way from my home on the Howard Gap Road to his cabin on the mountain, visit for a while and then walk home. In late years though I drive the jeep or truck to where the road dead ends and walk from there, stopping every little bit to catch my breath. I used these frequent stops as an excuse to admire the scenery in the valley below and the mountains beyond. Now I just admit the truth that age is catching up with me. Yet my old friend just keeps right on. He seems ageless.

These visits of mine on Good Friday started because Good Friday is the one day in the old man's life that takes precedence over all other signs that play such an important part in his life, such as the signs of the Zodiac, the light and dark of the moon, and so many others.

He puts great store on his garden and his gardening ability. It does not matter how late Good Friday comes or how early, as it has this year. It is the day to start planting his garden, especially his green beans, snap beans or as he always calls them, string beans.

On Good Friday he is in the cleared patch below his cabin bright and early with his work brute which in late years has always been a well broken steer or ox. It is hooked to a bull tongue plow for laying off the rows to plant. But on this Good Friday morning in 1972 the ground was white with an inch or so of snow and the ground under it was so wet from several days rain that I knew there would be no planting on this day.

I went to visit him just the same because I knew he would be expecting me and he would be expecting my usual Easter package which was always a poke full of chocolate and marshmallow Easter eggs. Soon after I started out it began to snow again and by the time I parked the jeep and started to climb to his cabin it had become a mixture of rain, snow and sleet.

When I came out of the woods to the edge of the clearing, I could see the old log cabin. The wind was blowing and I could see the smoke pouring out of the chimney at the end of the building. The smoke was rising only a few inches before the damp, moisture-laden wind caught it and swirled it low to the ground.

The pungent smell of the smoke from the oak, hickory and apple wood logs was like a heavy, heady perfume. As I stood there breathing deeply I thought how much so many people missed in these times of oil and gas furnaces. There is something unforgettable about the smell of the smoke from an open fireplace of mixed wood logs.

When I reached the cabin door I shoved it open, stepped in and slammed it shut against the wind. The old man was sitting in front of the hearth. He turned towards me, then back to the fire and spit a copious stream of tobacco juice that sent a shower of sparks up the chimney. Then he invited me to have a chair and set. I realized that he was depressed and dejected. I knew what the trouble was.

"Yep," he said, "I know it's Good Friday. The signs are just right for plantin' my string beans. Hit's not only Good Friday but hit's the light of the moon too and the two don't always hit together. That's the time to start plantin'."

I tried to cheer him up by telling him he ought to know it was too early to plant beans and if the weather had been fit they would have gotten killed. Here it was only the last part of March and we were bound to have plenty of frost before it warmed up. That got a rise out of the old man.

"Now listen here, young fellow," he began, "you can't tell me. I been plantin' beans on Good Friday since I can recollect and ain't never had any killed yet, whether it come late or early. My mammy did the same back in her day while Pap was off fightin' the Yankees and she had the raisin' of all the food for us young uns."

I kept quiet. I didn't want to get him stirred up by mentioning to him that I remembered several times in the years gone by when Good Friday came early and he planted his string beans only to have them killed by late frost.

CHAPTER 110

New Ground

I followed my old friend as he walked slowly up the trail that led to a field above his cabin. He stopped to point out a patch of land maybe a half acre or so in size. It was a freshly cleared patch that had "layed out" for a number of years. That is, it had not been cultivated or cropped but allowed to grow up in weeds, blackberry and dewberry briars, sassafras bushes and such.

The old man launched a stream of tobacco juice into space and watched it splatter on a large rock below.

"This here is goin' to be my tomator patch come springtime," my old friend said. He had spent the winter clearing the small patch with a mattox and grubbing hoe and had torn up the roots with his bull tongue plow, piling up the roots and brush to burn when the piles had dried enough to set on fire.

As we stood there I thought of the sweat and toil of mountain men, women and children through the years, clearing new ground to plant their crop of "tomators." As far back as I could remember it was always the custom. The practice had been handed down through the generations.

I started to tell him that new ground was not necessary now, what with the improved fertilizer, liming, the potent insecticides and fungicides. Farmers in the flat lands in recent years were raising tomatoes profitably year after year on the same land. Then it suddenly occurred to me. Why try to disillusion my old friend? He wouldn't believe me anyway; his father and grandfather always planted tomatoes in new ground. I had to admit to myself that through the years I had seen him raise some of the most beautiful, luscious and delicious tomatoes when others around him were failing with theirs that were not planted on new ground. He might just have something.

He pointed to the spot where he had piled the brush and burned it. He had already planted his tobacco seed to grow the plants he would need to raise his usual crop of tobacco for the home grown, home cured tobacco that he smoked and chewed. The seedbed was covered with what he called canvas. It was a thin, woven gauze that the old ones from the deep South can remember as mosquito netting.

"My pappy and grandpappy always told me to git your tobacco bed burned off and planted before February 14th to do any good," he said.

I asked him, "How come abody burns a tobacco bed?" He answered my question. "Why for two reasons. It heats the ground for one thing and then the fire kills all weed seeds in the ground and all the bugs."

Standing there by my old friend's tobacco bed, I told him I had been talking to Ben Blackwell a few days ago and that Mr. Blackwell said that he could remember when he was a boy everybody got together on the back side of Big Hungry. They would cut and haul wood to burn off a big bed so that everybody was always in a rush to get things ready by February 14th.

"Why was that?" I asked my old friend. "Why was February 14th so important?"

The old man didn't answer for a moment, spit a stream of tobacco juice plum across the tobacco bed, turned and squirted another stream down the hill. "Because my pappy and grandpappy told me."

We turned and walked down the hill to his cabin. The wood in the fireplace had burned to a bed of glowing hot coals. The old man put some ground up coffee in a smoke blackened pot, poured in water and hung the pot on a hook over the coals. "I'll just bile us a little coffee," he said.

While waiting for the coffee water to boil I asked him what was causing the mild winter weather.

"Hit beats me," he replied. "Things is all anti-godlin. A body can't go by the signs no more. Folks a meddlin' in things they go no business a doin', like goin' contrary to the Good Book. Folks foolin' around and trompin' on the moon."

He suddenly changed the subject like old ones are apt to do. "Yep, I recollect that fellow Ben Blackwell when he warn't nothin' but a nubbin of a boy helpin' with them tobacco beds back yander. I knowed his pappy, too." "I ain't seen hide nor hair of Ben in years but I heard tell he done pretty well sellin' automobiles and sech."

CHAPTER 111
Springtime Advice

I walked up the trail that led to the cabin of my old friend who lives alone on the side of the mountain. It was a beautiful day; the sky was clear and the sun was hot for the time of year. Going up the path with the southern exposure I quickly broke into a sweat. I found my old friend in his cleared patch below the house. He was planting his garden.

When I walked up we exchanged greetings. I asked him what he was planting.

He leaned on the hoe handle and mopped his face with a red bandana handkerchief. "Corn," he answered. "It's late to be plantin' corn but I had to wait until the signs was right. Should have planted when the dogwood first bloomed but the moon wasn't right. It's best to plant corn when the dogwood blooms but it must be on the new moon. The moon just now newed. Corn planted in the new moon when the dogwood is in bloom will grow straight and tall and it'll make two ears to every stalk."

The old man paused to bite off a chew of his home grown twist of tobacco that he cured himself.

"Young folks don't pay no mind to the signs now days," he sighed and spit a stream of tobacco juice. "And it's a pity if I do say so. Take that manure on this ground I'm plantin', I hauled it and scattered it on the old moon. Manure scattered on the old moon will hold its strength to go into the ground and its strength will stay there until the crop needs its."

My old friend wanted to get on with his planting but he also wanted to talk so I asked him a leading question, and he started again. "I plant my okra, beans and such that bear above the ground on the light of the moon on the increase, when the sign of the Zodiac is in the arms. That way things will yield double." He chuckled. "And you be sure to stoop low, or better yet crawl on your knees, when you go to plant your okra. That way it won't grow too tall."

"Now my taters and any other root crops, I plant on the dark nights when the signs in the legs. Folks would make a heap more stuff if they planted by the signs like they did in the old days."

I knew I should go and let the old fellow get on with his work before the signs changed on him so I began to take my leave.

As I started towards the path that led through the woods to where I had parked the jeep, he had to get in a parting piece of advice.

"Have you had your spring tonic yet?" When I turned back towards him and told him I had not he shook his head. "You go dig you some sassafras roots and boil up some sassafras tea. Drink it every day for about three weeks and you'll lose some of that fat around your middle." He chucked and spat. "Nothin' like sassafras tea in the springtime to perk abody up and take off that winter roll of fat."

I assured the old man that I would do that as soon as I got home. I turned and hurried down the path before he offered me more advice.

CHAPTER 112

Indian Summer

It was an ideal fall day. The sky was blue as only our Blue Ridge Mountains' sky can be at this time of the year. There was a gentle breeze blowing. It was an ideal day to visit my old friend who lives alone in his log cabin on the side of the mountain. Although it was well up into October there had not been a real killing frost, only a scattering frost here and there in the low places. All fall the weather had been unseasonably warm. I figured it was time for a visit to my old friend to get his weather forecasts for the approaching winter months.

For those of you who have never heard or read about my visits to the old man, I think I should introduce you. He lives alone on the south side of the mountain, just below the top, in his log cabin which is close to 200 years old. It was built by his grandfather who was one of the first pioneers to come into the area. How old he is I don't know and I don't think he really knows himself. When I was a boy I thought he was an old man already but as I look back over more than half a century I can see little change except for his gray hair and a step that is not quite as pert as it was in past years. His eyes are bright blue and the youthful twinkle is still in them; an inheritance from his Scotch ancestors. There on the side of the mountain he "tends his patches of cleared land and scratches out a livin'," as he puts it.

I drove the truck up the rough, twisting mountain road to where it dead ended. I started to walk the path through the woods that led to the cabin above. Years ago there had been a crude road that could be negotiated by an ox cart or a sled but the road had been abandoned and only a foot path was there now. There had been a time when I walked up the mountainside without stopping. As the years went by I began to stop a time or two on my way up while I admired the scenery below in what my old friend referred to as the flat lands. Now I stop, several times, and have to admit that I stop to catch my breath and rest my creaking joints and aching muscles.

When I reached the edge of the cleared land I could see the old log cabin with the smoke curling lazily out of the mud-daubed rock chimney. To one side was the log building that served as a barn and beyond that was the pig pen where my old friend always kept a couple of shoats fattening until the first cold spell came along and he could butcher. Near by were stacks of hay, corn, fodder and tops. The old man still cut his corn tops and pulled fodder, cured his hay and stacked it as his father and grandfather did.

My old friend was sitting in a chair leaning back against the south side of the cabin in the warm sun. His old felt hat was tilted over his eyes to keep off the glare of the sun. When I walked up and spoke the old fellow pushed his hat back and motioned to an empty chair beside him. "Set," he said.

Before I forget it, the two chairs and several others in the cabin were made by my friend's grandfather. Darkened by age, the frames were made of hickory and the seats were woven white oak splints. Those chairs were heavier than the so called kitchen chairs of today. They must have been well over a hundred years old.

When I sat down he started the conversation. "Knowed you was a comin'; my nose been itchin' all morning." My old friend believes in the signs and through all the years I have visited him, I have never surprised him because some sign or another had warned him that I was coming. The warm sun of Indian summer caressed us as we leaned back against the cabin. The only sounds were the calls of the unseen birds in the woods below and the splashing of the nearby stream from the spring above the cabin as it raced down the mountain to the flat lands below.

Before I sat down I handed him the usual present that I always brought him; a few good cigars, a package of fine pipe tobacco and several plugs of chewing tobacco.

The old man knew what was in the package; store bought tobacco, he calls it. Without looking in the bag he grunted an acknowledgement that I accepted as a thank you. He put the package on the ground by his chair; pulled a twist of his home grown, home cured tobacco out of the pocket of his bib overalls and tore off a mouthfull with his stubby, tobacco stained teeth.

To start a conversation, I asked him how he had been since my last visit. "Tolable, only tolable," he replied. Through all the years I have not known him to give any other answer in regard to his health. I asked him if he had ever seen it stay so warm so late in the season and without even a killing frost.

"What do you blame it all on?" I asked him.

The old man perked up. I was on his favorite subject and it was one he considered himself to be an expert on. "All of the signs are bad," he said, "and all point to a long cold winter."

Never seen so many foggy mornings and each one means a snow this winter. The mast is the heaviest in years; acorns, hickory nuts, black walnuts. I been settin' and watchin' the squirrels and chipmunks hidin' them away for when it snows."

The old man threw away his used wad of tobacco and tore off a fresh chew. "One of the surest signs," he said, "is the wooley worms. There's been the most and the fattest I ever seen. Some folks call them caterpillars. There's one now," He pointed to a large black and brown one lazily crawling across the bare ground in front of us. He directed a stream of tobacco juice towards the wooley worm and that caterpillar never knew what hit him. The old man never misses.

He wiped his mouth with the back of his hand. "Another sign," he began, "of a long cold winter is the golden rod bloomed earliest I can recollect." He shook his head. "I ain't never seen the sight of spiders in the house. When spiders start webbin' up in the corners so early and the cricket starts chirpin' a body better look out."

He stopped talking and when I glanced over to where he sat beside me I saw that he had slipped into a doze there in the warm autumm sun, as old ones have a way of doing. Suddenly his head jerked up. "Son", he said, "them things used to be signs but a body can't depend on them no more for sure. This trompin' around on the moon has got things all anti-godlin."

CHAPTER 113
Jeremiah Jones

The cold, northwest wind howled around the old log cabin on the side of the mountain. The sound made a body think of the folktales brought to these mountains by the first settlers that came here from Ireland and Scotland; the folk tales of the banshee, those legendary female spirits and ghosts whose wailing was supposed to forewarn families of the approaching death of one of the members. In the pioneer days, tales of the banshee were common here in our mountains and were handed down through the generations. Many a pioneer boy or girl sat close to the hearth fire and shivered with delightful fright while one parent or another told tales of the banshee as the winter wind howled outside; almost too frightened at the end to climb the ladder to the cold loft, jump into the cornshuck mattress bed and pull the quilt over their head to shut out the imaginary eyes peering from the ridge pole above.

Added to the howling winds now was the whistling caused by the wind blowing through the few cracks that had begun to appear between the logs where the dried mud had fallen out and had not been replaced as quickly as in the years gone by when my old friend was much younger.

The fired blazed warm, bright and cheerful as I sat there by the hearth in the late afternoon, not too long ago. The howling of the wind and the crackling and popping of the open fire were the only sounds in the ancient cabin because my old friend dozed, as he often did between spells of conversation.

An unusual hard gust of wind rattled the hand-rived white oak shingles on the roof. The old man's head jerked up and as if he was reading my thoughts he said, "Back in my young days when us young uns huddled around the fire of a night and the wind howled like it's doin' now we would say it was old man Jeremiah Jones wailin' and weepin' for his lost grandson."

When he saw the questioning look on my face, he said, "What? You mean to say I never told you that before? Well, I do say! Folks here abouts done all forgot about it. Guess I am the only one left in these parts that knows about it." I knew then it would be a spell longer before I could make my departure and it would be cold and dark when I made my way down the mountainside.

My old friend fell silent then, nodded a time or two and began. "It all happened a long time ago before there was many folks in these parts; so long ago that I can't separate what I knowed first hand myself and what my daddy told me. His name was Jeremiah Jones, or least ways that's what he claimed."

"No," he replied to a question I interrupted with. "No, he was no kin at all to the Jones hereabout now. There was plenty of folks back there then that doubted his true name was Jones but they let it go."

"Where he come from nobody ever learned for certain. He was not a man to talk much or to mix with folks. Sometimes from the little he said a body got the idea that he come to these parts from Virginia and then again maybe from Tennessee. The first it was knowed he was in these parts was when word got around that a family was livin' along the creek up the hollow a ways in a lean-to. Folks was curious. We knowed that a body couldn't get through a winter like we had back in them days livin' in a lean-to."

"Some of us boys begun to drop by one or two at a time when we were out huntin'. That's when we learned there was a young woman with him. She was a pretty thing with big sad brown eyes and she had a right young baby boy she fretted with all the time."

"The man claimed they was his daughter and grandson, her bein' a widow woman. While there was some talk among folks, his story was accepted."

My old friend paused, "Put another log on that fire, son," he said. When I did it sent a shower of sparks up the chimney. The old man bit a big chew of store-bought tobacco that I had brought.

"It turned out that Jeremiah Jones had bought the tract of land along the creek there and was fixin' to build a log cabin, clear a patch of land and settle there. There wasn't much to talk about in these parts back then and whenever folks met all the talk was about the man, the girl and the baby and how he could never get a cabin built before winter set in."

"There come an early cold spell that fall. Some of the boys had been huntin' up on the mountain and come back down the hollow where Jeremiah Jones was plannin' to put up his cabin. He hadn't made even a beginning of a start. They found him and his daughter huddled around a fire in front of the lean-to tryin' to keep warm. The girl was holdin' the baby and it was cryin' so pitiful like. After warmin' their hands and passin' the time of day the boys went on and got to takin' among themselves."

"The upshot of it was that they decided to set a day and pass the word to all the men in the settlement. They would go up the hollow and build this man and his daughter a cabin. The women folks would cook up a mess and go along and make a time out of it. That's how them folks got their cabin built afore the winter set in."

"They was grateful and thanked everybody nice like. As time went by folks quit droppin' by. The girl and her baby never went far from the cabin and the man scarcely ever visited other folks in the settlement. By now Jeremiah's head had turned white and the baby wasn't a baby no longer. He was a right friendly little shaver; blue-eyed and curly haired. They called him Billie Boy. When he got to be twelve years old or there abouts, the mother up and took sick sudden like and the first thing the neighbors knew she was dead."

"After that the man and his grandson became inseparable. The old man worshipped the ground that boy walked on. Back in them days the creek was full of fish. All the branches and creeks hereabout was. Any day it was fittin' Jeremiah Jones and his grandson could be seen fishin' one place and another."

"It made a right smart pretty picture; the curly headed, bright eyed boy and the silvery haired old man with his gray beard, each with a fishin' pole walkin' the creek banks. Then there came what we uns always called the June freshet."

"Folks now don't never hear the word freshet but when I was a boy and growin' up we always had a spring freshet and a fall freshet; sudden rains that fell heavy, filled up the creeks and overflowed the bottoms. The spring freshet come late that year, not until June and it was the worst ever in these parts and that's why folks ever afterwards always called it the June freshet. Well, that day the sun come up clear and warm. The old man and boy was seen as usual to start up the creek a fishin'. Long about noon, the blackest cloud rolled across the top of the mountain and with a crash and rumble of thunder that shook the ground, the clouds busted wide open. In no time a wall of water came rushin' down."

"Nobody knows exactly what happened. Sometime later the old man was found near dead in the top of a tree. There was no sign of the boy. A search party was got together and for several days they searched up and down the creek."

"No sign of the boy was ever found and what became of his body no one ever did know. All we could get out of the grandfather was that he saw the boy swept out of sight by that wall of water."

"From then on, Jeremiah Jones was tetched in the head. He kept to hisself. He got him a real mean dog. He fished from daylight to dark. Us young uns got to be scared of him but we couldn't help hidin' in the bushes to spy on him. He was always talkin' out loud to hisself. As time went on the old man talked more and more, from what we could hear. The old man had it in his mind that his grandson had been turned into a fish back there when the freshet hit and if he could only hook the fish that had been Billie Boy he would have his grandson back."

"By now he had let his snow white hair and beard grow long. It was all tangled like. He looked now like a wild man. Must have got deaf too because us boys could now creep up close. When he caught a fish he would hold it up close to his eyes and examine it good while it wiggled and squirmed. Then we young uns could hear him talk out loud, 'No! No! Tain't Billie. Tain't Billie. Strange where that boy is.' "

"There come a spell when nobody saw the old man. One day his dog turned up right here. Crawled up on the porch and lay there on his belly and scratched at the door. He acted cowed like and whined pitiful. All the meanness was gone out of him; he looked like he was beggin' with his eyes. When I throwed him some cold corn pone and meat scraps he wolfed 'em down. Some of us went up the hollow to the cabin. The door was shet tight. We called and knocked but there was no answer and nary a sound from inside."

"There was bound to be something wrong, so we decided, and busted the door open. Found the old man lyin' in the floor in front of the cold fireplace. He was dead. When the word spread the neighbors got together and buried him below his cabin on the creek bank where he could hear the water that he loved to fish in rushin' by. The bushes and briars begun to grow up and the old cabin begun to fall in. One night it burned down and nobody ever found out how it caught fire, because by now it had got around that the deserted old cabin was haunted. If a body goes pokin' around through the tangled bushes up there he might find a crumblin' pile of rocks where the chimney was."

"After a while folks out possum or coon huntin' at night began to tell things. On a moonlight night sometimes fishin' alone or with his grandson could be seen Jeremiah Jones. That's been a long time ago, son, and I'm the only one left that knows about it. And folks back there then begun to say when the wind howled and whined like it's doin' out there now that it was old Jeremiah Jones grievin' for his curly headed grandson and the boy's pretty, sad-eyed mother."

CHAPTER 114

Leather Britches

The old man was crumbling some of his home grown, home cured, twisted tobacco in the palm of his hand. He reached over for his vile smelling corncob pipe and began to fill it with the crumbled tobacco. He only gave me a contemptuous grunt when I remarked about how it would smell when he got it lighted. He leaned over and picked up a red hot ember on the edge of the hearth and put it to his pipe. How he does it without blistering his fingers I have never been able to figure.

The earlier mixture of sleet, snow and rain had now changed to a steady patter of rain on the hand-rived shingles that roofed his cabin. I glanced at my watch and was surprised that it was already noontime. I pushed back my chair and mentioned I had better be on my way while I could before the weather got worse. He insisted that I stay and have a bite. He pointed to two smoke blackened pots hanging from hooks over each side of the large fireplace where the red hot coals were glowing.

"I reckon as how you would come up today so I put your name in each of them pots." He leaned over and took the lid off each pot in turn. There was chicken and dumplings in one and in the other there were leather britches with a big slab of fatback and part of a home cured and smoked ham hock.

The aroma that surged out of those pots when he took off the lids was mouth watering. It was mighty easy to sit back and accept that invitation to "set and eat."

For the enlightenment of those who may not know, leather britches was a staple winter food in our mountain homes long before pressure cookers for canning and electricity for deep freezers for preserving food were known. String beans were picked when the beans had filled the pods. The beans, pod and all, were strung with a thread and needle in long chains and were then hung in a dry, warm place to dry out. These dried beans in their hulls were called leather britches. The day before they were to be eaten, the leather britches were soaked all day and night in a pot of water. They were started to boil early the next morning with a hunk of fatback or better still a large chunk of ham hock. By midday dinnertime, they were ready to serve and they sure made good eating. Leather britches are practically unknown in this generation and are seen now only on the dinner table of an old one who clings to the way of his or her ancestors.

A plate of my old friend's chicken and dumplings, leather britches and a big slab of crackling bread washed down with several glasses of cold, home-churned buttermilk makes mighty good eating if a body does not have to watch the calories.

CHAPTER 115
Dancing Flames

I walked up on the porch and knocked on the cabin door of my old friend who lives alone on the side of the mountain. I got a loud "Come!" from inside. I have never known my old friend to open the door for a visitor. It is always a hearty "Come!" because the door is never locked. There is no lock on any of the cabin doors; only latches with draw strings hanging outside to lift the latches. Of course he has bars on the inside that he can drop across the doors at night to keep intruders out, if he ever thinks to drop them in their slots which I have never known him to do.

When I walked in he greeted me. "Well, son, what brings you up here in all this mess?" I always feel flattered when he calls me "son" because in the more than 60 years I have known him he has always done this and now after all these years it makes me feel young.

I didn't tell him so but for the past few years when the weather takes a turn for the worst and especially in the wintertime I worry about my old friend.

Saturday morning when it started snowing he was the first thing I thought about.

The road to his cabin ends before it reaches his place on the side of the mountain and you have to walk through the woods for quite a distance on a trail to reach his patch of cleared land where the cabin sits. I have snow tires on the farm truck but the snow was driving in from the east and northeast and it looked as if it had set in for all day and maybe longer. As extra precaution I put the heavy truck chains on the back wheels.

When I reached the end where the road dead ends I turned the truck around so that when I started home I would have a down hill drag. I walked the half mile or so through the woods and when I reached the clearing I could see the cabin and the smoke curling up out of the chimney so I knew things must be all right.

The only heat my old friend has is from a big open hearth fire which he keeps heaped with logs from daylight to dark. Just before going to bed which he does not too long after dark sets in, he banks the fire with ashes so that come daylight all he has to do is stir the embers, throw on a few pine cones and fat pine splinters. He piles on the dry logs again and is all set for another winter day.

As I crossed the cleared patch and crunched through the snow to his doorsteps I could see the porch half full of wood stacked high with well seasoned logs. Some of them were pine but mostly they were hickory and oak for long burning and a hot fire. To one side there was a good sized stack of apple wood that he had cut and hand sawed from his apple orchard; the trees so old and neglected that they had ceased to bear fruit that was edible or marketable.

Apple wood was his favorite wood and he used it only on special occasions. He has told me all through the years of our friendship that smoke from apple wood smells different from all other smoke and the wood makes a brighter flame with so many different colors.

"The flame from apple wood dances and my grandma told me when I was just a young un that fairies dancin' in the flames made it do that and I have always believed her."

The following Index is for all three volumes of "Banks of the Oklawaha". Each entry has the volume number preceding the page, e. g. A. B. McClellan Co. II 367 denotes page 367 in Volume II.

Hood, Lemuel III 90
Hood, W. A. II 45; III 121
Hood School II 89; III 90
Hooper's Creek I 69, 88, 309; II 78, 80, 82, 112, 329-330, 351
Hoots, W. M. II 351
Hoots family III 87
Horace III 104-105
horse jockeys III 145
Horse Pen Gap III 169
Horse Pen Mt. III 169
Horse Shoe I 67-70, 142, 196-199, 201, 225, 243, 283, 364; II 24-25, 173, 175, 209-210, 320-322, 338, 404; III 153, 209, 215-216, 244
Horse Shoe Bend Farm II 210
Horse Shoe Cheese Coop III 215-216
Hosea Lake II 147
hotels *See specific names.*
See also inns & boarding houses.
hound dogs III 153-154
The House of Seven Gables II 127-130, *ill* 130
Houston, Flake II 243
Houston, Sam I 102; III 60
Howard, Furman I 277; III 60
Howard, George E. III 182
Howard, Port I 81
Howard, Captain Thomas I 49, 55; II 9, 17, 189, 405; III 13-15, *ill* 14, 190
Howard, Tom II 122-124
Howard's Gap I *ill* 48, 55, 88; II 18, 184; III 13-15, *ill* 14, 190
Howe, Elizabeth I 29
Howe, Jennie II 281
Howe, Louise I 29
Howe, Dr. W. B. W. II 51; III *ill* 167, 168
Howe, W. B. W. I 29; III 168
Howe Estate I 29
Hoyt, Goold III 5
Hudgens, Mrs. Frank III 127
Hudgins, A. E. II 340
Huggins, Jesse Pritchard III 22
Huggins, Mrs. Jesse Pritchard III 21-22
Huggins, Linell III 178
Huggins, Mingus I 318
Huggins Building I 284
Huggins family I 37; III 178
Hughes Mill III 22
Humphrey Hill III 127
Hunklary Hill III 127
Hunnicutt, Ed III 208
Hunt, Mrs. R. L. I 303
Hunter, F. V. II 38
Hunter, John II 110-111; III 173
Hunter's Pharmacy I 210; II *ill* 47, *ill* 56, 283, *ill* 284; III 138, 142
Hunthurst I 303
hunting II 165-166; III 153-159, 175, 176, 180

Huntsinger, Belle Whitesides I 42; III 108
Huntsinger, Gene I 42
Hutcherson, Bob I 156
Hyatt, Jacob III 5-6, 9
Hyder, Doc II 38
Hyder, H. D. I 227
Hyder, Henry I 195; II 351
Hyder, Rosie III *ill* 92
Hyder, Walt III 48
Hyder Building II 351; III 48
Hyman, John D. I 104
Hyman, V. L. II 45; III 121
Hyman Heights II 50

ice cream factory III 216
Immaculata School II 36
Imperial Hotel I 255, 257
Indian Camp Creek II 87
Indian Cave II 275; III 138, *ill* 139, 140
Indian Cave Lodge I 295-297, *ill* 296; III 138-141
Indian Cave Park I 295-296; III 139
Indian Cave Park Hotel II 275
Indian Hills II 146
Indian Jack II 18-19
Indians I 60, 87, 157, 248-249, 251, 343; II 5-19, 73, 99-100, 107-109, 163, 359; III 6, 13-16, 21-24, 110, 156, 169, 173, 181, 185, 190, 191, 192
See also Cherokee, Chickasaw & Creek Indians.
Ingersoll, Judge I 193
Ingils, John I 262
Ingles Supermarket II 244
inns & taverns, early I 25-26, 31, 40; II 78, 80; III 53, 55, 190, 221
Inter-Urban Car Line II 342-343
iron forge II 103-105, *ill* 104
Island Forge II 24
Island Fork Bridge I 201
Israel, Frank III 137, 147
Israel, J. A. II 339
Israel, Joe III 129
Israel, T. B. II 278
Israel, Big Tom I 172
Ives, J. Cason I 243; III 178
Ives, Mrs. J. Cason I 243
Ives, Bishop L. S. III 18
Ivy Knob III 198
J. C. Penny Co. store I 147, 266; II 59, 285; III 70
J. H. Stepp & Sons, Inc. I 227
Jack-in-the-bush II 273-274
Jackson, Andrew III 15, 225, *ill* 226
Jackson, B. B. (Brownlow) I 212-213, 315; II 45, 342; III *ill* 201, 204
Jackson, Brownlow III 244-245
Jackson, Earle III 260
Jackson, Eliza II 187
Jackson, J. P. II 43

Mill Spring *(Cont'd)*
8, 13
Miller, Andrew I 12
Miller, Captain II 151
Miller, David I 69
Miller, David III 74
Miller, Hubert (Bert) E. III *ill* 254, 255-256
Miller, John I 66, 179
Miller, Norman, Sr. I 211
Miller, Norman, Jr. III *ill* 254, 255-256
Miller, Otis I 255; II 32-33
Miller, Theodore E. III *ill* 254
Miller, Tom III 75
Miller, William D. II 180
Miller, Winfield (Win) D. III *ill* 254, 255-256
Miller's Hill II 151
Miller's Laundry I 211: III 256
millers III 98, 214
Mills, - - - - - I 255
Mills, Albert II 370
Mills, Ambrose I 7-8, 15, 17, 34, 87; II 163
Mills, Amelia I 17, 20
Mills, Eleanor I 10, 55; II 163, 405; III 109
Mills, Eleanor I 10, 13, 119
Mills, Eleanor I 10, 13, 119
Mills, Elizabeth I 10
Mills, Erwin II 295
Mills, George I 115-119; III 252
Mills, John I 10
Mills, Mabel I 117-118
Mills, Marvil I 10
Mills, Mr. I 175-176
Mills, Mourning I 10
Mills, Mourning Stone I 7
Mills, Phalby I 10
Mills, Sarah I 10, 14
Mills, William I 7-12, 13-15, 17, 20, 34, 43,
51, 53, 55, 79, 119; II 17, 163, 359, 405;
III 8, 109, 158
mills I 7, 87; II *ill* 75, 163; III 115, 122, 173,
179, 221
See specific names.
Mills Gap I 10, 17; II 17, 184
Mills River I 10; II 14-15, 63, 93, 103, 150,
184, 218, 412; III 93, 122, 172, 207-208,
215
Valley I 20, 34, 64-65, 83, 88, 142, 179-
181; II 92, 103-105, 151, 161, 381-382;
III 27, 57, 171, 193, 207
Mills River Academy I 68, 179-181; II 92;
III 27, 74
Mills River Community House I 180
Mills River High School I 181; III 57
Mills River Lions Club III 207-208
Mills River Presbyterian Church I 180; II 92
Mills River Recreation Park II 332; III 172
Mills River School I 180-181; II 151; III 57
Mimosa Inn II 7, 11, *ill* 163
Miss America II *ill* 82
Miss Kate II 244-245

Mitchell, Aiken I 175
Mitchell, Irene III 86
Mitchell, Judge I 193
Mitchell, Nannie III 86
Moffitt, Vernon I 201
Moland, Mrs. George III 206
Moland-Drysdale Corp. III 256
Molyneau, Edmund III 115, 150
Montgomery, Luella I 131-132
Montgomery, Robert I 131-132
Moon, Reedy Patch Hill III 108-109
The Moon-Eyed People I 3-4
Moore, Adam III 173
Moore, Bob III 242-243
Moore, Charlie II 288-289
Moore, Mrs. Charlie E. III 260
Moore, Frank II 220
Moore's Grove Methodist Church I 18; II 174
Moorse, James II 370
Moreno, Albert III 133
Morgan, Charlie I 303
Morgan, Clyde R. III 60-62
Morgan, Gen. Daniel I 142
Morgan, Evangeline III 61
Morgan, Fannie Levi III 60-62
Morgan, Jim I 256
Morgan, Preacher I 82
Morgan, Robert Ray III 61
Morgan's Mill II 254-257 *ill* 255
Morganton III 240
Morris, A. C. II 339
Morris, Amanda II 184
Morris, Billy II 164
Morris, Carl II 184
Morris, Jim II 184
Morris, King II 37
Morris, Richard II 184
Morris, Captain W. G. B. II 184
Morrison, Gov. Cameron II 134
Morrison, Claude II 147-150, 225; III 182-
183
Morrison, Daniel Lafayette (Fate) II 255
Morrison, David S. II 372-373
Morrison, Emily Jones II 255
Morrison, Lillie Hill III *ill* 85
Morrison cabin II 255
Morrow, J. C. I 212-213
Morse Brothers III 37
Morton, Harry III 56-57
Moses (Hebrew Patriarch) III 60-61
Moses, Judge John L. I 193
Moss, D. H. (Doc) II 55, 57
Mother's General Store I 321
Moultrie, Lavinia III 67-70, *ill* 69
Mt. Gilead Church II 109; III 171
Mt. Hebron I 125, 128-129, 296-297; II 275;
III 138-139, 141, 179
name of, III 139
Mt. Hebron Tower II *ill* 275; III 139
Mt. Moriah Church I 59; II 18; III 110, 164

Rutherford County I 24-25, 33-34, 63, 80,
    83-84, 88, 103, 165-168; II 177, 200,
    247; III 249-250
Rutherford County Home III 249-250
Rutherfordton I 52, 85; II 87, 177, 200; III
    10, 126, 127
Rutledge, Frederick III 115

Sackett, Augustus III 5-8
Saconon I 317; II 71, 73, 75
St. James Episcopal Church III 98
St. John Episcopal Church III 178
St. John in the Wilderness I 25, 75, 122; II
    129; III 17-19, *ill* 19, 67, 118, 133
    name of, I 25
St. John's Hotel I 174, 255, 257-259, *ill*
    259; III 42, 125
St. Mary's Chapel II *ill* 90
St. Paul's Episcopal Church I 12, 51; II 224;
    III 163
Sales, Mrs. J. C. II 242
Salisbury III 28, 66, 134
Salley, Dr. E. McQueen II 52
Sally Capps Branch I 30; III 20
Salola Inn II 175, *ill* 276, 278; III 110
Saluda I 131, 157; II 100, 101, 127-130,
    135, 137, 147, 149, 162-163, 205-206,
    219-220, 312, 372; III 28, 30, 222, 242,
    252, 268
Saluda Cottages I 29
Saluda Gap I 40, 88, 97, 104, 145-146; II
    184
Saluda Grade I 191; II 205-206, 207; III
    252, 268
Saluda Mts. II 166
Salvation Army II 371
Sam II 405-406
Sample, Ann III 204-205
Sandburg, Carl I 29, 111, 151, 300
Sanders, Mamie II 187
Sandifer, Elizabeth Graham II 247
Sandifer, Mrs. George Campbell II 338
Sandifer, Joseph R. (Sandy Joe) II 246-248;
    III 150
Sandifer, Mrs. Joseph R. II 248
Sandifer, Dr. Joseph T. II 247
Sandifer, Norma III 204
Sandifer, Sarah II 338; III 204
Saratoga Chip Factory I 218-219
Saunders family II 127
scarifying I 334
Schain, H. J. II 293
Schenck, Dr. Carlos A. II *ills* 379, 380, &
    383, 380-383
Scott, John I 320
Scott, Josiah I 201
Scottsburg I 201
scrofula I 154-157
Scruggs, John E. II 180
Seagle, Catherine II 90

Seagle, Charles II 90
Seagle, John II 90
Seagle, Lucy II 94
Seagle, Mary Drake II 87-90
Seagle, Mary Kent II 90
Seagle, Nathan Drake II 89-90
Seagle, Phillip II 87-90
Seagle, Richard II 90
Seagle, Thomas II 90
Seagle Chapel II *ill* 90
Seigle, Sam III 225
Seniard Creek III 172-174
Seniard Mt. III 172
Sentell, William I 38
Sentell family III 178
Sentell Mill III 179
Sentelle, Dick II 49
Sentelle, Elizabeth I 37-38
Sentelle, Jesse II 322
Sentelle, Richard I 38
Sentelle, Samuel I 38
Sentelle, William I 12, 35-39
Senter, William I 38
Sentle, Richard I 38
Seven Months a Prisoner I 125-129
Sevier, John II 245
Sevier, Rev. Dr. Joseph II 245
Sexton, Bale I 206
Shanghai (School) I 181; III 174
    name of, III 174
Shannhouse, Hazel Shepherd III 73
Sharp, Mrs. III 83-84, 166
Shaw family I 214; II 14-17
Shaw's Creek I 214; II 15
Shaw's Creek Baptist Church II 15, 146
sheep III 177-178, 195
Shepherd, Arthur II 368; III 73
Shepherd, Catherine II 281; III 73
Shepherd, F. G. III *ill* 135
Shepherd, Flave III *ill* 130
Shepherd, Hazel III 73
Shepherd, Jesse Merrill III 71-73, *ill* 72, 180
Shepherd, John Patton III 73
Shepherd, Kate III 73
Shepherd, Louise III 73
Shepherd, M. M. III 73
Shepherd, Mrs. M. M. III 73
Shepherd, Marian III 73
Shepherd, Martha III *ill* 71, 73, *ill* 135
Shepherd, Nanna III 73
Shepherd, Nimrod III 180
Shepherd, Ruth III 73
Shepherd, Thomas II *ill* 48; III 71, 73, *ill* 130
Shepherd, Mrs. Thomas II 51; III 73, *ill* 130
Shepherd, V. C. V. (Vol) II 299, 368; III 73,
    143
Shepherd, Mrs. V. C. V. II 368; III 73
Shepherd, William III 73
Shepherd Spring III 179-180
Shepherd's & Sentelle's Grocery Store II 55

Frank FitzSimons – Author